A Will In Massachusetts

2nd Edition

SIMPLE, PRACTICAL THINGS A RESIDENT OF MASSACHUSETTS CAN DO TO

- PRESERVE ASSETS
- AVOID PROBATE
- AVOID GUARDIANSHIP
- PROVIDE FOR HEALTH CARE
- PROVIDE FOR THE FAMILY'S CARE

By AMELIA E. POHL, ESQ.
and Massachusetts Attorney
JAMES A. MILLER

EAGLE PUBLISHING COMPANY OF BOCA

EAGLE PUBLISHING COMPANY OF BOCA
4199 N. Dixie Highway, #2
Boca Raton, FL 33431 E-mail: info@eaglepublishing.com

Printed in the United States of America
ISBN 1-932464-18-2
Library of Congress Catalog Card Number: 2002094112

A Will Is Not Enough In Massachusetts

2nd Edition

CONTENTS

Introduction

Over the years, as we practiced law, we noticed that the questions people have about Wills, Trusts, powers of attorney, avoiding probate and guardianship, preserving assets, providing health care for themselves and their families, are much the same client to client. Many people are concerned about who will control their finances should they become too aged or too ill to do so themselves. Of even more concern is their health care:

Who will make my medical decisions if I can't do so myself?
How can I pay for my health care?
How much and what type of insurance should I have?
How can I avoid guardianship?

Others worry about the care of family members. Those with minor children worry:

Who will care for my minor child if I become incapacitated or die?

Is there a way to make sure my child has enough money to see him through college?

Those with elderly parents worry:

How can I manage my parent's finances should my parent become too aged or ill to do so?

Can my parent qualify for MEDICAID?

If my parent dies, will I need to go through Probate?

Is there a way to avoid Probate?

We agreed that a book answering such questions would be of service to the general public. We wish to thank all of the clients, whom we have had the honor and pleasure to serve, for providing us with the impetus to write this book.

James A. Miller, Esq.

JAMES A. MILLER is the Managing Attorney of the LAW OFFICES OF JAMES A. MILLER. The office is staffed with experienced attorneys and paralegals trained in the complex areas of Probate Trust and Medicaid Law. The aim of each member of the firm is to help the client accomplish his Estate Planning goals and to take the mystery out of the planning process.

JAMES A. MILLER is highly committed to providing his clients with comprehensive planning services. A solid legal education, including a Juris Doctorate from Suffolk University School of Law, where he graduated Cum Laude, is the foundation for Mr. Miller's innovative approach to helping families plan for a comfortable, crisis-free inheritance. Attorney Miller has been providing Elder Law and Estate Planning services to his clients since 1994. These services have reached thousands of people concerned about protecting their families from the devastating legal effects of disability and death. Mr. Miller is a member of the National Academy of Elder Law Attorneys and of the Massachusetts Bar Association and Worcester County Bar Association.

JAMES A. MILLER is also a member of the AMERICAN ACADEMY OF ESTATE PLANNING ATTORNEYS.

About the Academy

The American Academy of Estate Planning Attorneys is a member organization serving the needs of legal professionals concentrating on Estate Planning. Through the Academy's comprehensive training and educational programs on state-of-the-art Estate Planning law and techniques, it fosters excellence in Estate Planning among its members and helps them deliver the highest possible service to their clients. The Academy provides its members with excellent legal education, and top notch practice management support. In addition, each member is required to attain thirty-six units of continuing legal education in tax and Estate Planning annually.

The American Academy of Estate Planning Attorneys serves law firms in over 150 geographic areas in forty-four states. Clients who chose an attorney who is a member of the Academy can feel confident that they have an attorney who is dedicated to bringing them the highest quality of service.

The Academy is also committed to educating consumers on vital Estate Planning issues that touch their lives. Through its series of publications, educational programs and its consumer Web site, the Academy seeks to create a public armed with the information they need to become wise consumers of Estate Planning services.

THE AMERICAN ACADEMY OF
ESTATE PLANNING ATTORNEYS
http://www.aaepa.com

Amelia E. Pohl, Esq.

Before becoming an attorney in 1985, AMELIA E. POHL taught mathematics on both the high school and college level. During her tenure as Associate Professor of Mathematics at Prince George's Community College in Maryland, she wrote several books including:

Probability: A Set Theory Approach,
Principals of Counting
Common Stock Sense.

During her practice of law Attorney Pohl observed that many people want to reduce the high cost of legal fees by performing or assisting with their own legal transactions.

Attorney Pohl found that, with a bit of guidance, people are able to perform many legal transactions for themselves. Attorney Pohl utilizes her background as teacher, author and attorney to provide that "bit of guidance" to the general public in the form of self-help legal books that she has written. Because there is such variation in the laws from state to state, each book written by Attorney Pohl is state specific.

With the assistance of an attorney licensed to practice in the given state, Amelia Pohl is currently "translating" this book for the remaining states.

Call EAGLE PUBLISHING COMPANY OF BOCA at (800) 824-0823 to learn of the availability of this book for any other state.

ACKNOWLEDGMENT

Many thanks to Massachusetts attorney KATHERINE T. LANTZ, JR. for her review of the Medicaid chapters of this book, namely Chapters 10 and 11. Ms. Lantz is a partner of THE LANTZ LAW FIRM, INC.

THE DESIGN ARTIST

LUBOSH CECH designed the cover of this book. Lubosh Cech is the founder of OKO DESIGN STUDIO located in Portland, Oregon. He designs promotional materials for print and digital media. He has received numerous awards for both graphic design and painting. For more information about Mr. Cech and the OKO Design Studio visit his Web site. http://www.okodesignstudio.com

The photograph on the cover is that of Cape Ann, Massachusetts. The photographer is C. Borland of PhotoLink.

Reading the Law

Where applicable, we identified the state statute or federal statute that is the basis of the discussion. We did this as a reference, and also to encourage the reader to look at the law as it is written. Prior to the Internet the only way you could look up the law was to physically take yourself to the local courthouse law library or the law section of a public library. Today all of the state and federal statutes are literally at your finger tips. They are just a mouse click away on the Internet. To look up a statute all you need is the address of the Web site and the identifying number of the statute.

FEDERAL STATUTES
http://www4.law.cornell.edu/uscode

MASSACHUSETTS STATUTES
http://www.mass.gov/legis/

Massachusetts laws are organized into some 282 chapters. Each chapter is further divided into sections. We have identified the Massachusetts law by Chapter and section. For example, (GLM 112:84) refers to Chapter 112, Section 84 of the General Laws of Massachusetts.

To look up a statute all you need do is go to the Web site and then to the General Laws section. Once at the Search Page you can type in the Chapter and the section within that Chapter.

If you come across a topic you think is important, you may find it both interesting and profitable to read the law as it is actually written.

When You Need A Lawyer

The purpose of the book is to give the reader a basic understanding of Massachusetts law as it relates to Wills and other methods of Estate Planning. It is not intended as a substitute for legal counsel or any other kind of professional advice. If you have a legal question, you should seek the counsel of an attorney. When looking for an attorney, consider three things:

EXPERTISE, COST and PERSONALITY.

EXPERTISE

The state of Massachusetts does not have a program to certify that an attorney is specialized in a particular area of law. This being the case, an attorney in Massachusetts may not represent to the public that he/she is certified by the state as a specialist in any given area of law. Attorneys are allowed to state that they concentrate on certain areas of law or that they limit their practice to an area of law.

The Massachusetts Bar has a Lawyer Referral Service. They can refer you to an attorney in your area who practices the type of law that you seek. There is a minimal fee for the initial half hour consultation. You can call the Lawyer Referral Service at (800) 392-6164. Out of state call (617) 338-0500. The Massachusetts Bar Association has a Web site with a list of Lawyer Referral Services throughout the state.

THE MASSACHUSETTS BAR ASSOCIATION
http://www.massbar.org/

One of the most reliable ways to find an attorney is through personal referral. Ask your friends, family or business acquaintances if they used an attorney for the field of law that you seek and whether they were pleased with the results.

It is important to employ an attorney who is experienced in the area of law you seek. Your friend may have a wonderful Estate Planning attorney, but if you suffered an injury to your body, then you need an attorney who is experienced in Personal Injury. Before employing an attorney for a job, ask how long he has practiced the type of law you seek and what percent of his practice is devoted to that type of law.

COST

In addition to the attorney's experience, it is important to check what it will cost in attorney fees. When you call for an appointment ask what the attorney will charge for the initial consultation and the approximate cost for the service you seek. Ask whether there will be additional costs such as filing fees, accounting fees, expert witness fees, etc. If the least expensive attorney is out of your price range then you can call the Massachusetts Bar Association at (800) 392-6164 for the telephone number of the Legal Aid office nearest you.

There are Legal Aid offices and Public Service Programs that can assist with special problems. You can find a comprehensive list of Legal Aid Offices and Public Service Programs at the Massachusetts Bar Association Web site given on the previous page.

PERSONALITY

Of equal importance to the attorney's experience and legal fees, is your relationship with the attorney. How easy was it to reach the attorney? Did he promptly return your call or did you have to go through layers of receptionists and legal assistants before being allowed to speak to the attorney? If you had difficulty reaching the attorney on your first call, you can expect similar problems should you employ that attorney.

Did the attorney treat you with respect? Did the attorney treat you paternally with a "father knows best" attitude or did he treat you as an intelligent person with the ability to understand the options available to you and the ability to make your own decision based on the information provided to you?

Were you able to understand and easily communicate with the attorney? Was he speaking to you in plain English or was his explanation of the matter so full of legalese to be almost meaningless to you?

Do you find the attorney's personality to be pleasant or grating? If you come away from your first visit feeling annoyed or uncomfortable, then he is not right for you. Find another attorney. It is worth the effort to take the time to interview as many attorneys as it takes to find one with the right expertise, fee schedule and personality for you.

The Organization of the Book

Many people who have a Will think they have their affairs in order, reasoning that should they die everything will go to the people named in the Will and somehow things will all be taken care of. But this is a simplistic view. There are many more things to consider.

1. What exactly will your beneficiaries inherit?
2. How will your property be transferred?
3. Can you (should you) avoid Probate?
4. Can you avoid a challenge to your Will?

The first four chapters of this book deal with these basic issues. Once you read these chapters you will have an understanding of what will happen to your property should you die, regardless of whether you do, or do not, have a Will.

The rest of the book deals with things a Will cannot do:

Chapter 5. Manage your personal debt
Chapter 6. Limit your business debt
Chapter 7. Provide care for a minor or disabled child
Chapter 8. Appoint someone to make your health care decisions should you be unable to do so
Chapter 9. Appoint someone to handle your finances should you be unable to do so
Chapter 10. Help you qualify for MEDICAID should the need arise
Chapter 11. Protect your home should you need to apply for MEDICAID
Chapter 12. Help your family settle your Estate.

A Will can't do these things but you will be able to do so once you read these chapters and understand what options are available to you under Massachusetts law.

GLOSSARY

This book is designed for the average reader. Legal terminology has been kept to a minimum. There is a glossary at the end of the book in case you come across a legal term that is not familiar to you.

FICTITIOUS NAMES AND EVENTS

The examples in this book are based loosely on actual events; however, all names are fictitious; and the events, as portrayed, are fictitious.

MALE GENDER USED

Rather than use he/she or himself/herself, for simplicity, we used the male gender.

Your Financial Check-up 1

To understand why ***A Will is Not Enough in Massachusetts*** you need to know what a Will can and cannot do. One thing a Will can do is make a gift of all you own (your ***Estate***). One of the things a Will cannot do is preserve and protect your property during your lifetime. For that, you need to think about risks to your property (poor investments, theft, loss through acts of nature, etc.) and what you can do to minimize or eliminate such risks. In other words, you need an ***Estate Plan*** for the care and management of your property during your lifetime.

The average person may be thinking "I don't have an Estate — never mind an Estate Plan." But you do. Everyone who owns property, has an Estate Plan. You may not have verbalized your Estate Plan, or even thought about it, but it's there none-the-less. Take the case of the college student purchasing his first car. If his parents bankroll the purchase, the son may offer to hold the car jointly with them. In such case, the son's Estate consists of his car. His Estate Plan is to hold the car jointly with his parents so that they will own the car should anything happen to him.

This may not be the best Estate Plan. Holding the car jointly with his parents may make them liable for injuries or damages should the car be involved in an accident. If the young man's parents are familiar with Massachusetts law, they would be wise to refuse the offer and reassure their son "You can make a Will and make us the beneficiary of your car. But even if you die without a Will, we are your heirs under Massachusetts law. Either way, we will inherit the car. Just make sure to drive carefully and carry enough car insurance."

This is a better Estate Plan. It gives the young man maximum control over his Estate (i.e., his car) during his lifetime. He can sell the car, mortgage it, or trash it, all as he sees fit. If he follows his parent's advice, of driving carefully and purchasing sufficient insurance, his Estate will have maximum protection. If he dies without a Will, and is single and without children, under the MASSACHUSETTS LAWS OF DESCENT AND DISTRIBUTION, his parents will inherit his Estate. And that is just the way the son wants things at this stage of his life.

Simple situation, simple Estate Plan. But, for most of us, life isn't all that simple. We may own many items of value and have loved ones who rely on us. At some point in our lives, we need to ask:

> *How can I make sure that my property will be inherited by my choice of beneficiary?*
>
> *How can I arrange to have my property inherited quickly and at minimum cost?*
>
> *How can I achieve these goals and yet have maximum control and protection of my property during my lifetime?*

We will explore the different ways to answer these questions so that you can decide on an Estate Plan that is best for you. But before doing so you need to know what property you own; i.e., how much your Estate is worth. If you are married and your spouse handles all of the finances, it may be that you have no idea of the value of your Estate.

That was the case with Kristin. She met Matt when they were both at the pinnacle of their careers, but they had no more insight into their precarious position than fireworks in a summer sky just before self-destruct.

Kristin was a model. Not the best, nor the most beautiful, but she made a comfortable living. She moved in a circle of famous models. She reflected off of their radiance, making her appear more attractive than she actually was.

Matt worked in middle management for one of those high tech companies. Like Kristin, he was not particularly gifted but he happened to be in Silicon Valley just at the time the high stakes investors were showing extraordinary, if not misguided, confidence in the industry. The good times were rolling. It never crossed Matt's mind that this would one day end. He spent the money as fast as it came in.

Kristin was impressed with the lavish gifts Matt gave to her. She, and her family, thought she made quite a catch when she announced her engagement. After the wedding she continued to model, but it took a lot of traveling and Matt resented her time away. Eventually, she agreed to stop working altogether. After all, why should she, the wife of a wealthy man, need to continue with the rigors of a model's life of diet and exercise?

Matt never told Kristin about his financial difficulties. All she knew was that he was drinking quite a bit. Her suspicion that he also was into drugs was verified when he died, suddenly, because of an overdose. Her shock and sadness turned to anger when she discovered that all he owned was mortgaged and he was heavily in debt. He even borrowed money from her family without her knowledge!

Matt's creditors took it all. The house, the boat, the Porsche, everything. If only Kristin had investigated the true state of their finances, she could have arranged to set aside the money she earned prior to her marriage and not end up as she did, a destitute widow, past her prime.

DETERMINING YOUR NET WORTH

Even if you are single you may not know the value of your Estate because you have not taken the time to actually sit down and figure it out. To get maximum benefit from this book, you need to take a few minutes to determine your ***Net Worth*** i.e. the current value of your Estate.

ASSETS

$______________	Cash (certificates of deposit, bank accounts, etc.)
$______________	Tangible personal property (jewelry, motor vehicles, private art, stamp or coin collections, etc.)
$______________	Cash value of insurance policies
$______________	Securities (stocks, bonds, etc.)
$______________	Cash value of pension plans, IRAs, etc.
$______________	Cash value of a partnership or other business interest
$______________	Real property (residence, time share, lot, condo, cooperatives, etc.)
$______________	TOTAL VALUE OF ASSETS

It may be that you have a loan on your car or home, or any of the above items. You need to subtract away monies you owe to get the bottom line value of what you own:

LIABILITIES

$______________	Private loans
$______________	Mortgage Balance
$______________	Credit card debt
$______________	Car loan or car lease balance
$______________	TOTAL LIABILITIES

A simple subtraction gives you the value of your Estate.

ASSETS — LIABILITIES = NET WORTH

If you are married and hold all property jointly with your spouse, divide by 2 to get the value of your own Net Worth.

Your Net Worth is the value of all that you own, and that is how much your beneficiaries can inherit. Who will inherit your property depends on how your property is ***titled*** (held or owned).

There are three basic ways to title property:

- ⇨ in ***your name only*** - or -
- ⇨ ***jointly*** with another - or -
- ⇨ ***in trust for*** another.

The way your property is titled determines who will inherit that property:

> Property held in your **name only** will be inherited by the beneficiaries named in your Will.
> If you do not have a Will, the property will go to your heirs according to the Massachusetts Laws of Descent and Distribution.
>
> Property you own **jointly** will go to the surviving joint owner(s) of that property.
>
> Property you hold in **Trust** will go to those you name as the beneficiary of the Trust.
>
> NOTE ⇨ If you are married, your spouse may have rights in your property, regardless of the way your property is titled.

We will examine each of these types of ownership in detail so that you can give yourself an Estate Planning check-up, i.e., you can check whether the way you are currently holding your property accomplishes your Estate Planning goals.

MINE, ALL MINE

There's much to be said about holding property in your name only and not jointly or in trust for another. There's maximum control. You can sell it, trade it, mortgage it, with no one to account to, or ask "may I?" How you protect your assets depends on how much security you require. Again, it's all up to you.

As discussed, there are three things to consider when setting up an Estate Plan:

CONTROL	How to control and protect your Estate during your lifetime.
BENEFICIARY	How to be sure your Estate goes to the beneficiary of your choice.
COST	How to transfer your Estate to your beneficiaries at lowest cost.

Holding all of your property in your name only should give you maximum control and protection; but such an Estate Plan may present problems with the cost of transferring your property upon your death. More than likely it will take some sort of court procedure to transfer that property once you die. The name of the court procedure is ***Probate***. In Massachusetts, Probate is conducted in the Probate and Family Court Department of the Trial Court (GLM 211B:1). We will refer to the court that handles Probate as the ***Probate Court***. We will refer to property that is transferred to your beneficiary by means of a Probate procedure as your ***Probate Estate***.

Probate can be expensive, so if you keep all of your property in your name only there could be a significant cost to transfer your property to the beneficiary of your Estate.

Holding property in your name should not create a problem with having your choice of beneficiary inherit your Estate, provided you have a valid Will. But if you die without a valid Will the Probate Court will use the Massachusetts Laws of Descent and Distribution to determine who inherits your property. Of course it could be that the beneficiaries of your Estate under the Laws of Descent are exactly who you would have wanted, had you taken the time to prepare a Will. To help you determine if this is the case, we will take a few pages to explain the Law. Those who have a Will might be tempted to skip over the section, but, this information is good to know in the event someone in your family dies in Massachusetts without a Will. Once you read this section you will know whether you have a right to inherit his property.

THE FAMILY'S RIGHT TO INHERIT

The Commonwealth of Massachusetts recognizes the right of the family to inherit property left by the ***decedent*** (the person who died); so the Laws of Intestate Succession cover all possible relationships beginning with the surviving spouse. In order for the spouse to inherit property under the Laws of Descent, the state of Massachusetts needs to recognize the union as a valid marriage.

Who Is Your Spouse?

In this era of people challenging the concept of the family unit, those of a philosophical bent may ponder the meaning of marriage. Is it a union of two people in the eyes of God? Is it even a union? Maybe it is just a contract between two people. Regardless of your philosophy, if you die without a Will, the state will distribute your property according to the laws of Massachusetts; and the laws of the Commonwealth determine whether you are married.

SAME SEX MARRIAGES

In 1998, the federal government passed the Defense of Marriage Act, saying that for purposes of federal law, marriage is a legal union between one man and one woman (28 U.S.C. 1738C). However, for purposes of state law, whether you can marry, who you can marry; and how you can marry, are determined by the laws of the state in which you live.

Massachusetts has a unique history on the issue of same sex marriage. In 1999, the Massachusetts Supreme Judicial Court ruled that the City of Boston had the right to define the terms "domestic partners" and their "dependent" for the purpose of extending health benefit coverage. The opposition argued that this was tantamount to legalizing same sex marriages. None-the-less, the Court ruled in favor of the City of Boston (*Connors v. City of Boston*, 430 Mass. 31 (1999), 714 N.E.2d 335).

In November, 2003, the Court took a more aggressive position and said that denying couples of the same sex the right to marry was a violation of their equal rights protection under the Massachusetts Constitution. The Court suspended their ruling for six months in order to give the Legislature time to pass laws enabling people of the same sex to marry in the state of Massachusetts (*Goodridge v. Department of Public Health*, 440 Mass. 309 (2003)).

That dead-line came and went with no action from the legislature. As of the time we went to print in April, 2006, the ruling of the Court still stands and there still is no Massachusetts law that either bans or allows same sex marriages. Couples of the same gender, can and do, obtain licenses to marry in the Commonwealth of Massachusetts.

Because of the Defense of Marriage Act, federal laws do not apply to married couples of the same gender. Many states have passed laws stating that a same sex marriage is not valid in that state, regardless of whether the marriage is valid in any other state.

In Massachusetts, state laws relating to a married couple apply regardless of whether the parties are of the same or opposite gender. But because the Massachusetts legislature has not passed new laws relating to same sex marriage, certain laws relating to a husband and wife may no longer apply. We will call these laws to your attention as they relate to topics covered in this book.

BEING MARRIED IN MASSACHUSETTS

To be married in Massachusetts means that a couple have obtained a *Certificate of Intention* to marry from the Clerk or Registrar of the Court, and then after three days, but not more than 60 days, they solemnized the marriage by a state or religious ceremony (GLM 207:20, 207:28, 207:38). The age of consent remains as it was under English Common Law, namely 12 for a female, 14 for a male, but people under the age of 18 may not marry unless the marriage is authorized by a Probate or District Court (GLM 207:25).

Massachusetts law prohibits the marriage of people:

- ☒ who are currently married to another (GLM 207:4)
- ☒ who are related closer than cousin (GLM 207:1, 207:2)

As of July, 2006, there are is prohibition against incestuous same sex partners. There is no law that prohibits the marriage of a man to his brother, or a woman to her daughter. This is one of those areas that will need to be revised, when and if, the laws relating to same sex marriage are passed by the legislature.

PARTIES RELATED THROUGH MARRIAGE

Massachusetts state specifically prohibits the following unions: a man cannot marry his stepmother; stepdaughter; step-granddaughter, mother-in-law, grandmother-in-law, grandfather's former wife. He cannot marry his grandson's former wife, but there is no prohibition against marrying his son's former wife i.e., his daughter-in-law (GLM 207:1, 207:3, 207:4).

There are similar prohibitions for a woman, with two exceptions — a woman cannot marry her former son-in-law, but she can marry her father-in-law (GLM 207:2).

THE COMMON LAW MARRIAGE

A Common Law marriage is one that has not been solemnized by ceremony. It is more than just living together. The couple must agree to live together as man and wife, and then publicly hold themselves out as being married; i.e., tell friends and family that they are married. Many states no longer recognize a Common Law marriage as being valid, and have passed laws to that effect. Although there is no specific law in Massachusetts that bars a Common Law marriage, courts have ruled that a Common Law marriage entered within the state of Massachusetts is not valid (*Commonwealth v. Munson*, 127 Mass 459). The surviving partner of such a union can inherit property as a beneficiary of the decedent's Will, but cannot inherit under the Massachusetts Laws of Descent and Distribution.

GOING OUT OF STATE WON'T WORK

A resident of Massachusetts who is prohibited from entering into a marriage for any of the above reasons (age, relationship to fiance, etc.) cannot marry in another state just to circumvent Massachusetts Law. If a union is banned in Massachusetts and the couple goes out of state to marry, that union will be considered to be null and void in the Commonwealth (GLM 207:10).

The same rule applies to residents of another state who marry in Massachusetts just to avoid the laws of the state of their residence. Specifically, if a couple who live in another state come to Massachusetts to marry because such union is banned in their home state, the Commonwealth will not consider their union to be a valid marriage (GLM 207:11)

Who Is Your Child?

Medical technology has made important contributions to solving the problem of infertility. There are all sorts of solutions, from hormone therapy, to sperm banks that provide donations anonymously, to frozen sperm or ova to be thawed and used at a later date, to women who become a surrogate or gestational mother. Solving a set of medical problems opened the door to a new set of legal problems. Used to be, the only question was "Who's the father? Now it could well be "Who's the mother?

To answer these questions, the Commonwealth of Massachusetts has laws that establish the parentage of children whose conception was assisted by medical technology. We will examine the law as it relates to the right of the child to inherit property.

CHILD OF ASSISTED CONCEPTION

A child born to parents using any form of assisted conception, has the same right to inherit from his parents as a child conceived the old fashioned way. A child conceived by means of artificial insemination, born to a married woman with the consent of her husband, is the legal child of both parents (GLM 46:4B). If the husband did not know or consent to such assisted conception, he can *petition* (ask) the Court to terminate his parental rights and responsibilities. If the husband is successful, the child will not be able to inherit from the husband, nor from his family.

FROZEN SPERM AND THE AFTERBORN CHILD

Under Massachusetts law a child conceived prior to death and born to the surviving spouse after the death, has the same right to inherit as any other natural child of the decedent (GLM 190:8). But suppose the child was conceived after death. Does that child have the same rights?

That question is becoming more of an issue as couples are freezing sperm, ovum or pre-embryo (fertilized cell) for use at a later date. Often the procedure is done to protect the cell from damage during cancer treatments. If the treatment is unsuccessful, the surviving parent may decide to go ahead with the pregnancy using the frozen reproductive cell. This raises issues of whether the surviving parent has the right to do that without the written consent of the deceased donor; and whether a child born of such procedure is entitled to inherit from the deceased donor.

The issue of inheritance has important consequences, not only on the state level but on the federal level as well. A minor child who lost a parent is entitled to Social Security benefits, but those benefits are based on the state's *Laws of Intestate Succession*. In Massachusetts, those Laws are called the Laws Of Descent and Distribution. Section 216 of the Social Security Act provides "a child's insurance benefits can be paid to a child who could inherit under the State's intestate laws." Specifically, a child cannot receive Social Security benefits, unless the child is entitled to inherit under the state's Laws of Intestate Succession."

The issue was brought before the Massachusetts Supreme Judicial Court in 2002. The case involved twins born to a woman two years after her husband died from leukemia.

The husband had his sperm frozen before starting his cancer treatment. The treatment was not successful and he died within the year. His wife used the sperm to conceive the twins after his death. She applied for Social Security benefits for herself and her twins. The U.S. District Court rejected the claim saying that the children did not qualify for benefits because they could not inherit under Massachusetts Laws of Descent. She appealed, and the District Court asked the Massachusetts Supreme Judicial Court to settle the matter. The Supreme Judicial Court ruled that a child conceived and born after the death of a parent can inherit, provided it is proven that the decedent is the genetic parent and had consented to posthumous conception and to the support of any resulting child (*Woodward v. Commr. of Social Security*, SJC-0840 (Mass. January 2, 2002)).

This being the law in Massachusetts, if you decide to freeze your reproductive cells, it is important that you express, in writing, whether you want your cells used after your death and whether you intend that a child born of the reproductive cell be entitled to inherit your Estate. For those who are married, it is important that your spouse join in the writing and agree to honor your wishes. That written agreement should include a provision about what will be done with the cells in the event of a divorce or the death of either party.

Still another legal issue raised because of modern technology is the question of the rights of the Surrogate mother as opposed to the rights of the biological parent who contracted with the Surrogate to bear his/her child.

THE SURROGATE PARENT

A case brought before the Supreme Judicial Court asked whether an agreement for adoption between a surrogate mother and the genetic father of her child was legally enforceable. The woman agreed to have his child and after the birth arrange for him to adopt the child. Once the child was born she changed her mind and the genetic father sued for adoption of the child. The Court found that the agreement between the surrogate and the genetic father was not enforceable because the agreement for adoption was made before the child was born. Under Massachusetts law (GLM 210:2), an adoption agreement is not valid unless is signed on or after the fourth day following the child's birth (*R.R. v. M.H.*, 426 Mass. 501 (1998), 689 N.E.2d 790).

Under current Massachusetts law, the child of a surrogate mother, is the natural child of the mother. If the mother is married and her husband agreed to the procedure, then he is the legal father (GLM 46:4B). After birth, the surrogate parents can agree to the adoption of the child by the intended parents. Adoption is necessary, regardless of whether either (or both) of the intended parents happen to be the genetic parent of the child.

THE ADOPTED CHILD

An adopted child has the same rights to inherit property from his adoptive parents as does a natural child. Whether the adoptive child can inherit from his natural parents depends on the circumstances of the adoption. If one of the child's parents dies, and the child is later adopted by a stepparent, the child still retains full rights of inheritance from both of his natural parents, and their respective families. But if a Court terminates the rights of his natural parent(s), the right to inherit property from his natural parents, and from their relatives, also terminates (GLM 210:7, 210:8).

THE NON-MARITAL CHILD

A child born out of wedlock has the right to inherit from his/her father and the father's relatives, provided

- ☑ the father acknowledged the child as his own - or -
- ☑ paternity was established by a court of law in this or any other state (GLM 190:7).

If the decedent denied his paternity, it will take a Court procedure to establish (or disprove) paternity. If you want to establish paternity, you need to consult with an attorney experienced in this type of litigation. If DNA tests need to be conducted, and the family plans to cremate the decedent, you may need to have your attorney move quickly to bar cremation until the matter is settled.

NO SHARE FOR NEGLECTFUL FATHER

If a child born out of wedlock dies, and his father did not treat the child as his own or was not determined to be the child's father by a Court, neither the father nor his relatives can inherit anything from the child (GLM 190:6).

Now that we know who is considered to be your spouse and your child in the Commonwealth of Massachusetts, we can examine their right to inherit your property.

Should you die with property titled in your name only, and without a Will, then the state of Massachusetts provides one for you in the form of the Laws of Descent and Distribution. Once your debts, funeral expenses, and the cost of the Probate procedure is paid, whatever is left (your net Probate Estate) is distributed as follows:

SINGLE WITH DESCENDANTS

If you are single and are survived by ***descendants*** (children, grandchildren, great-grandchildren, etc.), your descendants inherit your Probate Estate in equal shares, ***by right of representation*** (GLM 190:1, 191B:1). Representation is one of those legal terms that is best explained through example:

Suppose you are single and are survived by four children, Ann, Barry, Carl, David. If you do not have a valid Will, each of your children will inherit 25% of your net Probate Estate. If Ann dies before you, leaving no descendants, your Probate Estate will be divided equally among your surviving children, i.e., Barry, Carl and David each receive one third share of your Probate Estate.

Suppose instead that only Carl and David survive you. If Ann died leaving one child and Barry died leaving two children, your Probate Estate is divided into 4 equal shares — one for each surviving child and one share for each deceased child who left descendants. Carl and David each inherit their 25% share. The share intended for Ann, namely 25% of your Probate Estate, is given to her child. The share intended for Barry is divided between his two children. Each gets half of the 25% or 12 1/2% of your net Probate Estate.

MARRIED WITH DESCENDANTS

If you are married and have children, your spouse gets half of your Probate Estate and your children inherit the other half, in equal shares, by right of representation.

NO SPOUSE, NO DESCENDANTS

If you have no surviving spouse and no surviving descendants, your Probate Estate goes to your parents equally or to the survivor of them. If neither parent survives you, your Probate Estate goes to your brothers and sisters, equally, by right of representation.

There is no distinction between full blood siblings or half blood siblings. For example, if you have one brother with the same set of parents, and another brother with the same father and a different mother, both brothers inherit an equal amount (GLM 190:4).

If you are not survived by a sibling, or any of their descendants (nephews, nieces, great nieces or nephews, etc.), your Estate goes to your nearest living relative, i.e. your *next of kin* (GLM 190:3).

SPOUSE, NO DESCENDANTS, BUT RELATIVES

If you have no descendants, but you are survived by a spouse and *kindred* (blood relatives), your spouse gets the first $200,000 of your Probate Estate and half of anything over that value. Your next of kin inherit the other half in the same manner as just described, i.e. your parents share the other half. If only one parent is alive, that parent gets the entire inheritance. If no parent survives you, half of your Probate Estate is inherited by your brothers and sisters, in equal shares, by right of representation.

THE COMMONWEALTH: HEIR OF LAST RESORT

In Massachusetts, property that is either unclaimed or abandoned, goes to the state, so if you die without a Will and you have absolutely no next of kin, or if you have a Will but no beneficiary can be found, then the Commonwealth of Massachusetts "inherits" your Probate Estate. The only exception is for a veteran who dies while a member of the Soldier's Home in Massachusetts. In that cases the inheritance goes to the legacy fund or legacy account of the Soldier's Home (GLM 190:3).

IT ISN'T ALL THAT SIMPLE

The explanation in this book of the Massachusetts Laws of Descent and Distribution is abridged. We gave examples up to niece and nephew. Beyond that things get complicated. GLM 190:3 reads:

> If he leaves no issue, and no father, mother, brother or sister and no issue of any deceased brother or sister, then to his next of kin in equal degree; but if there are two or more collateral kindred in equal degree claiming through different ancestors, those claiming through the nearest ancestor shall be preferred to those claiming through an ancestor more remote.

You might think you could puzzle this out if only you knew what a "degree" means. The next section 190:4 reads:

> Degrees of kindred shall be computed according to the rules of the civil law.

Now you are probably thinking "Well I guess lawyers understand all this." But to a lawyer it just means that if someone dies without a Will and several distant heirs all make claim to the property, he is going to spend a lot of time doing research in the law library.

CALL YOUR LEGISLATOR

The Massachusetts Laws of Descent have a long history spanning hundreds of years. It was the job of the lawyer to puzzle out the meaning of the statute and then explain that meaning to his client. But now we are in the age of information. The laws that we must follow (both state and federal) are on the Internet. Citizens can easily access state and federal statute and read the laws for themselves. But what good is easy access to the law if the statutes are written in a manner that defies comprehension by the average citizen?

The Massachusetts Laws of Descent are unnecessarily complex. Many other states have written or revised their Laws of Descent so that the average citizen can read and understand the law. It is time to contact your legislator and demand that the Massachusetts Laws of Descent be revised so that a resident can understand exactly how his property will be distributed if he neglects to write a Will, or if, for some reason, the Court determines that the Will he left is not valid.

Meanwhile, don't be a victim of the system. You don't need to let the Commonwealth decide who and how much goes to your family members. You don't need to take the chance of having your property go to someone you may not even know or like. To avoid these problems., all you need to do is prepare a Will according to Massachusetts law and your property will be inherited the way <u>you</u> want.

See Chapter 4 for a discussion of how to prepare a Massachusetts Will.

THE COST OF PROBATE

Holding property in your name only gives you maximum control and protection during your lifetime. If you do not like the way your property will be distributed should you die without a Will, then you can control who inherits your property by preparing a Will. But there is still the question of what it will cost to transfer your Estate to your beneficiaries. In all probability, a Probate procedure will be necessary. How much of your Estate will need to be spent to Probate your Estate?

THE SMALL ESTATE

There is no need to be concerned about the cost of Probate, if you own a car (whatever the value) and other personal property in your name only worth no more than $15,000. Your property can be transferred to the person you name to serve as Executor of your Will, or if no Will, whoever volunteers to settle your Estate by paying bills, and then distributing whatever remains to the proper beneficiary. This ***Informal Administration*** is allowed when:

- ⇨ the Probate Estate consists of a car and other personal property worth no more than $15,000 and
- ⇨ the decedent was a resident of Massachusetts, and
- ⇨ at least 30 days passed since the date of death, and
- ⇨ no one has started a Probate procedure.

Forms to complete the Informal Administration can be obtained at the Probate Court in the county of the decedent's residence. Whoever volunteers for the job of settling the Estate is required to send a copy of the death certificate and completed Probate form, by certified mail, to the DIVISION OF MEDICAL ASSISTANCE (GLM 195:16, 195:16A).

The Division has the right to file a claim for reimbursement of monies paid by the state for Medical Assistance given to the decedent. We will discuss the state's right to recover funds in Chapter 11.

Once the forms are properly completed, notice is sent, and the filing fee paid, the *Registry of Probate* will provide documents giving the Volunteer authority to take possession of the property (MCL 195:16, 195:16A).

Things are not so simple if you leave real property or personal property in excess of $15,000, in your name only. There will need to be a full Probate procedure in order to transfer your Probate Estate to the proper beneficiary.

The root of the word Probate is "to prove." It refers to the first job of the Probate Court, that is, to examine proof of whether the decedent left a valid Will. The second job of the Probate Court is to appoint someone to settle the Estate. It will be his job to pay outstanding bills and then distribute whatever is left to the proper beneficiary.

If you leave a valid Will naming someone to be Executor of your Estate, the Court will appoint that person for the job and issue *Letters Testamentary* giving him authority to administer the Estate. If you die without a valid Will, the Probate Court will appoint someone to be the *Administrator* of your Estate and issue *Letters of Administration.* Massachusetts Courts usually refer to these Letters as "certified" copies of Appointment.

For simplicity, we will refer to the person appointed by the Court to settle the decedent's Estate as the ***Personal Representative.***

The full Probate procedure is involved and time consuming; not to mention, expensive. The Probate procedure takes at least a year, and can last longer, if the Estate is large, or some dispute arises. Someone must be appointed by the Court to serve as Personal Representative. Whoever is named as Executor of the Will gets the job. Massachusetts statute gives an order of priority for appointing a Personal Representative for those who die without a Will, with the spouse having top priority (GLM 193:1).

Your Personal Representative must take possession of your Probate Estate. He must prepare an inventory of the Estate and where necessary, employ an appraiser to evaluate the property (GLM 195:6). If the Personal Representative determines that there is not enough money to settle the Estate, he will report that fact to the Court. The Court may decide to appoint two or more *Commissioners* whose job it will be to examine all of the *claims* (demands for payment) and present a list of the amounts owed to the Court. The Commissioners will set a time and place to receive all claims against the Estate. Notice will be sent to all known creditors to submit their claims to the Commissioners. If the Court does not appoint any Commissioner, the Court will instruct the Personal Representative to give notice to the creditors of the time and place where their claims will be examined (GLM 198:2, 198:3, 198:4, 198:5).

It is the responsibility of the Personal Representative to see that the Probate procedure is conducted properly. If the Personal Representative makes a mistake then he may be responsible to pay for that mistake. For example, if he pays a debt that did not need to be paid — or if he transfers property to the beneficiaries too quickly and there were still taxes due on the Estate, he may be personally responsible to pay for such error (GLM 195:17).

To avoid mistakes, the Personal Representative needs to employ an attorney to guide him through the process. It then becomes the attorney's job to see to it that the Estate is administered according to Massachusetts law and without any personal liability to the Personal Representative. Attorney's fees are a proper charge to the Probate Estate.

PERSONAL REPRESENTATIVE'S FEES

The Personal Representative is entitled to reasonable compensation for his efforts. Compensation for the Personal Representative is subject to the Court's approval. (GLM 206:16).

The Massachusetts legislature has not set guidelines for what fees are considered to be reasonable, but Massachusetts Courts have ruled that when awarding fees, the Probate Court must take all of the facts into consideration including:

- ⇨ the size of the Estate
- ⇨ the legal questions involved
- ⇨ the time required to complete the work
- ⇨ the Personal Representative's skill and ability
- ⇨ the amount usually paid for similar work
- ⇨ the results accomplished

(*McMahon v. Krapf*, 323 Mass. 118, 80 N.E.2d 314 (1948).

Attorney's fees are also subject to the Court's approval. The Court will use much the same factors as above described to determine what represents a reasonable fee for the attorney (GLM 215:39A).

The Personal Representative and attorney's fees are significant charges to the Probate Estate; but they are not the only charges against the Estate. A Probate proceeding can incur some or all of the following expenses:

- *$$* Court filing fees
- *$$* The cost of a bond that the Court may order for the protection of your Probate Estate
- *$$* The cost of notifying your creditors which may include publishing notice, or mailing notice to them by registered or certified mail
- *$$* The cost of an appraisal
- *$$* Accounting fees to prepare an inventory, and account for monies spent during Probate
- *$$* The cost of transferring property to the proper beneficiary; i.e., recording fees, broker fees to sell securities or real estate.

Once the above costs, Personal Representative fees, attorney fees, taxes and all valid claims are paid, the Personal Representative will distribute whatever is left to the proper beneficiary and then close the Estate.

You may be thinking that Probate is a good thing to avoid. Why should your Personal Representative go through all that effort to settle your Estate? Why should your beneficiaries wait months or maybe years, and pay all these fees to inherit your Estate?

There are ways to arrange your Estate so that your beneficiaries can immediately inherit your Estate without incurring unnecessary costs. In the next two chapters we will examine different methods that can be used to achieve this goal.

Is Probate Necessary? 2

Many people think that only wealthy people need to make plans to avoid Probate, yet each year, beneficiaries of relatively modest estates, spend thousands of dollars to settle an Estate. A bit of Estate Planning could have eliminated most, if not all, of the cost (and hassle) suffered by those families.

It is not difficult to arrange your finances to eliminate the need for Probate if you have a small Estate and only one or two beneficiaries. All you need do is title your property so that it automatically goes to your beneficiaries. There are many ways to arrange your finances to achieve this result. The most common method is to hold property jointly with another. Such an arrangement is the Estate Plan of choice for most married couples. Husband and wife often hold all of their property jointly, so that the surviving spouse has complete and immediate access to their property without any need for Probate.

Holding property jointly may not be the most desirable method for the single person, or for the surviving spouse who is now single. There are other ways to ensure that your property is inherited quickly and without cost to your heirs. In this chapter we explore the pros and cons of different methods of holding property so that it can be transferred without the need for Probate.

PROPERTY OWNED JOINTLY

Bank accounts, securities, motor vehicles, real property can all be owned by two or more people. If one of the owners dies, the survivor(s) continue to own their share of the property. Who owns the share belonging to the decedent depends on Massachusetts law and how ownership of the property was set up.

THE JOINT BANK ACCOUNT

When a bank account is opened in two or more names, the owners of the account sign an agreement with the bank stating who is to have access to the account during the lifetime of the account owners; i.e. whether each owner has full authority to make a withdrawal, or whether two signatures are required. In Massachusetts, unless the agreement with the bank states differently, there is a ***right of survivorship***, meaning that the survivor owns the account and is free to withdraw all of the money (GLM 167D:5). However, if Estate Taxes are due on the transfer, the surviving owner is responsible to pay those taxes. See Chapter 3 for a discussion of Estate Taxes.

The benefit of a joint account is that the surviving joint owner inherits the money in the account immediately and without the need for Probate; but, as with any Estate Plan, convenience needs to be measured against potential problems. For example, suppose all you own is a bank account and you want whatever you have in this account to go to your child should you die. You might think that a simple solution is to make your child joint owner of the account, but first consider risks associated with a joint account.

⌧ OVERREACHING

Making your child a joint owner of the account gives the child free access to the account. Monies may be withdrawn without your knowledge or authorization. You may be thinking that couldn't happen because you would immediately know of the withdrawal, and you could force the child to return the money. That may be true when you are healthy and alert. But in this ever aging society, it is likely that you will live to an advanced age and not be as aware as you are today. And if you have two children and decided to hold your account jointly with them, then there may be a problem with how the funds are distributed should you die.

That was the case with Amanda. All she had when her husband died, was a bank account worth $50,000. She wanted to be sure that the money would go to her two sons, Robert and Leon, without the need for Probate. She went to the bank with her two sons and opened a new survivorship account with all three names on the account as joint owners.

Several years passed without incident. As Amanda aged, her health began to fail, and she became more and more dependent on Robert. She needed his assistance to take her to the doctor, to do her shopping, and of course take care of her finances. Robert had a wife and two children, so it was hard for him to care for his family and his mother as well. Leon was single, yet he never seemed to have the time to help care for his mother. And Robert resented that.

Finally, Amanda died.

After the funeral, Leon asked Robert about the bank account "Didn't Mom have a joint account in our names?"

“Yeah, but I closed it out. There was only a few thousand left, and I used it for her funeral.”

Leon thought it strange that all of the money was gone, so he went to the bank and asked to see the record of withdrawals. He found that over the last two years Robert had written several large checks to himself. There was only $7,000 left in the account when Robert closed it out, within a week of her death.

Leon fumed for several weeks before he brought up the subject. Robert’s face flushed when Leon asked about the money. Leon did not know if it was from anger or embarrassment. He soon learned that it was both when Robert asked “Where were you for the past two years? You never once helped. Did you know she became incontinent at the end? Who cleaned up? Not you. She blessed me every day. She often said she would have been dead long ago if it wasn’t for me. She wanted me to have that money!”

“Mom never said anything to me about wanting you to have the money. She never asked for my help and neither did you. It isn’t right for you to throw this up to me now.”

The boys never spoke of the money again. But then there were few times that they ever spoke to each other after that.

Overreaching isn’t the only problem with a joint account, there is also the problem of liability.

☒ POTENTIAL LIABILITY

If you hold a bank account jointly with your adult child and that child is sued or gets a divorce, then the child may need to disclose his ownership of the joint account. In such a case, you may find yourself spending money to prove that the account was established for convenience only and that all of the money in that account really belongs to you.

Because of these inherent problems, you might want to hold the funds so that your beneficiary does not have access to the monies unless you die while the account is open. You can do so by opening a ***Beneficiary Account***.

THE BENEFICIARY ACCOUNT

As explained, the terms of a bank account are established when a bank account is opened. Your agreement gives directions about who can access your account during your lifetime, but it can also give directions about what to do with the account should you die. If you hold the account in your name only and do not give any such directions, then should you die while the account is open, the monies in your account will become part of your Probate Estate and will be distributed in the same way as any other item that you hold in your name only.

One way to avoid Probate of the account, yet retain full control of the account during your lifetime, is to name one or more persons to be the beneficiary of your account. There are two forms of beneficiary account. Your contract with the bank can direct your bank or credit union to hold your account ***In Trust For*** ("ITF") a beneficiary that you name (GLM 171:40, 167D:6).

THE IN TRUST FOR ("ITF") ACCOUNT

Under Massachusetts law, unless your contract with the bank or credit union says differently:

⇨ The beneficiary does not have access to the account during your lifetime.

⇨ You, as the owner of the account, have complete control over the account. You can add to it or close it or change beneficiaries without asking anyone's permission to do so (GLM 167D:6, 171:40).

THE PAY ON DEATH ("POD") ACCOUNT

Massachusetts statute does not provide for an In Trust For account to be held for the benefit of more than one person. It may be that you wish to hold an account for the benefit of two or more beneficiaries. Your bank may offer other plans such as a ***Pay On Death*** ("POD") account.

For example, a POD account can be set up as:
Eldon Connors POD Betty Connors and Fred Conners, JTWRS

This is short-hand for:
"Eldon Connors Pay On Death to Betty Connors and Fred Conners as Joint Tenants With Right of Survivorship."

The agreement with the bank will say that Eldon is the owner of the account. On his death, the money is to go to Betty and Fred. If either of the beneficiaries of the account should die before Eldon, the account will go to the surviving beneficiary.

THE TRANSFER ON DEATH SECURITY

The Massachusetts law for securities is similar to the statute for bank accounts. You can hold the security in beneficiary form by instructing the holder of the security to Pay On Death or to TRANSFER ON DEATH ("TOD") to a named beneficiary (GLM 201E:106, 201E:401).

As with the Pay On Death account, the Transfer On Death designation has no effect on the ownership of the security until the owner of the security dies. The security can be held jointly with another with instructions that once both owners of the security die, the security is to be transferred to a named beneficiary. For example, suppose a security or a brokerage account is titled: TANYA BEDDIE TOD JEB BEDDIE

Jeb does not have any right to the account while Tanya is alive. Once Tanya dies, all Jeb need do is produce a certified copy of the death certificate and the security or brokerage account will be transferred to him. If Jeb dies before Tanya, and Tanya makes no other provision for transfer to a beneficiary, the security will becomes part of Tanya's Estate (GLM 201E:107, 201E:201).

You can use these Beneficiary Accounts (*In Trust For, Pay On Death, Transfer On Death)* to transfer your bank accounts and securities to your beneficiaries without the need for Probate. More importantly, a Beneficiary Account affords you maximum control and protection of those funds during your lifetime.

CAUTION NO CREDITOR PROTECTION

Property held in beneficiary form, i.e. "In Trust For" or in a POD or TOD account, does not belong to the beneficiary until the death of the owner of the account, and maybe not even then, if there is not enough money to pay for the monies owed by the decedent. Creditors of the owner of the account can demand that the monies in the account be used to pay claims against the decedent's Estate. If the Court orders that an allowance be given to the surviving spouse or minor children for their maintenance during the Probate procedure, and there is not enough money in the Probate Estate to pay for that allowance, then securities with a TOD designation can be used to pay the allowance.

In order to use the funds in the TOD account, the decedent's creditor (or surviving spouse or child) needs to make a written demand to the Personal Representative of the decedent's Estate. The Personal Representative must, within one year from the date of death, seek a Court order requiring the TOD account be used to pay for the debt or the allowance (GLM 196:2, 201E:302, 201E:402). The beneficiary of the decedent's account can take possession of the property, but would be wise not to spend the inheritance until the year has passed or until the beneficiary is sure that the Personal Representative does not need the money to settle the decedent's Estate.

If you are setting up a beneficiary account, and creditor protection is of concern to you, the joint account might be a better way to go. As we will see in Chapter 5, if an account is owned *jointly with right of survivorship*, the property belongs to the surviving owner immediately upon death. Creditors of the deceased joint owner cannot demand money from the account.

REAL PROPERTY OWNED JOINTLY

If you own real property together with another, who owns the property upon your death depends on how the current owner is identified on the face of the deed. The top paragraph of the deed should identify the person who transferred the property to you. That party is called the ***Grantor***. The person to whom the property was transferred is called the ***Grantee***. The deed might read something like:

> ROBERT TRAYNOR, a single man,
> of Essex County, Massachusetts,
> for consideration of $200,000, paid
> grants to JAMES CODY, a married man
> and JAMES CODY, JR. a single man,
> as **JOINT TENANTS**,
> of Suffolk County, Massachusetts,
> with warranty covenants . . .
> the land in Suffolk County
> with legal description
> . . .

In Massachusetts, property held as JOINT TENANTS means that the Grantees have rights of survivorship (GLM 184:7). Should either Alfred or Robert die, the survivor will own the property 100%. Nothing need be done to establish that ownership, but the name of the deceased joint owner remains on the deed. See page 38 for an explanation of what documents can be recorded so that anyone who examines the title to the property will know that the survivor is now the sole owner of the property.

DEED HELD AS TENANTS IN COMMON

There are no rights of survivorship if the Grantees of a deed are identified as ***Tenants In Common***. Each person owns his own share of the property. Unless the deed indicates differently, they each own an equal share. If one owner dies, his share will go to the beneficiary of his Will. If he died without a Will, the Laws of Descent and Distribution determine who inherits his share. A Probate procedure will be necessary in order to transfer the decedent's share of a Tenancy In Common to the new owner.

NO SURVIVORSHIP UNLESS STATED IN THE DEED

A deed to two or more people is a Tenancy In Common unless the deed specifically indicates a joint tenancy. For example, there are rights of survivorship if the Grantees are identified as:

"Harold Krol **jointly** with Sylvia Rodrigues"

or

"Harold Krol and Sylvia Rodrigues in **Joint Tenancy**"

or

"Harold Krol and Sylvia Rodrigues **or the Survivor**."

But a deed to "Harold Krol and Sylvia Rodrigues" without any word of survivorship, is a Tenancy In Common (GLM 184:7).

Best to consult with an attorney if there is any question in your mind about how to interpret the deed.

DEED OWNED BY HUSBAND AND WIFE

If a married couple hold property as follows:

TODD AMES AND SUSAN AMES, TENANTS BY THE ENTIRETY

when one spouse dies, and providing they are married at the time of death, the surviving spouse owns the property 100%. If the deed does not say TENANTS BY THE ENTIRETY, or does not say that they are JOINT TENANTS, they own the property as TENANTS IN COMMON (GLM 184:7).

DEEDS PRIOR TO FEBRUARY 11, 1980

Under the English Common Law, a Tenancy by the Entirety was a Joint Tenancy modified by the Common Law theory that a husband and wife are one. With a joint tenancy each partner owns their own share of the property until death, when the surviving owner owns it 100%. With a Tenancy by the Entirety, each owns 100% of the property both before and after death. In 1980, the Massachusetts legislature passed a law stating that if a married couple own real property as Tenants By the Entirety then:

- ⇨ both husband and wife are equally entitled to the income and possession of the property;
- ⇨ if one spouse owes money and the property is the primary residence of the non-debtor spouse, the creditor cannot take the house as payment for the debt; however, both are equally responsible to pay for necessities furnished to either spouse or to a member of their family (GLM 209:1).

Massachusetts Courts ruled that the 1980 law created a new form of Tenancy By The Entirety, however, both the new and old form of Tenancy By The Entirety have rights of survivorship. If a Tenancy By The Entirety was recorded before February 11, 1980, no new deed need be recorded unless the couple wish to have the property changed to the new form of Tenancy By The Entirety (GLM 209:1A).

DEED WITH A LIFE ESTATE

A ***Life Estate*** interest in real property means that the person who owns the Life Estate has the right to live in that property until he/she dies. You can identify a Life Estate interest by examining the face of the deed. If somewhere on the face of the deed you see the phrase RESERVING A LIFE ESTATE, the Grantee cannot take possession of the property until the owner of the Life Estate dies. For example, suppose the granting paragraph of the deed reads:

> ROSE CAVALLO, a single woman,
> of Norfolk County, Massechusetts . . .
> for $10 and other good and valuable consideration
> paid by SALVATORE CAVALLO, JR. a married man
> of Norfolk County, Massachusetts,
> with warranty covenants the land in
> . . .
> RESERVING A LIFE ESTATE TO ROSE CAVALLO
> . . .

Rose is the owner of the Life Estate. Salvatore is the owner of the ***Remainder Interest***. Rose has the right to occupy the premises during her lifetime or to rent it out and receive the income from the property. During Rose's lifetime, Salvatore has no right to the possession of, or the income from, the property. Once Rose dies, Salvatore will own the property and is free to take possession of the property and to lease, sell or transfer it, as he sees fit.

If you are an owner of the Life Estate interest, upon your death, no Probate procedure will be necessary to transfer the property to the owner of the Remainder Interest.

AN INVISIBLE LIFE ESTATE

In Massachusetts, your surviving spouse has a Life Estate in real property that you own as an *Estate Of Homestead.* Your surviving spouse can continue to live in that home until she remarries or dies. If you are survived by a minor child and no spouse, your child can live in the home until the child reaches the age of 18 (GLM 188:1, 188:4).

You can create an Estate of Homestead in one of two ways. You can have the deed that transfers the property to you identify the property as being Homestead property, or you can have a *Declaration of Homestead* recorded with the *Registry of Deeds*. A mobile home can be held as an Estate of Homestead by filing a Declaration of Homestead with the city or town Clerk's office in the city or town where the mobile home is located (GLM 188:2).

DOWER RIGHTS

In addition to the Life Estate in your Estate of Homestead, your surviving spouse has rights of ***Dower***. Dower rights evolved from the English Common Law. The corresponding rights for husbands are known as *Curtesy* rights. In Massachusetts, both Dower and Curtesy rights are the same, namely a one-third Life Estate interest in real property owned by the deceased spouse — not including "wild land," i.e., undeveloped land that is not used with a farm or residence (GLM 189:1, 189:3). If you are married and you own real property that is not also in your spouse's name, then unless your spouse signs a document giving up Dower rights, should you die, your spouse will be entitled to claim a *Tenancy In Dower* in your property regardless of whether you own the land in your name only, or jointly with another, or as a Tenant In Common, and regardless of whether your Will gives that property to someone who is not your spouse.

Probate will not be necessary if you own property in Massachusetts:

- ➪ as Joint Tenants - or -
- ➪ as Tenants By The Entirety - or -
- ➪ as the owner of a Life Estate.

As explained, in each of these cases, upon your death, the surviving owner will own the property 100%, however your name remains on the deed. The Massachusetts Registry of Vital Records is responsible to issue the death certificate, but not to publish it or make it part of the public record. If the surviving owner wishes to transfer the property, he will need to produce a certified copy of the death certificate at closing.

To make the death known to the general public the surviving owner can have his attorney prepare and record a document called a ***Deceased Joint Tenancy Affidavit***. An *Affidavit* is a written statement sworn to before a Notary Public. The Deceased Joint Tenancy Affidavit identifies the property, giving the property address, the Permanent Real Estate Index Number, and the full legal description of the property. A certified copy of the death certificate is attached to the Affidavit. Once the Affidavit is recorded with the Registry of Deeds in the county where the property is located, anyone who examines the title to the property will learn of the death and know who now owns the property (GLM 183:5A).

WHEN PROBATE IS NECESSARY

If you own Massachusetts property in your name only, or as a Tenant In Common, it will take a Probate procedure to transfer property to your intended beneficiary. As explained in Chapter 1, the type of Probate procedure depends on the size of your Estate.

OUT OF STATE PROPERTY

This chapter relates only to real property you own in the Commonwealth of Massachusetts. If you own property in another state or country, the laws of that state or country determine who has the right to inherit your property.

RIGHT OF SURVIVORSHIP

Whether or not there is a right of survivorship depends on the laws of that state. Some states require that the deed specifically state that there is a right of survivorship. In such states, a deed held as Joint Tenants (and no stated right of survivorship) is the same as a Tenancy In Common. Other states are like Massachusetts, in that a deed that identifies the owners as Joint Tenants has a right of survivorship even though the deed may not specify such right. If you own out of state property jointly with another, it is important that you check with an attorney in that state to be sure that your share of the property will go to the person of your choice.

SPOUSAL RIGHTS

Many states have laws similar to Massachusetts that give a surviving spouse rights in real property owned by a decedent spouse. If you are married and own property in another state, it may be that your spouse has rights in that property even though only your name appears on the deed. That may be the case in Community Property states (Arizona, California, Idaho, Louisiana, Nevada, New Mexico, Texas, Washington and Wisconsin). In other states, there may be Dower or statutory rights. In the next chapter, we will discuss the rights of a surviving spouse in real property located in Massachusetts. If you are married, and own property in another state, you need to determine the rights of your spouse in that state as well.

Still another concern is whether a Probate procedure will be necessary to transfer out of state property that you own to your beneficiary. Each state is in charge of the way real property located in that state is transferred. Most state laws are similar to Massachusetts, namely, property with a right of survivorship or property in which you hold a Life Estate interest are transferred without the need for Probate. Property you own as a Tenant In Common or in your name only may require a Probate procedure in order to transfer the property to your beneficiary.

If you own property in your name only in this state and in another state, upon your death it may be necessary to have a Probate proceeding in Massachusetts, and an *ancillary* (secondary) Administraton in the state where the property is located. This can double the cost of Probate.

Still another problem with out of state property is the matter of taxes. Some states have an inheritance or transfer tax. Estate and Inheritance Taxes may be due in the state where the property is located as well as in Massachusetts. It may be necessary to file a tax return in two states. In addition to increased taxes, this can significantly increase the cost of accounting fees.

If you own property in another state, it is important to consult with an attorney to learn the answers to all of these questions, namely:

Who will inherit my property under the laws of the state where it is located?

Will a Probate procedure be necessary to transfer that property to my beneficiaries?

What taxes will need to be paid in that state?

If you find that Probate will be necessary to transfer real property that you own in Massachusetts or elsewhere, you may decide that the cost of Probate is too expensive. You may be tempted to go for the quick fix of having the deed to the property changed so that you are joint owners with the intended beneficiary of the property; or you may decide to transfer the property to your intended beneficiary and keep a Life Estate for yourself.

This will avoid Probate, but it may not be the best Estate Plan because you will not have maximum control over the property during your lifetime. If you hold real property as a Joint Tenant or as a Life Tenant, you will not be able to sell that property during your lifetime without getting permission from your beneficiary. And if the beneficiary gives permission and the property is sold, the beneficiary will have the legal right to share in the proceeds of the sale.

You may be thinking "I can make my son joint owner of my home and avoid any need for Probate. I trust him to do what I want with the property. If I decide to sell, I know he won't ask for any part of the proceeds regardless of his legal right to those funds."

And all that may be true, but it may cost you more in taxes to sell your property than if you kept the property in your name only.

Under today's law, you can sell your home without paying a Capital Gains Tax, provided you lived there for 2 of the prior 5 years and the Capital Gains on the sale is not greater than $250,000 ($500,000 if married). If you sell your home after making the Life Estate transfer (or making your child a Joint Tenant), then unless your child occupies the home as his primary residence, his share of the property is subject to a Capital Gains Tax.

If your son does not take his share of the proceeds, then why should he pay any Capital Gains Tax?

In such case, you'll be the one to pay the tax on your son's share of the proceeds.

Is there a better way to avoid Probate?

Maybe. Read on.

How To Avoid Probate 3

TRUE OR FALSE?

( ) If you have a Will, then Probate will be necessary.

( ) Probate will be necessary if you don't have a Will.

( ) Probate is necessary if you own property that is worth more than $15,000.

If you answered false to all of the above, you are either a lawyer, or you carefully read the last chapter.

All of these sentences are false because all of your property may pass to your beneficiaries automatically, without the need for Probate, such as property held jointly or in a Pay On Death account. The point we were trying to make is:

> Whether Probate is necessary has nothing to do with whether there is a Will, or even how much money is involved. The determining factor is how the property is titled (owned).

There are three basic ways to title property:

- in your name only
- jointly with another
- in trust for another

Chapter 1 examined the pros and cons of holding property in your name only, with the biggest "con" being that Probate may be necessary.

In Chapter 2 we noted that holding property jointly with another solved the Probate problem, but at the sacrifice of the control and protection offered by keeping property in your name only. In this Chapter we examine another option which may be the solution to these problems, namely the REVOCABLE LIVING TRUST (also known as an *Inter Vivos Trust*).

A Revocable Living Trust is designed to care for your property during your lifetime and then to distribute your property once you die without the need for Probate. You may have been encouraged to set up such a Trust by your financial planner, attorney, or accountant. Even people of modest means are being encouraged to use a Trust as the basis of their Estate Plan. But Trusts also have their benefits and drawbacks. Before getting into that, let's first discuss what a Trust is and how it works.

To create a ***Revocable Living Trust***, an attorney prepares a Trust Agreement in accordance with the client's needs and desires. The "Agreement" refers to the fact that the person creating the Trust (the *Settlor* or *Trustor)* is contracting with someone to be the ***Trustee*** (manager) of property placed in the Trust. By signing the Trust Agreement, the Trustee agrees to manage the Trust property according to the directions given in the Trust Agreement.

If the Settlor places property into the Trust, he is also referred to as the *Grantor*. We will refer to the Revocable Living Trust as the "Living Trust" or just the "Trust" and the person who sets up and funds the Trust as the "Settlor." Usually the Settlor appoints himself as initial Trustee so that he is in total control of property that he places into the Trust. In such case he signs the Trust Agreement as the Settlor and also as the Trustee who agrees to follow the terms of the Trust Agreement. The Trust Agreement also appoints a ***Successor Trustee*** to take over the management of the Trust property should the initial Trustee resign, become disabled or die.

Once the Trust document is properly signed, the Settlor can transfer property into the Trust. The Settlor does this by changing the name on the account from his individual name to his name as Trustee. For example, if Elaine Richards sets up a Trust naming herself as Trustee, and she wants to put her bank account into the Trust, all she need do is instruct the bank to change the name on the account from Elaine Richards to:

ELAINE RICHARDS, TRUSTEE OF THE ELAINE RICHARDS
REVOCABLE LIVING TRUST
UNDER AGREEMENT DATED April 12, 2006.

If Elaine wants to put real property that she owns into the Trust, she can have her attorney or a title insurance company prepare and record a new deed with the owner of the property identified in the same manner, i.e.

ELAINE RICHARDS, TRUSTEE OF THE ELAINE RICHARDS
REVOCABLE LIVING TRUST
UNDER AGREEMENT DATED April 12, 2006.

The Trust Agreement states how property placed into the Trust is to be managed during Elaine's lifetime. Elaine, as Trustee, controls the Trust property. For example, monies she keeps in a Trust bank account can be withdrawn or added to in the same manner as if the account were in her name only.

Because the Trust is revocable, Elaine can cancel the Trust and have the Trust property put back into her own name. If she does not revoke the Trust during her lifetime, once she dies the Trust becomes irrevocable. Her Successor Trustee is required to follow the terms of the Trust Agreement as it is written. If the Trust says to give the Trust property to certain beneficiaries, the Successor Trustee will do so; and in most cases without the need for Probate.

If the Trust directs the Successor Trustee to continue to hold property in Trust and use the money to take care of a member of Elaine's family, the Successor Trustee will use the Trust funds to care for the family member in the manner described in the Trust Agreement.

A Living Trust has many good features.

☆ AVOID PROBATE

As discussed in Chapter 1, Probate can be time consuming and expensive. Both the Personal Representative and his attorney are entitled to payment for their services. These fees can be significant. It may be necessary to hire accountants and appraisers, as well. If you have property in two states, then two Probate procedures may be necessary (one in each state) and that could have the effect of doubling the cost of Probate. If the Trust is properly drafted and your property placed into the Trust, there should be no need for Probate. Upon your death, your Successor Trustee can transfer property, in this or any other state, to the beneficiary of your Trust.

☆ AVOID A CHALLENGE TO YOUR ESTATE PLAN

A Trust operates much like a Will because it provides for the distribution of your Estate when you die. Unlike a Will, it is not subject to Probate, so no Court is charged with the duty of "proving" that your Trust is valid. Your Successor Trustee can distribute your property as you direct, without asking anyone's permission to do so, and without giving the Court or any outside party an opportunity to examine the document. This does not mean that your Estate Plan cannot be challenged; but if the Trust is drafted according to Massachusetts law, and not with the intent of ripping off your creditors, or cutting off your spouse's right to inherit, it will be very difficult for anyone to challenge the document.

☆ PRIVACY

Your Trust is a private document. No one but your Successor Trustee and your beneficiaries need ever read it. When opening a bank account in the name of the Trust, the bank might ask for a copy of the Trust Agreement, but all they need is basic information about the Trust such as the date of execution of the Trust; the Trust tax identification number; the identity of the Settlor, the current Trustee, the identity of Successor Trustee and the beneficiaries of the Trust, etc. You attorney can prepare a *Certificate of Trust* to give to the bank that contains this basic information.

If you have a Will, once it is admitted to Probate it becomes part of the court records. Anyone can examine the court records, read your Will and see who you did (or did not) provide for. Other Probate documents such as the inventory of your Probate Estate, creditor's claims, etc. are also open to public scrutiny. In some states, court records are now available on the Internet!

LEASE SAFE DEPOSIT BOX AS TRUSTEE

Another privacy issue is what happens to the contents of your safe deposit box, should you become disabled or die. If you hold a safe deposit box in your name only, once the bank (or other safe deposit box lessor) learns of your death, access to the box is restricted. It may take a Probate procedure for your family to gain access to the box.

By leasing the safe deposit box in your capacity as Trustee, you can avoid the need for Probate, just to examine the contents of the box. You can instruct the bank that upon your death or disability, your Successor Trustee has full authority to enter the box and remove any and all of the items from that box.

☆ CARE FOR FAMILY MEMBER

You can make provision in your Trust to care for a minor child or family member after you die. If your family member is immature or a born spender, and you are concerned that he may spend, within months, what it took you a lifetime to earn, you can have your attorney prepare a Trust that will spread the inheritance over an extended period of time. Your Trust can direct the Trustee to give a certain amount of money every 5 or 10 years; for example you can direct the Trustee to give part of the gift when the beneficiary reaches 25, another amount when he reaches 35, and then 45, etc.

If your beneficiary has a creditor problem, you can set up a ***Spendthrift Trust***. You can direct your Successor Trustee to use the Trust funds for your beneficiary's health care, education, and living expenses, and nothing else. With a properly drafted Spendthrift Trust provision the Trust funds should be protected from the claims of the creditors of the beneficiary. An important exception is money owed by the beneficiary for alimony or child support. A Massachusetts court ruled that a beneficiary of a Trust who is entitled to receive income from the Trust must make support payments as ordered by the Court. If the beneficiary has no other source of income, the Trustee will need to use the income and/or principal from the Trust to make those payments (*Cooper v. Cooper*, 680 N.E. 2nd 1173 (Mass.1997)).

NO CREDITOR PROTECTION FOR SETTLOR

Although you can set up a Spendthrift Trust for the benefit of a family member, you cannot set one up for yourself. Property you place in your Revocable Living Trust is freely accessible to you. It is likewise accessible to your creditors both before and after your death. If you die owing money, your Personal Representative can request that Trust funds be used to pay for those debts. If no Probate procedure is necessary, your creditor can demand payment from your Successor Trustee, provided the demand is made within one year from the date of your death (GLM 197:9).

☆☆ AVOID GUARDIANSHIP

Once you have a Trust, you do not need to worry about who will take care of your property should you become disabled or too aged to handle your finances. The person you appointed as Successor Trustee will take over the care of the Trust property if you are unable to do so. If you do not have a Trust, and become incapacitated, a court may need to appoint a *Guardian* or *Conservator* to care for your property. The cost to establish and maintain the guardianship or conservatorship is charged to you. As we will see in Chapter 9, such legal procedures can be expensive; and once established cannot be terminated unless you die or are restored to health (GLM 201:13).

With all these perks, you may be ready to call your attorney to make an appointment to set up a Trust, but before doing so there are a few things you need to consider.

THE CONS

⌧ COMPLEXITY

A Trust is a fairly complex document, often more than 20 pages long. It needs to be that long because you are establishing a vehicle for taking care of your property during your lifetime, as well as after your death. Your Trust may be written in "legalese," so it may take you considerable time and effort to understand it. It is important to have your Trust document prepared by an attorney who has the patience to work with you until you understand each paragraph of the document and are satisfied that what it states is what you really want.

⌧ COST

Because of the thoroughness of the document and the fact that it is custom designed for you, a Trust will cost much more to draft than a simple Will. In addition to the initial cost of the Trust, it can be expensive to maintain the Trust should you become disabled or die. Your Successor Trustee has the right to charge for his duties as Trustee, as well as to charge for any specialized services performed. A financial institution can charge to serve as Successor Trustee, and also charge to manage the Trust portfolio. If you decide to have a financial institution serve as Trustee, then it is important that you compare the fee schedules of different institutions.

You can choose an attorney, or an accountant, or a financial planner, to serve as Trustee, but this may create a conflict of interest because the professional can use his position as Trustee to generate fees for himself or his firm.

If you decide to appoint a professional as Trustee you should have a fee agreement stating what will be charged for his duties as Trustee and what will be charged for professional work done on behalf of the Trust. The fee agreement should be included in the Trust document with a provision that whoever accepts the job of Successor Trustee, agrees to accept the fee as provided in the Trust document.

You may decide to appoint your spouse or a family member as Successor Trustee, who may want little, or no, compensation. Regardless of who you choose to be Successor Trustee, you need to come to a fee agreement. The agreement can be for a set amount or a percentage of the value of the Trust, or other method to be used to determine his compensation.

Under Massachusetts law, if you do not make written provision for fees, your Successor Trustee is entitled to be compensated in the same manner as any fiduciary, such as a Personal Representative (GLM 206:16). If the beneficiaries of the Trust think the Trustee is charging too high a fee, they can ask the Court to determine an appropriate fee (GLM 203:12). But that will probably trigger an expensive legal battle. It is better that you set the fee. Hopefully, that will head off unnecessary legal fees.

⌧ PROBATE MIGHT STILL BE NECESSARY

The Trust only works for those items that you place in the Trust. If you own property in your name only, then upon your death, a Probate procedure might be necessary in order to transfer the property to your beneficiary. For example, if you purchase a security in your name only, without a "Transfer On Death" designation to a beneficiary or to your Trust, then a Probate procedure may be necessary to determine who should inherit the security.

The attorney who prepares the Trust usually creates a safety net for such situations. He prepares a Will for you to sign at the same time you sign the Trust. The Will makes your Trust the beneficiary of your Probate Estate. If you own anything in your name only, should Probate be necessary, the Will directs your Personal Representative to make that asset part of your Trust by transferring the asset to your Successor Trustee. Your Successor Trustee will add that asset to your Trust (GLM 203:3B).

The Will prepared by the attorney is called a ***Pour Over Will*** because it is designed to "pour" any asset titled in your name only, into the Trust. Having a Pour Over Will ensures that your property will go to the beneficiaries named in your Trust. But the downside of holding property in your name only is that a full Probate procedure may be necessary just to get that asset into your Trust. If avoiding Probate is your goal, holding property, in your name only, defeats that goal.

You can ensure that a Probate procedure will not be necessary by transferring your assets into your Trust during your lifetime, but if you neglect to put something into your Trust, the Pour Over Will stands by to transfer that asset into your Trust.

☒ YOU MAY NEED YOUR SPOUSE'S PERMISSION TO TRANSFER PROPERTY INTO YOUR TRUST

Most married couples prepare a Trust as part of their overall Estate Plan. Sometimes a married person has a Trust that was prepared prior to the marriage, or he may decide to create a Trust to care for children from a previous marriage. In such case, it may be necessary to have the spouse agree, in writing, to transfers into the Trust. The reason is two-fold. As explained in the last chapter, your spouse has the right to claim a Tenancy In Dower in real property you own as of the date of your death. This means that if you transfer real property into your Trust, your surviving spouse has the right to demand a Life Estate in one-third of all of the real property you own— not including undeveloped land (GLM 189:1, 189:3).

DEFEATING DOWER RIGHTS

There are ways to defeat your spouse's Dower rights. One way is enter into an *Antenuptial* (Premarital) or *Postnuptial* (Marital) Agreement giving up those rights (GLM 189:8, 209:25). If you are living separately for "justifiable cause, your spouse is not entitled to Dower rights, provided a Probate Court enters a judgment saying that you have been deserted (GLM 209:36). Still another way is to state that the amount left to your spouse in your Will is intended to be given in place of the Dower (GLM 191:17).

If your spouse is not satisfied with that amount, he/she can demand an ***Elective Share*** of all of the property (real and personal) that you own as of the date of your death. The Elective Share depends on the value of your Estate and whether you are survived by kinsfolk (GLM 191:15).

SURVIVED BY SPOUSE AND NO KINSFOLK

If you are survived by a spouse and no descendant or other blood relatives, your spouse is entitled to $25,000 plus half of the remaining value of your property. The other half goes to the beneficiaries of your Will, or Trust.

SURVIVED BY SPOUSE AND DESCENDANTS

If you are survived by descendants, your spouse is entitled to one-third of your Estate.

SPOUSE, NO DESCENDANT, BUT OTHER KINSFOLK

If you are survived by kinsfolk but no descendants, your spouse gets $25,000 plus half of all of the property that you own.

In all of these cases, if the Elective Share is worth more than $25,000, your spouse is entitled to $25,000 outright with the income for life from the remainder of that Elective Share (GLM 191:15).

For example, suppose, you leave $300,000 worth of securities to your children and make no provision for your spouse. Your spouse can file a demand in the Registry of Probate for an Elective Share of one-third of the securities ($100,000). Your spouse is entitled to take $25,000 in securities outright and the income from the remaining $75,000 worth of securities for life. Once your spouse dies, your children will inherit the securities.

TRUST PROPERTY SUBJECT TO ELECTIVE SHARE

Massachusetts Courts have ruled that property contained in the decedent's Revocable Living Trust must be included when determining the Elective Share for the surviving spouse, so even if the securities are held in your Trust, your spouse is still entitled to an Elective Share of those securities (*Sullivan v. Burkin*, 390 Mass. 864,(1984), 460 N.E.2d 572).

☆ ⌦ THE TRUST IS LEGALLY ENFORCEABLE

Any beneficiary of the Trust can petition the Court to settle a dispute arising out of the administration of the Trust. For example, if the Trustee is not properly administering the Trust, the beneficiaries can ask the Court to remove the Trustee and appoint another to serve as Successor Trustee (GLM 203:12). The Trustee also has the right to petition the Court for authority to do certain things which may or may not be authorized in the Trust document. For example, the Trustee (or even a beneficiary) can ask the Court to issue an order giving the Trustee authority to terminate the Trust and distribute the Trust property to the beneficiaries (GLM 203:25).

We gave this section a cross and a star, because the right to have a Trust enforced or administered by a court is a double edged sword. It is great to have the Court protect the rights of your beneficiaries, but the cost of a Court battle could be greater than using Probate to transfer your Estate. Worse yet, your beneficiaries are at a disadvantage because the Trustee can charge the legal expenses to your Trust (GLM 215:39B).

The beneficiaries must pay for their legal battles out of their own pocket. Even if the beneficiaries win the argument, the Trustee's legal fees are paid from the Trust, so there is just that much less for your beneficiaries to inherit.

TAXES AND YOUR TRUST

Putting property into a Revocable Living Trust does not shield that property from taxes. All of the property held in a Revocable Living Trust is taxed as if the Settlor were holding that property in his own name. If the property earns income, income taxes will be due, and at the same rate as the Settlor would have paid if he had no Trust. Once the Settlor dies, both the federal and state government have the right to impose an ***Estate Tax*** on property transferred to a beneficiary as a result of the death.

All the property owned as of the date of death becomes the decedent's ***Taxable Estate.*** This includes *real property* (residential lots, condominiums, etc.) and *personal property* (cars, life insurance policies, business interests, securities, IRA accounts, etc.). It includes property held in the decedent's name alone, as well as property that he held jointly or in Trust. It also includes gifts given by the decedent during his lifetime that exceeded the ***Annual Gift Tax Exclusion.*** Up to the year 2002, that value was $10,000 per person, per year. The Annual Gift Tax Exclusion was adjusted for inflation in 2002 to $11,000 and again in 2006 to $12,000 (26 U.S.C. 2503(b)).

For most of us, this is not a concern because a federal Estate Tax does not need to be paid unless the decedent's Taxable Estate exceeds the federal ***Estate Tax Exclusion*** amount. That value is currently two million dollars and is scheduled to go even higher.

YEAR	ESTATE TAX EXCLUSION AMOUNT
2006-2008	$2,000,000
2009	$3,500,000

Under current law, the federal Estate Tax is scheduled to be phased out in the year 2010, but reinstated once again in the year 2011 with an Estate Tax Exclusion Amount of $1,000,000 — unless lawmakers change the tax law once again.

THE MASSACHUSETTS ESTATE TAX

Under the law, as in effect in June, 2006, Massachusetts Estate Taxes are due whenever the decedent's Taxable Estate exceeds $1,000,000 (GLM 65C:2A).

NO TAX FOR SURVIVING SPOUSE

Both state and federal government do not tax property passing to the decedent's spouse who is a U.S. citizen. However, once the surviving spouse dies, all of his/her Estate is subject to Estate Taxes. Setting up a Revocable Living Trust can significantly reduce the amount of state and federal Estate Taxes that may be due once the surviving spouse dies.

A TRUST TO REDUCE ESTATE TAXES

Under current law, Estates of those who die in 2010 are exempt from federal Estate Taxes, but in 2011, the Estate Tax is scheduled to be reinstated and Estates worth more than $1,000,000 will once again be subject to a sizeable Estate Tax. A couple with an Estate in excess of a million dollars can reduce the risk of an Estate Tax by setting up "His and Her" Trusts so that each person can take advantage of his own Estate Tax Exclusion Amount.

For example, if a husband and wife own two million dollars, they can separate their funds into two Trusts each valued at one million dollars. The Trusts can be set up so that a surviving spouse can use the income from the deceased partner's Trust for living expenses. In this way, their standard of living need not be reduced by separating their funds into two Trusts.

If they do not wish to separate funds, they can set up a single Joint Trust that separates into two Trusts once one partner dies. Again, the surviving spouse is free to use the income from both Trusts. Once both partners are deceased, the beneficiaries of their respective Trusts will inherit the funds, hopefully with no Estate Tax due.

If the couple makes no Trust provision, and they hold their property jointly, the last to die will own the two million dollars with only one Estate Tax Exclusion available. If lawmakers do not change the tax law, and the surviving spouse dies in 2011, or later, everything over one million dollars will be subject to both state and federal Estate Taxes. A Revocable Living Trust is a relatively simple way for a married couple to reduce, if not eliminate, the need to pay Estate Taxes.

However, as explained on the next few pages, there is still the problem of the federal Gift Tax and the Capital Gains Tax.

THE UN-UNIFIED GIFT TAX

As explained, up to 2002, the federal Annual Gift Tax Exclusion was $10,000. It increased to $11,000 in 2002, and then to $12,000 in 2006. The IRS keeps a running count of amounts you give to someone that exceed the Annual Gift Tax Exclusion that is effective in the year of the donation.

Although you are required to report a gift that exceeds the Annual Gift Tax Exclusion, no tax need be paid unless that running total is more than the federal lifetime Gift Tax Exclusion. That amount is currently one million dollars. If your running total does not exceed the Gift Tax Exclusion amount during your lifetime, once you die, the cumulative value of gifts you reported to the IRS will be added to your Taxable Estate.

Until the Estate Tax law was changed, the Gift and Estate Tax were unified. No Gift Tax needed to be paid unless the total value of the taxable gifts exceeded the federal Estate Tax Exclusion amount. In 2004 that changed. The Estate Tax Exclusion amount went up to $1,500,000, but the amount for the Gift Tax Exclusion remained at $1,000,000, so they now are no longer unified.

To summarize:
If you make a gift to anyone that is greater than the Annual Gift Tax Exclusion for that year, you must report the gift to the IRS. The IRS keeps a running count of gifts you made in excess of the Annual Gift Tax Exclusion. In 2004, if that sum exceeds $1,000,000, you will pay a Gift Tax on any amount that you give that is over the Annual Gift Tax Exclusion. The Estate Tax is scheduled to be repealed in 2010, but not the Gift Tax.

Massachusetts does not have a Gift Tax at this time.

The current federal Estate tax is scheduled to be phased out in the year 2010, but a new Capital Gains Tax is scheduled for 2010 that may prove even more costly than the Estate Tax. The new Capital Gains Tax is related to the way inherited property is evaluated by the federal government. Real and personal property is inherited at a "stepped-up" basis, meaning that if the decedent's property increased in value from the time he acquired it, the beneficiary inherits the property at its fair market value as of the decedent's date of death. For example, if he decedent bought stock for $20,000 and it is worth $50,000 as of his date of death, the beneficiary will take a step-up in basis of $30,000; i.e. the beneficiary inherits the stock at the current $50,000 value. If the beneficiary sells the stock for $50,000, he pays no Capital Gains Tax. If the beneficiary holds onto the stock and later sells it for $60,000, the beneficiary will pay a Capital Gains Tax only on the $10,000 increase in value since the decedent's death.

Up to 2009, there is no limit to the amount a beneficiary can take as a step-up in basis. But in 2010 caps are set in place. The decedent's Estate will be allowed a 1.3 million dollar step-up in basis, plus another 3 million for property passing to the surviving spouse (26 U.S.C. 1022(b)). The new law could result in significant Capital Gains taxes that the beneficiary must pay. For example, suppose in 2010 you inherit a business from your father that he purchased for $100,000 and it is now worth 2 million dollars. There is a capital gain of 1.9 million dollars, but you are allowed a step-up in basis of only 1.3 million. If you sell it for 2 million dollars $600,000 of your inheritance will be subject to a Capital Gains tax.

We will discuss methods of reducing the Gift Tax and the Capital Gains Tax in Chapter 7.

MAYBE A WILL IS BEST AFTER ALL

Although many methods can be used to transfer property without the need for Probate, it may be each method has a downside that is objectionable to you. Maybe you don't have enough money at this time to warrant the cost of setting up a Trust. Holding property jointly with another may raise issues of security and independence. Holding property so that it goes directly to a few beneficiaries in a Pay On Death account may not be as flexible as you wish. This may be the case if you want to give gifts to several charities or to a minor child.

For example, you can hold all your property so that it goes directly to your son without the need for Probate. If you ask him to use some of the money for your grandchild's education, it may be that your grandchild gets none of the money because your son is sued or falls upon hard times. If you keep your property in your name only and leave a Will giving a certain amount of money to your grandchild, the child will know exactly how much money you left and the purpose of that gift.

After taking into account all the pros and cons of avoiding Probate, you may well opt for a Will and a Probate procedure. If you make such a decision, it is important to keep in mind that Estate Planning is not an "all or nothing" choice. You can arrange your Estate so that certain items pass automatically to your intended beneficiary, and other items can be left in your name only, to be distributed as part of a Probate procedure. By arranging your finances in this manner, you can reduce the value of your Probate Estate, and that in turn should reduce the cost of Probate.

In the next chapter, we discuss the Will as an Estate Planning tool.

Those of you who have a Will may be thinking that there is no reason to read the Chapter, but does your Will:

- Make provision for the amount to be paid to your Personal Representative?
- Make gifts of your personal property? (jewelry, car, etc.)
- Name a Guardian to care for your minor child?
- Make adjustment for gifts or loans that you gave to the beneficiaries of your Will?
- Give specific instructions about how your bills and taxes are to be paid; i.e., which of your beneficiaries will have his inheritance reduced in order to pay your debts and taxes?

Has your Will been prepared so that it will be difficult for anyone to challenge it?

Have you stored your Will so that it is safe AND easily accessible to you during your lifetime and to your Personal Representative after your death?

If you answered "Yes" to all of the above questions, then you can skip over to Chapter 5.

Your Will– Your Way 4

Many people decide that the Will is the best route to go but do not act upon it, thinking it unnecessary to prepare a Will until they are very old and about to die. But according to reports published by the National Center for Health Statistics (a division of the U.S. Department of Health and Human Services) 2 of every 10 people who die in any given year are under the age of 60. Twenty percent may seem like a small number until it hits close to home as it did with a young couple.

Alex and Cathy were an old-fashioned couple in a modern world. When they married, they knew they wanted a large family. There was no question that Cathy would stay home and raise the children while Alex went to work. Luckily he did very well as one of the managers of a string of restaurants. Better yet, he enjoyed his work. He loved to cook and would even take over the kitchen when he returned from work. That suited Cathy just fine because she had her hands full raising their three boys.

Cathy couldn't help thinking how lucky they were that morning as she fixed breakfast. A nice house. Healthy, if not rambunctious, boys. All in all, a comfortable marriage. Her only concern that day was the fact that Alex was flying off on a business trip. All this terrorist news made her nervous about flying. Alex reassured her that it was only an hour's flight, and besides he was flying the company plane and not a commercial airliner.

But it was not terrorists that brought down the plane, just a malfunctioning rudder.

THINGS A WILL CAN DO

Though we all agree that one never knows, still people put off making a Will, figuring that if they die before getting around to it, Massachusetts law will take over and their property will be distributed in the manner that they would have wanted anyway. The problem with that logic is the complexity of the Massachusetts Laws of Descent. It isn't too difficult to figure out who will inherit your property, if you are survived by a spouse, child, parent or sibling. But if none of these survive you, the ultimate beneficiary of your property may not be the person you would have chosen, had you taken the time to do so.

Others think that it is not necessary to have a Will because they have arranged their finances so that all of their property will be inherited without the need for Probate. But money could come into your Estate after your death. This could happen in any number of ways from winning the lottery and dying (of happiness, no doubt) to receiving insurance funds after your death. For example, if you die in a house fire, the company that insures your home may need to pay for damages done to the property. In such case, the funds will need to be paid to your Estate. A Personal Representative may need to be appointed and the insurance funds distributed according to Massachusetts law.

If you die without a Will, your Estate may be distributed differently than you would have wished. And there are other important reasons to make a Will.

APPOINT THE PERSONAL REPRESENTATIVE

An important reason to make a Will is to appoint the person of your choice to serve as Personal Representative. If you die without a Will, your surviving spouse has the right to be appointed to settle your Estate. If there is no surviving spouse, or if the spouse is unable or unwilling to serve, your next of kin have the right to be appointed as Personal Representative (GLM 193:1). By *next of kin,* we mean those people who inherit the property according to the Massachusetts Laws of Descent and Distribution. Usually the family agree among themselves who will serve as Personal Representative, but if there is a dispute, the Court will make the decision.

SET PERSONAL REPRESENTATIVE'S FEE

Once you decide on a Personal Representative, you need to check with that person to be sure that he is willing to serve in that capacity. And if so, then you should come to an understanding about how much compensation he will receive to settle your Estate. If you do not make provision for his fee, the Court will award the fee based on the guidelines described in Chapter 1 (GLM 206:16).

THE PERSONAL REPRESENTATIVE MAY SEEK MORE MONEY

You can put the amount of agreed compensation in your Will; however your Personal Representative can reject that amount and ask for more money. To avoid the problem, you can have your attorney draft an Agreement that you and your Personal Representative sign and attach it to your Will. Having a separate fee Agreement will not stop your Personal Representative from asking for more money, but with such an Agreement, the Court will not agree to the increase unless something unusual occurs (such as a law suit) causing much more work than the ordinary Probate procedure.

You also need to keep in mind that the Personal Representative's fee is just to administer the Estate. It does not include payment for professional work he may do while settling the Estate. For example, if you appoint your attorney as Personal Representative, he can agree to the amount stated in the Will for his role as Personal Representative, and then ask the Court to award him attorney's fees as well (GLM 215:39A).

The same goes for any other professional. If you appoint your accountant to serve as Personal Representative, he is entitled to receive compensation for his work as Personal Representative and also for any accounting work he does such as preparing and filing tax returns; preparing an inventory and doing an accounting for the beneficiaries. A financial planner who serves as Personal Representative may be compensated for his management of the Estate property (buying and selling securities, taking care of rental property, etc.) in addition to his fee to administer the Estate.

But the main problem with appointing a professional as your Personal Representative is the same as appointing a professional to serve as the Successor Trustee of your Trust; namely, that it creates a potential conflict of interest. The professional can use his position as Personal Representative to generate fees that might have been avoided had someone else settled the Estate.

When choosing a Personal Representative, consider the relationship of the Personal Representative to the beneficiaries and determine whether it would be better to appoint a non-professional for the job.

If you decide to appoint a professional for the job, have your compensation agreement state what will be paid for duties performed in the administration of the Estate as Personal Representative and what monies will be paid as compensation for any professional service he may perform.

MAKE GIFTS OF YOUR PERSONAL PROPERTY

Another benefit to making a Will is that you can make provision for who will get your personal property (computers, antiques, securities, boats, snowmobiles etc.). When making a Will consider making provision for your car. If you make a ***specific gift*** i.e. a gift to a named beneficiary of your Will, it will be relatively simple for your Personal Representative to transfer the car to your beneficiary. If you do not make a specific gift of your car, your Personal Representative will decide what to do with it. He may decide to sell it and include the proceeds of the sale in the Estate funds to be distributed as part of the Probate Estate; or he can give the car to one beneficiary of your Estate as part of that beneficiary's share of the Estate.

GIFTING PERSONAL EFFECTS

Many who have lost someone close to them report that the distribution of small personal items caused the greatest conflict. If you arrange your finances so that no Probate procedure is necessary, your next of kin will need to decide among themselves how to distribute your ***personal effects*** (clothing, books, music collection, etc.). Without guidance from you, and no Personal Representative with authority to make decisions, there could be disagreement and hard feelings over items of little monetary value, but much sentimental value.

If you make a Will, you can include a list of gifts of personal effects in your Will and your Personal Representative will distribute those gifts according to your list. Of course, it is not possible to make a list of each and every item you own; but you can instruct your Personal Representative to allow certain family members to take their choice of items not mentioned in your Will. If two or more family members want the same item, instruct your Personal Representative to use an appropriate lottery system (coin toss, high card in a cut of a deck of cards, etc.) to decide who "wins."

CAUTION YOU CAN'T GIVE WHAT YOU DON'T HAVE

You need to give considerable thought whenever you make a specific gift to someone. It could be that you no longer own the item at the time of your death. This could happen with property or money. For example, suppose you leave all of your Estate to your son, with a specific gift of $10,000 to each of your three grandchildren. Your son is the ***residuary beneficiary*** of the Probate Estate, meaning he gets whatever is left once all of the bills are paid and all of the specific gifts made. If the cost of your last illness leaves your Probate Estate with only $30,000 to distribute, would you want the grandchildren to get their gifts and your son nothing? The simple solution is to make all of them residuary beneficiaries by leaving each a percent of your Estate. For example, instead of making a specific gift to each grandchild you could leave 70% to your son and 10% to each grandchild.

NON-PROBATE TRANSFERS

You can make provision in your Will only for those items held in your name that do not transfer automatically to a named beneficiary upon your death. For example, a security with a Transfer On Death registration, the proceeds of a life insurance policy, Trust property and IRA accounts are all ***non-Probate*** assets because they will be inherited by your named beneficiary without the need for Probate. You have, in effect, already made a gift of these assets so unless you named your Estate as the beneficiary of these assets, they should not be mentioned in your Will (GLM 201E:302).

To do so might cause your Will to be challenged by whoever was named as the beneficiary of the non-Probate asset.

CHOOSE A GUARDIAN FOR YOUR MINOR CHILD

If one parent dies, it is the right and duty of the surviving parent to care for the child. But it could happen that both parents die before the child is grown. If you have a minor child, you can use your Will to name someone to serve as your child's Guardian in that event (GLM 201:3). You can even include a Trust in your Will, naming someone to serve as Trustee to care for property that you leave to your minor child.

See Chapter 7 for more information about how to make provision for the care of your minor child in the event of your incapacity, or death.

MAKE ADJUSTMENT FOR PRIOR GIFTS

With a Will, you can make adjustments for gifts or loans given during your lifetime. For example, if you have loaned money to a family member and do not expect to be repaid, then you can deduct the loan from that person's inheritance. Of course, it may be that you are not concerned with inequities. That was the case of an aged woman who had three children, Paul, Rita and Frank, her youngest. Frank always seemed to need some assistance from his mother. She often "loaned" him money that he never repaid.

Her other children were responsible and independent. Paul was married and had children of his own. He decided to purchase a house but was having trouble accumulating the down payment. His mother agreed to lend him the money. Paul and his wife offered to give his mother a mortgage on the property. The mother said a simple promissory note from Paul was sufficient, and she would have her attorney draft the note.

The attorney drafted the note but was concerned about the inequity. "You never made a Will. Were you to die, each of your children will inherit an equal amount of money. If Paul still owes money on this promissory note, he will either need to pay the balance to your Estate, or have it subtracted from the amount he inherits. All of the money you gave to Frank will not count towards his inheritance unless you make your intentions clear that you considered the money you gave to Frank to be an advancement of his inheritance You can do this by making an adjustment in a Will, or by having Frank give you a promissory note for any outstanding debts" (GLM 196:3, 196:5).

"It's O.K." replied the mother "I love all my children equally . . . some are a little more equal than others."

MAKE PROVISION FOR PAYMENT OF DEBTS

Most Wills contain an instruction to the Personal Representative to ". . . pay all the expenses of my last illness, funeral expenses, costs of administration, taxes and just debts. . . " Under Massachusetts law, paying all of your debts does not include paying off a loan on a gift made to a beneficiary.

For example, if you leave your car to a beneficiary, and you have a loan on the car, you need to specify whether you want the loan to be paid from your Probate Estate so that your beneficiary will inherit the car free and clear, or whether you want to have your beneficiary be responsible to pay off the loan. If you make no provision in your Will, then under Massachusetts law, your beneficiary will inherit the loan along with the car (GLM 191:23).

This same rule applies even if you do not make a specific gift of the item. For example, if there is a mortgage on your home, and you make no mention of who is to inherit the home, it will be inherited by your residuary beneficiaries; and they will be responsible to pay off the loan. They can use the Estate funds to do so, but if there is not enough money in the Estate to pay off the loan, whoever takes title to the property will need to pay the debt or make arrangements to refinance the property.

MAKE PROVISION FOR PAYMENT OF TAXES

Taxes are another concern for those Estates large enough to be subject to Estate Taxes. State and federal law require that Estate Taxes be paid by the beneficiaries of the Estate in proportion to the value received, unless the decedent made some other arrangements to pay for the taxes. If you make no provision for the payment of taxes, whoever inherits your property will pay a percentage of the taxes based on the amount they receive (GLM 191:1A).

The beneficiary must pay his share regardless of whether he inherits the property through a non-Probate transfer (joint owner, beneficiary of your Trust, beneficiary of a Pay On Death account, beneficiary of a life insurance policy, etc.) or as the beneficiary of your Probate Estate (26 U.S.C. 6324 (a)(2), GLM 65A:5). Each beneficiary who receives property that was included in your Gross Estate, is personally liable to pay their proportionate share. If Estate Taxes are not paid when due, the taxes become a lien on your Gross Estate (all the property you own at the time of your death) for ten years from the date of your death (GLM 65C:14).

If you do not want the beneficiary of a specific gift of land or personal property to be responsible to pay Estate Taxes, you can direct your Personal Representative to pay all of your taxes from your Probate Estate. This means that the amount that the residuary beneficiaries of your Probate Estate receive will be reduced by the amount of taxes paid.

Those who have a Trust can direct the Successor Trustee to use Trust funds to pay Estate Taxes. Again this relieves the beneficiary of a specific gift from paying an Estate Tax, but at the expense of the residuary beneficiaries of the Trust.

PREPARING YOUR WILL

After reading the last few pages you may be thinking that everyone should have a Will. And we would agree with your conclusion. Regardless of whether you arrange for all of your property to pass directly without the need for Probate; and regardless of whether you have a Trust, it is important to have a Will for all of the reasons just stated.

Anyone who is at least 18 years of age and of sound mind can make a Will (GLM 191:1). Courts have ruled that "sound mind" means that when you made the Will, you knew what you were doing (namely making a Will); and that you weren't suffering from a condition causing you to be delusional so as to affect the way you gifted your property. The Court will also look for evidence that you had "sound memory" meaning you knew what property you had and who of your relatives would, under ordinary circumstances, expect to inherit that property (*Tarricone v. Cummings*, 340 Mass. 758 (1960), 66 N.E.2d 737).

You may be thinking "That seems simple enough. I think I'll sit down and write one out." But preparing a Will is like figure skating. It is harder than it looks. A Will needs to be clearly worded. A sentence that can be read in two different ways can lead to a dispute over what you intended; and that could lead to a long and expensive Court battle.

Your Will needs to be prepared according to Massachusetts law, meaning that you sign the Will (or tell someone to sign the Will for you), in the presence of at least two witnesses, each who also sign the Will, who can testify that they saw you sign the Will, and you did so of your own free will and at the time you signed it, you knew what you were doing.

Neither of your witnesses should be a beneficiary of your Will unless there are two other, independent, disinterested witnesses to your Will. If there are only two witnesses, one of whom is a beneficiary of the Will, any gift made in your Will to that witness, or to his spouse, is ***void***; i.e., the gift is not legally enforceable (GLM 191:2).

The problem of having someone present who could directly or indirectly profit from your Will is that of ***undue influence***. Undue influence occurs when someone exerts such pressure on the Will maker so that he is not acting according to his own free will.

But undue influence is not easily proven. Massachusetts courts have ruled that to prove undue influence, it must be shown that:

- ⇨ the Will maker, because of age or infirmity was susceptible to undue influence
- ⇨ the Will maker made an "unnatural" disposition in his Will giving property to someone who had an opportunity to exercise undue influence; and who did, in fact, improperly use that opportunity to get the gift.

(*Heinrich v. Silvernail*, 23 Mass. App. Ct. 218 (1986), 500 N.E.2d 835).

Even if there is no undue influence, and your Will is clearly worded, properly signed and witnessed, it can still be challenged if you are married and did not make provision for your spouse as required by Massachusetts law. As explained in Chapter 3, your spouse has the right to an Elective Share of your Estate.

As explained in Chapter 3, your spouse has the right to inherit as much from your Estate as is allowed under Massachusetts law. If you attempt to give your spouse less than the statutory amount, then unless your spouse signed a Premarital or Marital Agreement giving up that right, he/she can challenge your Will. Your surviving spouse can ask the Court for an award of the Elective Share (GLM 191:15).

THE "FORGOTTEN" CHILD

Although your spouse has the right to elect against your Will, your child has no such right. You can give your child as much as you wish or nothing at all, but you must be specific. If you wish to disinherit a child, or even a grandchild, you need to identify the child and say that the omission is intentional. If you make no mention of your child, or grandchild, he can challenge your Will saying that you "forgot" to include him as a beneficiary. If the child or grandchild is successful, he will be entitled to inherit the amount he would have received had you died without a Will (GLM 191:20).

If you are concerned that someone may challenge your Will, it is important that you consult with an attorney who is experienced in Estate Planning. He will prepare the Will according to your wishes. If you meet with the attorney in the privacy of his office, and without anyone else present, it will be difficult to prove that someone was using undue influence to make you make gifts according to their wishes and not yours.

Once the Will is prepared according to your direction, the attorney can supervise the signing of your Will. He will see to it that your Will is signed and witnessed in the presence of two disinterested witnesses — usually members of his staff. Each witness will sign the Will next to your name as witness; and they will sign a separate paragraph before a Notary Public that says, they saw you sign the Will, and you did so of your own free will and at the time you signed it, you were 18 or older, and of sound mind. A Will signed in this manner is considered to be ***Self-proved*** meaning that it can be admitted to Probate without any further testimony from the witness as to its authenticity (GLM 192:2).

Should someone later challenge the Will, your attorney will be able to present proof to the Court that the Will was prepared exactly as you wished, and that no one was present to influence you. The attorney and the witnesses to your Will, can testify that you signed the Will willingly and that you were competent to know what you were doing when you signed the Will. You can even have your attorney include a ***no contest*** provision in your Will stating that if a beneficiary named in your Will challenges any provision in the Will, he will inherit none of your Probate Estate.

Such a provision is called an ***In Terrorem Clause*** because it is designed to cause fear (if not terror) in the heart of your beneficiary. Many states will not enforce such a clause, because they want people to have the right to challenge a Will, and let the Court decide whether that challenge is proper.

Massachusetts Courts have upheld a provision that bars a challenge to a Will (*Rudd v. Searles*, 262 Mass. 490 (1928), 160 N.E. 882). However, in that case, the Court found that there was no ***probable cause*** ** for the challenge. If a Court finds that there was a good reason for the challenge, such as a Will maker who was not of sound mind, or someone forcing the Will maker to sign the Will, the Court might allow the person who makes the challenge to inherit the Will maker's property.

Including an In Terrorem Clause in your Will should discourage your beneficiaries from filing frivolous law suits. But an In Terrorem Clause cannot guarantee that no one will challenge your Will. Anyone who makes the challenge understands that if he loses, there is the chance that the Court will find that there was no good reason for making the challenge in the first place. Should the Court reach that conclusion, the Court will uphold the penalty provision and the person who contests the Will will be barred from inheriting anything under your Will.

But the challenger also knows that if he wins, the Court must conclude that there was probable cause to bring the law suit. In that case, the In Terrorem Clause will not prevent him from inheriting property under your Will.

** Lawyer talk for "had good reason to do so."

STORING YOUR WILL

Once you sign your Will, you may wonder where to store it. If an attorney prepared your Will, he may suggest that he place it in his vault for safekeeping. By doing so, he ensures that your heirs will need to contact him as soon as you die. This does not mean that they are required to employ him should a Probate procedure be necessary. It only means that he has an opportunity for future employment.

But there are problems with such an arrangement. The Will could be lost or mistaken for another Will. That happened in at least one case. The attorney prepared Wills for two people with the same name and similar family circumstances. When one person died the attorney submitted the wrong Will to Probate.

If you decide to allow your attorney to store the Will, you need assurance that the attorney will be responsible for the document. You should get a receipt and something in writing that says:

⇨ The attorney accepts full responsibility for storage of the Will. Should it be lost or damaged, he will replace the document at no cost to you; and if you are deceased, he will, at no cost to your beneficiaries, present sufficient evidence to the Court to accept a valid copy of the Will into Probate.

⇨ There will be no charge to you, or your heirs, for the storage and retrieval of the document.

⇨ Should he sell his practice, retire, or die, he or the successor to his practice, will return the original document to you.

THE SAFE DEPOSIT BOX, SAFE BUT . . .

You might consider placing your document in a safe deposit box that you lease at a bank. The only problem with the bank safe deposit box is convenient access. If you hold a safe deposit box in your name only, should you die the bank will not allow anyone to access the safe deposit box without Court authority. Once a Personal Representative is appointed by the Court, he will have such authority and be able to remove the contents of the safe deposit box. If you arranged your finances to avoid Probate, it is self defeating to have entry to a safe deposit box trigger a Probate procedure.

For those who are married, the solution to the problem of accessing the safe deposit box after death, is to lease the box jointly with your spouse, such that each of you has free access to the box. Those who have a Trust can solve the problem by giving their Successor Trustee joint access to the safe deposit box. If you are single and do not have a Trust, you can lease the box jointly with a trusted family member. Of course, if privacy and security are important to you, that may outweigh any concern for the convenience of your beneficiaries.

STORE IT WITH THE COURT

Perhaps the best place to store your Will is with the Register of Probate in the county of your residence. The one-time fee for doing so is currently $5 (i.e., as of June 2006) (GLM 191:10). You are free to retrieve the Will from the Register in the event that you move or decide to change your Will.

Regardless of where you choose to store your Will, let your Personal Representative know that you have a Will and how to retrieve it in the event of your death.

I thought you said a Will is not enough

After reading this chapter, you may be thinking that the book is poorly named. After all, look at all the good things a Will can do:

- choose the person you want to settle your Estate
- arrange to have your Personal Representative settle your Estate for a reasonable fee
- give your personal items, including your car, to the person of your choice
- choose a Guardian for your child
- discourage a challenge to your Will.

But that is not all there is to an Estate Plan. A Will cares for your property when you are deceased, but it cannot provide for the care of your property in the event you become disabled. A complete Estate Plan provides for the care of your property during your lifetime and for the care of your person as well.

In these days of extended old age, many of us will need assistance with our health care and/or finances as we age. It is important to arrange to have someone manage finances and make medical decisions in the event that we are too aged or too ill to do so ourselves. These topics are covered in Chapters 8 and 9.

And a Will may be effective to transfer all that you own upon your death, but it cannot help your family pay for your debts. It may be that you have so many debts that your family is left with little or nothing. A complete Estate Plan provides for the financial well being of your family once you are deceased; and that is the topic of the next chapter.

Arranging To Pay Bills 5

You can think of your Estate Plan as being composed of two separate parts, a Lifetime Plan and an Inheritance Plan. Your Lifetime Plan provides for the care of your property during your lifetime, with the goal being maximum control and protection. Your Inheritance Plan provides for the inheritance of your property, with the goal being minimum cost and hassle to your beneficiaries. You could consider your Estate Plan to be a master plan that balances the goals of the Lifetime Plan with those of the Inheritance Plan.

When people consider their Inheritance Plan, they are mostly concerned about giving their possessions away. Many do not take into account how the bills they have accumulated will be paid once they are deceased, or even who will be responsible for paying those bills. Most of us do not worry about providing for the payment of our debts, thinking "I'll have that paid off long before I die." But with easily available credit, many are maintaining a high debt balance as a way of life. Paying off all of their loans is not a priority. Many will live their lives without ever being free of debt.

This does not imply that people do not know how to manage their funds. For many people (and corporations), it makes good sense to use other people's money to carry on business. In fact, great debt is a badge of honor for the wealthy. If a bank will lend you a million dollars, it means you have the means to repay that amount. Banks will not lend much money to those with few assets. Rich or poor, we all need to think about how our debts will be paid once we are gone.

WHO IS RESPONSIBLE TO PAY BILLS?

Suppose you die without funds, and owing money. Does the debt die with you or is someone else responsible to pay what you owe? If you are married, the first person the creditor will look to, is your spouse. To understand the basis of this expectation, you need to know a bit of the history of our legal system.

Our laws are derived from the English Common Law. Under English Common law, a single woman had the right to own property in her own name and also the right to contract to buy or sell property. When a woman married, her legal identity merged with her spouse. She could not hold property free from her husband's claim or control. She could no longer enter into a contract without her husband's permission.

Once married, a woman became financially dependent on her husband. He, in turn, became legally responsible to provide his wife with basic necessities — food, clothing, shelter and medical services. If anyone provided basic necessities to his wife, then, regardless of whether the husband agreed to be responsible for the debt, he became obliged to pay for them. This law was called the DOCTRINE OF NECESSARIES.

In the United States, a series of Married Women's Rights Acts were passed giving a married woman the right to own property. Massachusetts laws were passed giving a married woman the right to sue and be sued, work and be paid for her work, to contract in the same manner as any single woman (GLM 209:2, 209:4, 209:6). As Married Women's Rights laws were passed, states had to decide whether the Doctrine of Necessaries still applied— especially in light of the equal protection under the law.

Specifically, if a husband is responsible to pay for his wife's necessities, shouldn't his wife be responsibility to pay for her husband's necessities?

In some states, notably Florida, courts decided that neither partner was responsible to pay the other's necessities, unless they contracted or agreed to do so. But in Massachusetts they came to a different conclusion. The Massachusetts legislature passed laws stating that a woman has the right to own property, but a husband continues to be responsible to pay for his wife and family's necessities. Either party can purchase necessities for the family. If the contracting spouse does not have sufficient funds to pay for these items, the debt must be paid from property they own together as husband and wife. As explained in Chapter 2, property owned by the couple as Tenants by the Entirety after February 11, 1980 is available to pay for family necessities (GLM 209:1).

If there is no joint property, the husband remains liable to pay for the necessities from his ***separate*** property; i.e., property he owned prior to the marriage and that has not been co-mingled with marital property. The wife is liable for necessities purchased for the family from her separate property, but only if she knew or consented to the purchase, and she has at least $2,000 as her own separate property. Even if the wife is liable, under Massachusetts law that liability is limited to $100 per purchase of a necessity (GLM 209:7).

This right continues after death. If a husband dies and money is owed for family necessities, his Estate is responsible to pay that debt. If the wife dies, her Estate is limited to only $100 per purchase of a necessity. In these days of same sex marriage and equal protection under the law, it is questionable whether this law will continue to be enforceable in the Commonwealth of Massachusetts.

JOINT DEBTS

Which leads to the next question. Is anyone other than your spouse responsible to pay monies you owe? For joint debts, the answer is "yes."

A ***joint debt*** is a debt that two or more people are responsible to pay. Usually the contract or promissory note reads that both parties agree to *joint and several* liability, meaning they both agree to pay the debt and each of them, individually, agrees to pay the debt. A joint debt can also be in the form of monies owed by one person with payment guaranteed by another person. If the person who owes the money does not pay, then the *guarantor* (the person who guaranteed payment) is responsible to pay the debt.

Should one of the joint debtors die, then Massachusetts law provides that the debt must be paid from the decedent's Estate as if the contract (or judgment) were joint and severable, or as if the judgment were against the decedent alone (GLM 197:8). Of course if there are insufficient funds in the Estate to pay the joint debt, then the joint debtor remains liable to pay for the debt.

PAYING FOR NECESSITIES

Should you die, your hospital bills, nursing home bills, funeral expenses, legal fees for the Probate of your Estate are all debts of your Estate. They are not joint debts unless someone guaranteed payment for monies owed. Hospital and nursing home bills are considered to be necessities, so if you are married and there are insufficient funds in your Estate to pay for these bills, your spouse must use property owned jointly with you to pay for that debt (GLM 209:1)

JOINT PROPERTY BUT NO JOINT DEBT

Suppose you have a credit card in your name only, and you have a bank account together with your son. Should you die, can the credit card company require that your share of the joint account be used to pay the debt?

The answer to this question depends on how the joint property is titled. As discussed earlier there are different ways to hold property jointly with another. Courts in Massachusetts have ruled that property held jointly with rights of survivorship, belongs to the surviving joint owner as of the date of death and it is not available to pay the decedent's debts (*Weaver vs. New Bedford,* 140 N.E.2d 309, Mass (1957)).

If there is no right of survivorship, upon your death, your son will continues to own his share of the account. Your share of the account becomes part of your Probate Estate, and as such is available to pay your debts.

BUT NOT EXEMPT FROM UNCLE SAM

Bank accounts in the name of two or more persons with rights of survivorship, are payable to the surviving joint owner(s) (GLM 167D:5). The surviving owners have no obligation to use the joint account funds to pay the decedent's creditors because the funds are not part of the decedent's Probate Estate. However, the decedent's share of the joint account is included as part of the decedent's ***Taxable Estate***. If Estate Taxes are due to the federal or state government and there are no other funds to pay those taxes, the surviving owners of the joint account will need to contribute as much of the decedent's share of the account as is necessary to pay the tax bill (GLM 65A:5).

PAYING FOR CREDIT CARD DEBT

Most of us are wise enough not to hold a credit card jointly with a child, but holding a credit card jointly with a spouse is commonplace, especially if the card is being used to pay for necessities. If you hold a credit card with your spouse and you are concerned that it might be a struggle to pay it off should one of you die, consider purchasing credit card insurance to cover the debt.

Many credit card companies offer insurance policies and include the premium as part of the monthly payment. It benefits the credit card company to offer life insurance as part of the credit package, because they are assured of prompt payment should the borrower die.

In these days of high credit card interest rates, you might be struggling to pay your monthly credit charge. Adding still another charge to the account may not be an option, regardless of the security offered to your spouse. In such case, a better route might be for you to remove your name from the account and open a new account in your name only. This is especially important if you are using your credit card to pay for your business expenses, and not family necessities.

Still another reason not to hold a joint credit card is that each of you can establish your own line of credit in the event one of you retires or is out of work. Should the breadwinner of the family die, it may be difficult for the surviving spouse to establish credit if the spouse is retired and/or has no recent work record. It is easier for an unemployed spouse to establish a line of credit when he/she is married to someone who is working.

OTHER TYPES OF LOAN INSURANCE

Many mortgage companies offer mortgage insurance to their borrowers. Mortgage rates are currently low, so an additional charge for mortgage insurance on the life of the primary wage earner may be worth the effort. This is particularly the case with families raising children. With such insurance, the family can inherit the homestead free of debt. The monthly insurance charge may be a small price to pay to ensure that the children can continue to live in their own home until they are grown.

Car loan insurance is still another thing to consider. If a married couple purchases (or leases) a car, and one of them dies, it may be a struggle for the other to pay off the loan. This was the case with Eva and Howard. Both had to work to support their three children. They owned two well used cars. It seemed that one car or the other was always in the shop. When they saw a *NO INTEREST* advertisement for a new car, they decided the offer was too good to pass up.

The monthly payments were high, but it was their only luxury. With both their salaries, they were able to make the payments. When Howard had his first heart attack, he was out of work for several weeks so they struggled to keep the payments current. Howard worked in construction, and was anxious to return to work. The doctors advised that such work might be too strenuous for his weakened heart. Construction work was all Howard knew, and the pay was good, so he ignored the warning and went back to his old job.

The second heart attack was fatal, leaving Eva as the sole means of support for her family.

With Howard gone there was no need for two cars. Eva could not afford the payments on the new car anyway, so she decided to sell it. Unfortunately, what she could get for the car was significantly less than the balance owed. Once she fell behind in payments she decided to surrender the car rather than have them repossess it. She was sure they would understand, considering all that she had been through these past several months, not to mention that she was a widow with three small children.

They didn't understand.

The company took the car and then sued for the balance of monies owed. The judge was sympathetic, but under the law there is no "life is tough" defense. He ruled that Eva had to pay the monies owed; and, as per the terms of the loan agreement, she even had to pay the fees for the company's attorney and all court costs. What an emotional and financial nightmare!

The pity was, it all could have been avoided, had they worked payment of debts into their Estate Plan. Howard was the primary driver of the new car and the primary wage earner. All he had to do was put the loan in his name only, and take out loan insurance. Eva would have inherited the car, debt free. She could have kept it or sold it as she saw fit.

Even if Howard didn't purchase loan insurance, had he put the loan in his name only, the company could only have sued his Estate. They would not have been able to sue Eva personally (GLM 209:7).

The good part of purchasing loan insurance — be it credit card insurance, mortgage insurance or car insurance, is that you may be able to purchase the policy without taking a medical examination. The down side is that companies generally do not offer such insurance to those over the age of 65; and for those under 65 the cost of the insurance is a factor. It usually costs more to purchase loan insurance than a life insurance policy. Those in fairly good health need to comparison shop. If it is your goal to have insurance cover all of your outstanding debts, then the cost of a single life insurance policy may be much less than purchasing several loan insurance policies.

The Estate Planning strategy of purchasing life insurance to pay off all of your loans works best if you are married and your spouse is jointly liable for your debts. If you name your spouse as beneficiary of the life insurance policy, he/she can use the life insurance funds to pay off all monies owed. If you name your spouse (or anyone else) as beneficiary of your insurance policy, and that person has no legal obligation to pay your debts, none of your creditors can ask your beneficiary to use the insurance funds to pay your debts.

The only exception is purchasing a policy to defraud your creditors. If a creditor can prove that you bought the policy to avoid using those funds to pay monies owed to him, then a Court can order that whatever you paid for the policy, be paid to the creditor from the proceeds of the policy (GLM 175:125).

If you want the insurance funds used to pay your debts, then name your Estate as beneficiary of your policy. If you want someone to inherit money after you are gone, and you do not want those funds reduced by the cost of Probate or to pay off your debts, then naming that person as beneficiary of the insurance proceeds should accomplish your goal.

With or without debt, you may be wondering about life insurance — should you have it? How much is enough? The answer to these questions depends on the "sleep at night" factor, namely how much insurance do you need so that you won't worry about insurance coverage when you go to sleep at night? It is often more an emotional than a financial issue.

Some people have an "every man for himself" attitude and are content to have no life insurance at all. When they die, whatever they have, they have. And that is what their heirs will inherit. Others worry about how their loved ones will manage if they are not around to support them, and decide to purchase enough insurance to maintain their dependents in their accustomed life style. The same person may have different thoughts about insurance coverage as circumstances change — from no coverage in his bachelor days to more-than-enough coverage in his child rearing days to just-enough-to-bury-me in his senior years.

Insurance companies recognize that people's needs change over the years. Many companies offer flexible insurance coverage. As with any consumer item, it is a good idea to shop around.

ANNUITIES TO SPREAD THE INHERITANCE

In addition to the problem of how much life insurance to carry, there is the concern of how the monies will be spent. Leaving a large sum of money to a person who is less than prudent, may lead to a spending spree.

Most beneficiaries go through their inheritance within two years. For many, the reason the money is gone so soon, is that there just wasn't much money to inherit in the first place. But for others, it's a spending frenzy. Luckily, People's spending habits remain much the same throughout their lifetime. Some people are born squirrels, always saving for the winter. For others, it's

Earn-A-Penny Spend-A-Penny

Most of us fall somewhere in between. We are not extravagant in our spending habits, yet it is a struggle to save. But why should we struggle to purchase an insurance policy if the intended beneficiary will spend it all in a few months? If you want to leave an insurance policy benefit to someone you love, but the intended beneficiary is immature, or a born spendthrift, then a simple solution to the problem may be to purchase an ***Annuity*** rather than a life insurance policy with a single lump sum payment. You can purchase an Annuity from an insurance company so that upon your death (the ***Annuitant***) receives money on a regular basis (monthly, quarterly, yearly) rather than one large payment.

Hopefully, this regular source of income will encourage your beneficiary to think ahead, and learn to budget his finances.

THINGS THAT ARE CREDITOR PROOF

There are certain items that can be inherited by your beneficiaries free of the claims of your creditors. As discussed, the beneficiary of your life insurance policy inherits the proceeds of the policy free from the claims of your creditors. And that is so, regardless of the value of the life insurance policy. There are other items that can be inherited free of debt under Massachusetts law:

✧ THE HOMESTEAD ✧

As explained in Chapter 2, you can create an Estate Of Homestead by having your deed identify the property as your homestead, or you can have a *Declaration of Homestead* filed with the Registry of Deeds (GLM 188:2). The benefit of owning property as an Estate of Homestead is creditor protection. Up to $500,000 is exempt from the claims of the homeowner's creditors (GLM 188:1).

EXCEPTIONS TO THE RULE

The *Homestead Exemption* from the claims of creditor does not extend to taxes, delinquent payments for child or spousal support, monies owed prior to acquiring the homestead, mortgages or mechanics' liens on the property. It also does not extend to judgments against the homeowner that involves fraud, duress, undue influence, mistake, or lack of capacity.

Creditor protection continues for surviving spouse until he/she remarries or dies. If you have a minor child and no spouse, creditor protection is lost once the child reaches 18. And of course, if you are the sole owner of the property and not survived by spouse or minor child, creditor protection ends upon your death and your home can be sold to pay for monies you owe (GLM 188:4).

Only one homestead exemption is available for property held jointly. However, if you are 62 years of age or older, or if you meet the disability requirements for Supplemental Security Income ("SSI"), you are entitled to your own homestead exemption of $300,000. This means that a couple who own their home jointly, and who are both elderly, or disabled, are entitled to $600,000 of creditor protection for their Estate of Homestead (GLM 188:1A).

✧ HOUSEHOLD ITEMS ✧

Massachusetts statute (GLM 235:34) lists household items cannot be taken by creditors. The list includes:

- ⇨ household furniture, up to $3,000 in value
- ⇨ an automobile necessary for personal transportation or to maintain employment up to $700 in value
- ⇨ up to $300 in value of provisions (food, household items) for the family use
- ⇨ 2 cows, 12 sheep, 2 swine and 4 tons of hay
- ⇨ a bible, and other books up to $200 in value
- ⇨ a sewing machine, if in actual use by the family, up to $200 in value.

The Probate Court can also set aside other items of your personal property if it is needed by your surviving spouse. If you are single, up to $100 can be set aside for each of your minor children. This personal property is taken free of the cost of the Probate proceeding and free of your debts (GLM 196:2).

✧ GROUP INSURANCE PROCEEDS ✧

If you have a group annuity contract or a group life insurance policy as part of your employment, then the proceeds of such policies are creditor proof. The insurance proceeds are paid to you or the beneficiary of the policy free of your debt, with the exception of monies owed for child or spousal support. If you owe back support, the proceeds of the policy may be used to pay for those debts (GLM 175:132C, 175:135).

✧ BENEFITS FROM A FRATERNAL BENEFIT SOCIETY ✧

Any benefit that is payable by a fraternal benefit society (e.g., AARP, American Legion, Kiwanis, Lighthouse for the Blind, Rotary Club, etc.) is free of the monies owed by the decedent. In fact, benefits paid by a fraternal benefit society are free from the claims of the creditors of the member of the society AND from the creditors of the beneficiary (GLM 176:22).

✧ PENSION PLANS ✧

Annuities, pensions, profit sharing or other retirement plans regulated by the federal Employee Retirement Income Security Act of 1974, including Keogh plans and IRA accounts, and plans identified by the Internal Revenue Code of 1986 as 401(a) and 403(b) are creditor proof. Monies received by a beneficiary of such plans are protected from the decedent's creditor with the exception of monies owed by the decedent for child or spousal support, and monetary penalties for a crime. In general, income taxes are not paid when monies are placed in the fund but rather when monies are withdrawn from the account. Taxes must be paid regardless of whether the monies are withdrawn by the retiree or the person he named as beneficiary of the retirement plan (GLM 235:34A).

AN ESTATE PLAN FOR THE BANKRUPT

You may think the above title to be an oxymoron (a contradiction in terms). If a person is bankrupt, why plan for an Estate he doesn't have? But facts are, that people who file for bankruptcy are often quite wealthy and that is their downfall. Because they have substantial income or property, banks and people are willing to lend them money. If more money is borrowed than can be repaid, the unhappy result is bankruptcy. In the event you are concerned about meeting your responsibilities as parent or spouse, yet you enjoy a life style of financial brinksmanship, then consider investing in items that are "creditor proof."

That's exactly what Alan decided to do. Alan was astute, well aware of his strengths and weaknesses. He enjoyed his work and knew he had the capacity to earn large sums of money. But he also knew he was a gambler. Not the Las Vegas type, but a gambler in business ventures. "No risk, no gain" was one of his favorite sayings.

If you charted Alan's net worth over the years it would look like the peaks and valleys of the NASDAQ. Lots of high highs and low lows. Unfortunately, he married a woman who did not share his adventurous spirit. His wife became increasingly intolerant of their financial instability. She came to realize that this was his life style and things would never change. "All gamblers die broke," she said as she walked out the door with their 5 year old daughter in tow.

That, and the fact that he had to declare bankruptcy, brought Alan up short; and he began to be concerned about his future and that of his family.

Alan talked things over with his bankruptcy attorney "I am a good businessman, but not a clairvoyant. There was no way to predict the turn of events that led to this situation. But I know I will bounce back, and it will just be a matter of time before I am earning a good living. I also know that I am an entrepreneur and not a 9 to 5 type guy so this could happen again. What concerns me is how to provide some security for my child in case something happens to me before she is grown."

The attorney suggested "Your home is a great investment. You have an Estate of Homestead so up to $500,000 of its value is creditor proof, except for mortgages, taxes, and judgments against you that involve fraud and child or spousal support (GLM 188:1). In the event of your death, creditor protection continues until your daughter is 18, or so long as your spouse remains unmarried and continues to occupy the house (GLM 188:4) Because of the Homestead Exemption you can be assured that your daughter will have a decent place to live until she is grown. You could also purchase a life insurance policy naming your daughter as beneficiary. She will inherit the proceeds free of your debts. But I don't recommend you buy the policy right now. If you purchase the policy when you are insolvent (i.e., you owe more than you own), and then die, your creditors can demand that the monies paid for the policy (plus interest) be given to them and not to your daughter (GLM 175:125). But only the premium (what you paid for the policy) is at risk. If the premium is just a small part of the proceeds, then maybe this is not of concern to you. "

The attorney continued "A pension plan is an excellent Estate Planning tool. Not only are the funds protected from your creditors during your lifetime, but the monies can be inherited by your daughter free of your debts (GLM 235:34A)."

Alan was annoyed "You're saying that while I am alive, I can protect $500,000 of the equity in my home, and my retirement funds? What about all those millionaires who protect their money in Offshore Trusts? If I really hit it big, why can't I do that?"

"You could, but there are many drawbacks. Just to set up an Offshore Trust costs tens of thousands of dollars, not to mention how much it would cost just to maintain the Trust."

Alan said "Yes, but if I had millions of dollars that would not be a problem."

"True, but there are other considerations. Once you put your money into the Trust, you are essentially giving up control of that money."

Alan was skeptical "Oh come now. Why would anyone put his money where he can't get to it?"

The attorney explained "The Trust can be set up so that funds are available for whatever the millionaire wants. Usually funds are made available to support his family. Trust funds can be used to maintain the family home or yacht. Monies from the Trust can be used to pay for travel or for an expensive vacation. And of course the Trust would provide for the transfer of the property to the millionaire's beneficiaries, once the millionaire dies. What the millionaire can't do is be the Trustee of the Trust. The millionaire cannot be Trustee, because if he were, he would have control over the money, and his creditors could take legal action here in the United States to force him to use his Trustee powers to use that money to pay his creditors."

“How can they force the issue? Why couldn’t he, as Trustee, just refuse?”

“Remember, that as long as the millionaire is a citizen of the United States, and he is physically present in the states, he is subject to the laws of this country. If a creditor goes to Court and wins, the U. S. Judge could order the millionaire, as Trustee, to use Trust funds to pay that debt. If the millionaire-Trustee refused, the Judge could put him in jail for contempt of Court. No, for an Offshore Trust to work, the Trust must be a foreign Trust, that is, drafted according to the laws of a foreign country, Trust property must be located outside of the United States, and the Trustee cannot be a citizen of the United States.”

Alan said “Well I guess the millionaire might have a relative who is not a U.S. citizen to manage the Trust.”

The attorney agreed “Yes, or he could use a financial institution that does not do business in the U.S., to manage the funds. But there are other problems with an Offshore Trust. There’s the safety factor. Trust funds are kept outside of the United States. If the funds are kept in a foreign bank and the country suffers an economic collapse, then those funds could be lost.”

Alan wondered “Isn’t that much the same risk as money in a U.S. bank? Only $100,000 of the cash in a U. S. bank account is insured. If the bank fails, any money in that bank over $100,000 could be lost.”

The attorney disagreed “Our U.S government is stable, and we trust that they will regulate U.S. banks and keep our money safe. But that is not the case with other small countries. The government of a small country could collapse and the banks along with it.”

"But why keep money in a bank? Most millionaires have their funds invested in stocks and bonds, or in real property."

The attorney agreed "True, but real estate could be risky. If your Trust contains real property located within the United States, your creditor could go to a U.S. court and take that property."

Alan wondered "Couldn't the creditor take the overseas property as well?"

"He could, but it would be hard. For one thing he would need to find the property. And the Trustee is not about to tell him where it is, unless the creditor sues, and the laws of that foreign country require the Trustee to tell. Even if the creditor locates Trust property, whether it is stocks, bonds, or real estate, most Offshore Trusts are established in countries that are not creditor friendly. For example, if you set up an Offshore Trust in the Cook Islands, they will not accept a judgment that a creditor won in the United States. The creditor will need to employ a Cook Islands attorney to sue you all over again in the Cook Islands. That's expensive. And the Cook Islands have a higher standard of proof. Here in the U.S., all your creditor need do is show that you owe the money *by a preponderance of the evidence.* That's lawyer talk for "the jury must be more than 50% sure you owe the money." In the Cook Islands, the creditor's attorney must prove you owe the money *beyond a reasonable doubt* (Cook Islands, International Trusts Act of 1984 Section 13B(1)). That standard is the one we use here in the U.S. for criminal cases. In addition, the foreign country usually has a short Statute of Limitations, so if your creditor does not sue you in that country within that period of time, he cannot sue you at all."

Alan said "I can see why Offshore Trusts are so popular."

The attorney cautioned "But there are other problems. The U.S. considers transfers into and/or out of the Trust to be taxable. The IRS requires special tax returns to be filed for all foreign Trusts. In addition, the IRS looks closely at Offshore Trusts to determine whether they are fraudulent transfers, designed to avoid U.S. income taxes or U.S. Estate taxes. The IRS wants to be sure that the creditor the millionaire is avoiding isn't Uncle Sam!"

Alan said "Yes, but if you pay your taxes, that shouldn't be a problem. If I ever get to the point where I am that wealthy, I'll come back to discuss setting up an Offshore Trust."

The attorney refused "No, I'm just a country lawyer. If you want to go that route, you need a specialist — someone who has overseas connections, and who has experience in writing such Trusts. If you are serious about setting up an Offshore Trust, let me know and I will recommend someone to you."

"O.K. I will."

The attorney offered a final word of caution "If you are able to accumulate a significant amount of money, don't risk it all in a business venture. Limit the amount of money you can lose to just the money that you invest in business. Keep your personal funds separate and protected from your business debts. If you want to start a business, make sure that you cannot be personally liable for your business debts. You can avoid personal liability by forming a corporation, or a Limited Partnership, or a Limited Liability Company.** Stay away from a sole proprietorship or a business partnership."

** These topics are discussed in the next chapter.

Your Business Estate Plan 6

It would take a very thick book to do justice to the topic of Business Estate Planning. Estate Planning issues must be discussed for each type of business:

CONTROL	How to control and protect your business during your lifetime.
BENEFICIARY	How to be sure your business goes to the beneficiary of your choice.
COST	How to transfer your business to your beneficiary quickly and at lowest cost.

With just one chapter to devote to the topic, we can only provide the reader with an overview of the subject. Hopefully, the overview will give the reader some ideas that can later be pursued with a financial planner, or an attorney.

We have written this chapter for the reader who listed a business value as part of his Net Worth on page 4. People who are self employed, but who do not think of themselves as business owners, may profit from the information covered in this chapter, as well.

This chapter should also be of interest to someone who has the possibility of inheriting a business interest, such as the child of a small business owner, or perhaps the spouse of someone who is self employed. Even those who are thinking of starting a business, may find it worthwhile to take a few minutes to read this chapter.

Those who have no present business interest may want to skip this chapter and go on to Chapter 7.

Your business is your property, and as such it is included as part of your overall Estate Plan. But owning a business isn't as simple as just holding title to a tangible item such as a car or parcel of real estate. For example, if you own a business in your name only, i.e. as a ***sole proprietor***, there may be no single document that indicates ownership of your business property. If you are doing business under a name other than your own, you probably registered a Trade Name or Trade Mark with the OFFICE OF THE STATE SECRETARY of the Commonwealth when you applied for a business or occupational license (GLM 110B:1, 110B:2, 110B:4).

A Certificate of Registration issued by the State Secretary identifies you as the owner of the business, but it does not identify your business property. You could own a truck, computer, copier or other expensive business equipment. Title to that property is probably in your personal name.

Your business bank account may be in your name only, or in the Trade Name of the business with you alone as signatory on the account. Charge cards and business loans are either in your name only, or in the Trade Name with your name as guarantor.

If you want to leave your business to your son, how do you do it? Do you leave him the equipment used in the business? If you are doing business under your own name and not a registered Trade Name, how do you give him that name? And how do you handle business related loans? If you leave him the business, will he agree to be responsible for any outstanding business debt?

In addition to providing for the transfer of your business, you need to make provision for its operation in the event of your incapacity or death. If you do not make such provision, a Court may need to make that decision for you. In particular, if you become incapacitated, it may be necessary to have a Court appoint a Conservator to operate your business (GLM 201:16, 201:20). If you die, and have not provided for the transfer or continued operation of the business, the Court may authorize your Personal Representative to operate the business up to a year, or until it is transferred to the proper beneficiary (GLM 195:7).

A partnership can be even more complicated, unless there is a written partnership agreement that says how the business is to be transferred in the event that one of the partners dies. Even the transfer of a corporation can be a major headache if there are several shareholders and no shareholders' agreement to say how shares should be transferred in the event of the death of a shareholder.

For these reasons, it is important to think about an Estate Plan for your business. You need to ask yourself:

> *How can I have maximum protection and control over my business during my lifetime?*
>
> *How can I ensure that my business continues to operate in the event of my incapacity?*
>
> *How can I structure my business so that it can be transferred quickly and at minimum cost to my beneficiaries?*

We will examine each type of business ownership as it relates to these questions.

WHAT'S THE BEST TYPE OF BUSINESS OWNERSHIP?

Those who read the first five chapters know us well enough not to expect a definitive answer to the above question. Our job, as we see it, is to explain the rules of the game (i.e., Massachusetts law) to the reader. Once you know how things work in Massachusetts, you can make an informed decision as to the type of business ownership that best accomplishes your goal.

SOLE PROPRIETORSHIP
Maximum control — Maximum liability

You are the boss if you do business in your name only, but you take full personal responsibility for any loss suffered by the company; and as explained, you may need to consult with an attorney if you want to make arrangements for someone to take over your business should you become incapacitated or die.

Because of this personal liability issue, many people think it best to form a corporation as soon as they start up the business. That may not be the best strategy. It takes money to form a corporation. You may need to pay an attorney to set up the corporation. You will need to pay to file your Articles of Organization with the Office of the State Secretary. Each year you need to file an annual report and pay an annual filing fee (GLM 156B:6, 156B:13, 156B:109).

And there may be additional accounting fees. Each year you will need to file separate corporate income tax returns; one for the state and one for the IRS.

You do not need to pay filing fees to the Secretary of State to form a sole proprietorship, and you do not need to file separate income tax returns. You can include your business income as part of your personal income tax return and not go through the cost and hassle of filing a separate corporate return.

Another reason to start a business as a sole proprietorship is the risk of failure. Although every new business owner thinks his venture must surely culminate in riches, research conducted by the Brandow Company shows that only 55% of new businesses get to celebrate their third birthday (see their data at www.brandow.com). You can always form a corporation should your business succeed. If the business does not succeed, then at least you didn't waste time, effort and money to form a corporation.

But What About My Personal Liability?

Many people seek to limit their personal liability by forming a corporation, however, that doesn't always work in the real world. For example, if you wish to rent a store front or office space, an experienced landlord will allow you to lease the space in the corporate name, but he will require you to sign as a guarantor. Should the business fail, he will have the right to sue you, personally, for the full value of the lease. Once you have established a successful business, the landlord may agree to just hold the business liable; and in that case having a corporation instead of a sole proprietorship will limit your personal liability.

Regardless of what form of business ownership you choose, you can be held personally liable for any fraudulent or negligent act that you commit. The way to avoid personal liability for fraudulent acts is not to willfully (deliberately) deceive or cheat anyone.

Most of us are honest folk, but negligence is another matter. We all make mistakes. The way to limit your liability for negligence is to purchase insurance that provides protection for mistakes and accidents. For example, if you open a title insurance business, you can purchase an Errors and Omissions insurance policy to cover a loss caused by a mistake you might make in a title search. If you have a business involving the care of a person (adult or child day care center, nurse practitioner, etc.), it is important to have coverage for an injury to a client due to accident or negligence.

If you have a business location (a storefront or office) consider purchasing a comprehensive business insurance policy to cover injury to anyone who visits your business, as well as damages to the premises. For example, if you open a flower shop you can get insurance to cover an injury to a customer who slips and falls. The same policy can cover vandalism to your shop, such as a broken plate glass window. You can be compensated for loss should a storm cause the electricity to go out and your shipment of fresh cut flowers wilt for lack of refrigeration.

The purpose of any business insurance policy is to shift the risk of a business loss from your pocket to that of the insurance company.

And the downside is . . .

The problem with insurance is the greater the risk, the greater the cost. We all would like 100% insurance coverage, but few of us can afford the premium. What holds true for life insurance holds true for business insurance. The right amount of insurance coverage for you is the amount that allows you to sleep at night.

BUSINESS PARTNERSHIP
Shared control — Maximum liability

A business partnership is much like a marriage. You can both start out with the best of intentions, only to find that you are hopelessly incompatible. The break-up of a business partnership can be just as bitter and hotly contested as the breakup of a marriage. A properly drafted Partnership Agreement is a must — not only to set the terms of a dissolution, but to clearly state what is expected of each partner; i.e., how much each will contribute to the business venture in terms of effort or financing.

The Partnership Agreement should cover what will happen to the partner's share in the event of his incapacity or death. Most Partnership Agreements provide for an appraisal of the business and the buy out of the deceased (or disabled) partner's share. The Partnership Agreement may need to be backed up with financing. For example, you could sign a Partnership Agreement that requires the company to buy out your partnership interest should you become disabled or die. But what good is the Agreement if there is not enough cash in the company to pay for the buy out?

You will have better protection if the Partnership Agreement requires the company to maintain disability and life insurance to pay for the buy out. Many insurance companies offer Key man insurance. The policy is designed to compensate the company for the loss of someone who is essential to the continuation of the business. If sufficient insurance is purchased, the proceeds of the policy can be used to cover any loss suffered by the company and to buy out the share of the company that was owned by the deceased or disabled partner.

The sole proprietorship and the partnership are the earliest type of business organization. Massachusetts laws governing these types of business organizations have their roots in English Common Law. Common law requires the sole proprietor and each business partner to take full personal responsibility for the debts of the company. As people became ever more litigious (lawyer talk for "sue happy") businessmen sought to limit their liability and prevailed on the legislature to create a form of business ownership to limit that liability.

Legislatures in each state responded to that need by giving businessmen the right to create a company (the corporation) with an identity separate from the owners of the business. By doing business as a corporation, the businessman's liability is limited to the money he invests in the company. A person can sue the corporation for business debts, but not the owners of the corporation.

This does not mean that a corporate owner can use the corporation to do things that are fraudulent. If he does, he can be held personally liable but the Massachusetts Supreme Judicial/Appeals Court has ruled that they will "pierce the corporate veil" only if it is necessary to ". . . defeat fraud or wrong, or for the remedying of injuries. . ." Holding shareholders, directors or officers personally liable is done only in " . . . rare particular situations in order to prevent gross inequity." (*Gurry v. Cumberland Farms, Inc.*, 406 Mass 61 (1990)).

THE CORPORATION
flexible control — limited liability

Whoever forms a corporation (the *incorporator*) has maximum control over the corporation. He decides how the company will operate by having the Articles of Incorporation and the company By-laws prepared according to his specifications. He can keep full control of the company as the only shareholder, or he can distribute shares and give up as much control as he wishes. Transferring corporate ownership is simple. It is a matter of signing a stock certificate transferring the shares of stock in the company. You can have a Transfer On Death designation to a named beneficiary.

If you own shares of stock in your name only, without a TOD designation, your Personal Representative will transfer the shares to the proper beneficiary. But keeping shares in your name only may not be the best way to go if you own a majority of shares and operate the business yourself. If Probate is necessary, it may take several months before the shares are transferred to the proper beneficiary, meanwhile, someone needs to continue to operate the business. If you do not leave directions for the continuation of the business, the Personal Representative (or the Probate Court) may decide it is best to just sell the company and give the proceeds of the sale to your beneficiaries.

The better route is to have your attorney prepare a Revocable Living Trust and transfer the shares into the Trust. The Trust document can give your Successor Trustee specific instructions about how the business is to be managed or transferred should you become incapacitated or die. Still another important benefit is to avoid the need to Probate what may be your only valuable asset.

THE LIMITED PARTNERSHIP

Just as a sole proprietor can limit his liability by forming a corporation, the partners of a general partnership can limit their liability by converting the partnership to a ***Limited Partnership***. As with the corporation, the Limited Partnership is a creation of the legislature and is regulated by Massachusetts law. A *Certificate of Limited Partnership* must be filed with the Massachusetts Office of the Secretary of State (GLM 109:8).

The structure of a Limited Partnership differs from a general partnership. In a general partnership, each partner has full authority to conduct business on behalf of the partnership. Each partner is personally liable for monies owed by the partnership, regardless of whether that partner actually incurred the debt. The Limited Partnership has *General Partners* and *Limited Partners*. Only a General Partner has authority to conduct partnership business. A Limited Partner has no control over the management of the company and has no personal liability for company debts. However, the General Partner and the Limited Partnership itself can be sued for monies owed GLM 109:19, 109:24).

But even a General Partner can avoid personal liability by forming a corporation, and then letting the corporation serve as the sole General Partner. An unpaid creditor of the Limited Partnership can sue the corporate General Partner, but not the shareholders of the corporation. Liability can be limited to the amount of money invested in the business venture. None of the owners will have personal liability. Of course, as with the corporation, all parties can be held personally liable for fraudulent or criminal acts performed in their partnership capacity.

The astute reader might be wondering "Why would anyone form a corporation (and pay all of the costs to set up the corporation) and then make the corporation the General Partner of a Limited Partnership (after paying all that money to set up the Partnership)? If limited business liability is the goal, why not just form a corporation?"

Answers to those questions are many and in fact, far removed from the original goal of limiting the business risk of the partners to just the money they invested in the business. The Limited Partnership can be used as a means of transferring a family business to the children with some significant tax benefits. For example, suppose Mom & Pop run a small, highly profitable, rapidly expanding, gourmet chocolate shop. They have two children, both in college. Right now, the business is worth about $500,000, but they figure that by the time they retire, the business could be worth millions. If their children inherit the business at that time, there could be significant Estate Taxes due. Also, because they are making lots of money right now, they are paying very high income taxes.

Both problems can be solved with a Family Limited Partnership. Mom and Pop can be the General Partners of the company and retain total control. They can make each child a Limited Partner by transferring shares of the business worth less than the Annual Gift Tax Exclusion. The 2006 Exclusion is $12,000, so together Mom and Pop can gift shares of the partnership up to $24,000 per child, per year. By gifting a percentage of the business each year, the parents can eventually transfer all of the business to the children. When the parents die, there will be no Gift or Estate Tax because the children already own the business. Of course there is still the problem of the Capital Gains Tax should the children decide to sell the business.

Regardless of how much of the company they give away, Mom and Pop can keep total control of the company because they are General Partners. When the parents are ready to retire, one or both of the children can take over as General Partner — but if making chocolate is not their thing, the parents can arrange to have a corporation manage the Limited Partnership and the children continue to receive income as limited partners. As for the current income tax problem, the children, as limited partners, are entitled to receive income from the business. Income paid to the children and their parents is generally taxed at a lower rate than the taxes to just Mom and Pop. For example, suppose the company earns $100,000. Mom and Pop will pay a high rate of income tax if they are the only two partners in the company. If the children become partners, then each partner can earn $25,000 and the overall bill for income taxes will be smaller.

Still another important advantage of the Family Limited Partnership over the corporation is creditor protection for the children's partnership interest. For example, suppose one of the children becomes a dentist, gets sued for malpractice, and loses the case. If Mom and Pop had incorporated the business and given the children most of the shares of stock in the company, the creditor could take the shares to satisfy the judgment. The creditor could wind up owning the company! Not so, with a Limited Partnership interest. A judge could order that the income from the Limited Partnership be used to pay the judgment, but he could not order the Partnership share itself to be given to the creditor unless the Limited Partnership Agreement allows for such transfer or all of the partners agree (GLM 109:40, 109:41, 109:42). Not likely with Mom and Pop as General Partners. They might even decide to pay all of the income to themselves as salary and not distribute anything to the hapless creditor!

We used an actual business as an example to explain how the Limited Partnership worked. It didn't take Estate Planning attorneys long to figure out that the "family business" could be just income producing items (such as stocks and bonds) that Mom and Pop placed into the Limited Partnership. The family "business" could be just the business of earning income. In other words, the Family Limited Partnership (or even a Family Partnership) could just be a type of an Estate Plan created solely for the purpose of transferring assets to the children to avoid paying Estate Taxes, and to pay less in income taxes.

It didn't take the IRS long to challenge this method of Estate Planning. A series of IRS rulings and court cases followed, with the main issue being whether a bona fide business partnership existed.

There is a common sense rule of evidence that says "If it looks like a duck and walks like a duck, and quacks like a duck, it must be a duck." In 1946 the Supreme Court decided that whether a family partnership is really a business partnership for tax purposes, should be determined on a case by case basis; and that the IRS should use the "walk and quack" test. Only the justices said this in proper legal terms. They said to determine whether a partnership exists depends on "...whether the partners really and truly intended to join together for the purpose of carrying on a business and sharing in the profits or losses or both. And their intention in this respect is a question of fact, to be determined from testimony disclosed by their agreement, considered as a whole, and by their conduct in execution of its provisions" (*Commissioner v. Tower*, 327 U.S. 280 (1946)).

THE LIMITED LIABILITY COMPANY

The IRS continues to take a close look at family partnerships, and will challenge any tax break if the family partnership (limited or not) does not meet the basic requirement of being a bona fide business partnership. Perhaps in response to IRS challenges, in the 1990s each of the 50 states, and even the District of Columbia, passed laws enabling residents of their state to form a new business entity called a ***Limited Liability Company***. The name of the company must identify it as a Limited Liability Company "L.L.C." or "LLC" or a Limited Company or "L.C." or "LC. " (GLM 156C:3)

This new entity is not required to be a profit making venture. Under Massachusetts law it can be formed to ". . . carry on any lawful business, trade, profession, purpose or activity" (GLM 156C:6). A Massachusetts LLC is formed by filing a *Certificate of Organization* in the Office of the State Secretary.

The LLC combines the better features of the Limited Partnership and the Corporation. Like the corporation, it can be formed by a single person who sets the rules of the company when he forms the corporation. The set of rules is called an *Operating Agreement.* Members who join the company must agree to act in accordance with the Operating Agreement (GLM 156C:12)

The LLC can be run by a manager (who is not a member of the company) or it can be run by a member or members of the company. As with a corporation, all members have limited liability, regardless of whether that member happens to be managing the company.

As with a Limited Partnership, a creditor cannot take possession or control of a share of the company owned by a member. The most the creditor can do is get a court to assign income generated by that share to the creditor (GLM 156C:40).

Now Mom and Pop can form a LLC, give away some or all of the shares of the company during their lifetime, and still keep control of the company, and with no more personal liability than a non-managing member of the Limited Liability Company. Transfers into the Limited Liability Company can be made so that there are no Estate or Gift Tax consequences. Income can be distributed to the children, or not, as Mom and Pop see fit.

The skeptic is probably thinking "Maximum control, limited liability, easily transferred to my beneficiaries, no Estate Tax. This is too good to be true. There must be a catch somewhere."

And so there is. It's called the Capital Gains Tax. If you transfer property during your lifetime, that property is valued by the IRS as of the date of transfer. If you gift a share of the Limited Liability Company during your lifetime, your beneficiary will take your basis in the property (i.e., the value that you paid for your interest in the Company). If you sell the share to your beneficiary, his basis is the fair market value of the share as of the date of purchase. Either way, once the beneficiary decides to sell the property, there may be a significant Capital Gains Tax due. An experienced Estate Planning attorney should be able to suggest any number of ways to solve the problem, including purchasing life insurance to pay the tax.

INSURANCE TO PAY DEBTS AND TAXES

Regardless of what form of business ownership you have, you need to think about what will happen to your business in the event of your incapacity or death. And in particular, how company debts will be paid. If your business is highly leveraged (business talk for "owes lots of money"), you also need to consider how those loans will be paid should you become disabled or die. One solution is to purchase Key man insurance. As explained earlier, Key man insurance is protection for the company against the loss of a valuable employee. The company purchases the policy and the proceeds are paid to the company to compensate it for the loss; but ultimately the policy benefits those who inherit the business.

Taxes are still another concern. Your business may be worth millions on paper, and your Estate Taxes will be based on that value. Your heirs might be forced to sell the company just to pay the taxes, but without your leadership they may get only a fraction of the value of the company.

Even if the federal government decides to eliminate federal Estate Taxes, the state of Massachusetts, or any other state where you have a business location, may decide to levy an Estate or Inheritance Tax.

And there is still the problem of the Capital Gains Tax. No one in Congress is talking about doing away with the Capital Gains Tax — and that tax could be sizeable. One solution to the problem of an unknown Estate Tax and/or Capital Gains Tax is to purchase life insurance that can be used to pay for any Estate Tax that may be due upon your death and any Capital Gains Tax that may be due when your beneficiary sells the property he inherits.

That may sound like a good, simple, solution, but you need to think things through before calling your insurance agent. The first question being:

How much insurance should I purchase?
That is a tough question. If you are in good health, who knows what will happen before you die. Will your business increase in value or go bust? Will the federal government really do away with Estate Taxes or will they do nothing and allow the tax to be reinstated in 2011?

The last question is particularly troublesome. Under today's tax law, if you purchase a life insurance policy, or even control the benefits of the policy, all of the proceeds of the policy will be counted as part of your taxable Estate. You may be buying insurance just to pay more in taxes to Uncle Sam.

You don't need a soothsayer or psychic to solve the problem. A financial planner with access to computer generated models can predict your life expectancy, how much your business will be worth when you retire and even the probability that the economy will require Estate Taxes to be reinstated!

Suppose your financial planner predicts that Estate Taxes will be reinstated and that your heirs will probably need to pay one million dollars in federal and state Estate Taxes. If you purchase a million dollar insurance policy, the proceeds of the policy will be included in your Estate. If there is an Estate Tax of 40% your heirs will net only $600,000 of the million dollar policy, with the rest going to pay for Estate Taxes on the policy itself. Your heirs will need to come up with an additional $400,000 to make up for the original million dollars predicted as being necessary to pay your Estate Taxes. A solution to this dilemma is the IRREVOCABLE LIFE INSURANCE TRUST.

An ***Irrevocable Life Insurance Trust*** can be designed to provide money to pay any tax that may be due after your death. To be sure that the IRS does not count the proceeds of the Trust as part of your taxable Estate, the Trust must meet the following requirements:

- ⇨ The Trust must be irrevocable
- ⇨ You cannot be Trustee.

The Trust can be set up for the benefit of your child. In such case, the child can be Trustee of the Trust. The child, as Trustee, will purchase an insurance policy on your life. You may need to file a Gift Tax return if you give your child a large sum of money to purchase the policy. It is better to have the child purchase a policy that is paid in quarterly or annual premiums instead of a single lump sum payment. You can give the child an amount each year up to the Annual Gift Tax Exclusion ($12,000 in the year 2006) to pay for the premium. If you are married, you and your spouse can gift up to $24,000 per year without the need to file a Gift Tax return.

As tax laws change, the child/Trustee can use as much of the gift as is needed to purchase sufficient insurance to cover the taxes. The Trust can be set up to cover Estate taxes or Capital Gains taxes, or both. For example, the Trustee can purchase an insurance policy that pays a million dollars upon your death. Those insurance funds can be used to pay your Estate taxes. Should it happen that no Estate taxes are due, the Trustee can keep the monies invested until the business is sold. The Trust funds can be used to pay any Capital Gains Tax that may be due at that time. If monies are left over once all taxes are paid, they can be distributed to the named beneficiaries of the Trust.

Your attorney can design an Irrevocable Insurance Trust in any number of ways to meet the special needs of you and your family. For example, an Irrevocable Insurance Trust can be set up to solve problems described in the last Chapter. Alan wanted to leave insurance proceeds for his child but was concerned that the cash value of the policy could be taken by his creditors. A properly drafted Irrevocable Insurance Trust can solve such problem, because the Trust, and not Alan, is the owner of the policy.

Of course, it costs significant money to set up and maintain an Irrevocable Insurance Trust. Those who do not have concerns about creditors may wonder whether it's necessary to go through all that cost and bother if there will be no more Estate Taxes in the future. After all a simple life insurance policy can cover any Capital Gains Tax that may be due. But, as explained, the tax law as passed in 2001 reinstates the federal Estate Tax in 2011. If lawmakers take no further action, the Estate of anyone who dies on January 1, 2011, and thereafter is subject to a federal Estate Tax for an Estate over one million dollars.

Someone with an active imagination could envision the following scenario:

It is New Year's eve, 2010. A 97 year old lies sleeping, at his home, surrounded by his four grandchildren who are his sole heirs.

"He looks so peaceful."

"Yes. Surprising, considering that he has terminal cancer, failing kidneys and heart. His doctor says he can't last more than a few days. The doctor left a supply of morphine so that we can keep Gramps comfortable over the New Year's holiday. The doctor gave him a shot just before he left."

"The doctor said not to give Gramps another shot unless he was in pain. His heart is in such a weakened condition, he could easily overdose on morphine."

"Yes, of course."

"Too bad he didn't get a chance to do some Estate Planning before he had that stroke last year. "

"I thought his attorney took care of all that."

"His attorney suggested he set up an Irrevocable Insurance Trust to pay for any Estate Tax, but Gramps felt sure that Congress would pass a law that would permanently repeal the Estate Tax."

"I can't imagine Gramps coming to that conclusion. The economy is down and the government needs to raise taxes. It is easier for legislators to leave the law as written back in 2001, than take some affirmative action."

"Gramps was always a sharp business man, but in his later years his mind wasn't as clear as when he earned his five million dollars."

"Is that what we are going to inherit?"

"Not unless he dies before midnight. After midnight the Estate Tax is reinstated, and at a rate of 45%. Between state and federal taxes, we'll be lucky to come away with half a mill each."

"Gramps moved. I think he may be in pain."

"Yes, he does look uncomfortable."

"It isn't right to let him suffer like this."

"Yes, of course."

Continuing To Care 7

There are any number of reasons that people give for wanting to continue on with their lives. For the lucky ones, their main reason for living is that they are having a great time and don't want it to end. For many, it is more a sense of responsibility. During child rearing years the concern of the parent is what will happen to the child should the parent suddenly die. Once a child is grown, the roles often reverse, and it is the child worrying about what will happen to his parent if the child were not present to see to the care of the aging parent. Even pet lovers worry about what will happen to their pet should the owner no longer be around.

There is little that can be done to prepare those who depend on you for the loss of your companionship and emotional support; but there are many things you can do to provide financial support for those who rely on you. Even people of modest means can make financial provision so their loved ones will have an easy transition from being dependent to becoming self sufficient.

This chapter explains the many simple, and relatively inexpensive, things you can do to provide care for your loved ones should you not be present to do so yourself.

It doesn't happen very often, but both parents could die or become incapacitated before their child is an adult. Most parents don't want to think about, much less prepare for such a happening. But in this age of postponing parenthood, many parents are in their fifties and sixties and still raising children. The probability of a life threatening illness increases with age, so parents need to understand the importance of planning ahead.

Parents with dangerous occupations also need to provide for the care of their minor child in the event of the disability or death of both parents. It is surprising to think of how many of us are employed in high risk occupations. Construction workers, military personnel, firemen, state and federal law enforcement agents, and in this day and age, even postal workers face hazards on a daily basis.

Regardless of the parent's age or occupation, planning for the care of a minor child should be part of every parent's Estate Plan, not only because it is the responsible thing to do, but also because it is relatively simple and inexpensive to do.

A child must be cared for in two ways, the ***person*** of the child and the ***property*** of the child. To care for the person of the child, someone must be in charge of the child's everyday living, not only food and shelter but also to provide social, ethical and religious training. Someone must have legal authority to make medical decisions and see to the child's education. To care for the child's property, someone must be responsible to see that monies left to the child are used for the care of the child and that anything left over is preserved until the child becomes an adult.

A Guardian will need to be appointed to care for the person and property of the child in the event that both parents become incapacitated or die before the child is grown.

USING A WILL TO APPOINT A GUARDIAN

As explained in Chapter 4, each parent can use his Will to appoint someone to serve as Guardian of their minor child in the event that both parents die before the child is grown. It is a good idea for both parents to name the same person to serve as Guardian. If the child's parents appoint different people for the job and then die simultaneously, it will be up to the Court to decide who is best suited to be Guardian. If they do not die simultaneously, the Court will give top priority to the person named in the Will of the last parent to die (GLM 201:3).

It is important that you check with the person of your choice prior to making the appointment because should the need arise that person must be both ready and willing to take on the responsibility of raising your child. Have your attorney explain to your choice of Guardian what legal steps will need to be taken to become the legal Guardian of the child.

One problem with using a Will to appoint someone to be your child's Guardian, is that for the appointment to be effective, the Will must be admitted to Probate; i.e., the Court must determine that the Will is valid; and the person you chose as Guardian needs to file a petition to be appointed as the child's Guardian. It might take several weeks before that person has the legal authority to care for the child. A better solution is to appoint someone as a STANDBY GUARDIANSHIP PROXY who can immediately assume responsibility for the care of the minor child, should the need arise.

Parents can have their attorney prepare a document appointing a ***Standby Guardianship Proxy*** of their minor, or even unborn child, in the event they both become incapacitated or die. (GLM 201:2B). The parents need to sigm the Designation of Standby Guardianship Proxy in the presence of two witnesses — neither of whom is the Standby Guardianship Proxy. Only one parent needs to sign in the event that the other parent is deceased, incapacitated, or has had his parental rights terminated.

The appointment becomes effective upon any one of the following events:

- ➪ the death of the minor's parent(s)
- ➪ the consent of the minor's parent(s)
- ➪ the incapacity of the minor's parent(s) as established by the written certification of a licensed physician (GLM 201:2D).

The Standby Guardianship Proxy can immediately take over the care of the child in the event both parents are deceased or incapacitated or have had their parental rights terminated. However, within 90 days the Proxy must petition to be appointed as the legal Guardian of the minor.

If the Standby Guardianship Proxy does not apply to be Guardian within that time, and the parents are unable to care for the minor, upon petition by any interested party, the Court will appoint someone else for the job.

In the event that you did not appoint a Standby Guardianship Proxy, and you need someone to care for your child for a short period of time because you and the other parent are going to be absent, you can have your attorney prepare an ***Emergency Guardianship Proxy*** appointing someone to serve as the Emergency Proxy of the child.

Both parents must sign the document unless one of them is deceased, or has his parental rights terminated, or whose whereabouts are unknown (GLM 201:2G).

The Emergency Proxy can take over as soon as the document is signed or at a later specified date. For example, suppose you need to go into a hospital and expect to remain there for a few weeks. You can give the Emergency Proxy authority to care for your minor child for up to 60 days, beginning with the day you enter the hospital.

Court authority is not necessary for the Proxy to be effective, however, if the Proxy needs to continue to care for the child beyond 60 days, and you are unable to sign a new Proxy, the Proxy must apply to the Court to extend the time, or if necessary, be appointed as the child's legal Guardian (GLM 201:2H).

Appointing a Standby Guardianship Proxy or an Emergency Guardianship Proxy does not change your rights as a parent. While you are able, you and the Proxy will care for the child together (GLM 201:2D). You are free to revoke the appointment at any time and appoint another Proxy — or none at all (GLM 201:2F). You will need to revoke the Proxy in writing, and send a copy to anyone who might rely on the document to care for your child (GLM 201:2E).

THE BEST CHOICE OF GUARDIAN

Many parents never get around to appointing a Guardian for their minor child because they cannot come to an agreement as to the best choice of Guardian. "I think my mother should be Guardian. After all she raised me, and I turned out fine" can signal the opening salvo of a lengthy, and often unresolved battle. Not being able to agree on a choice of Guardian should not discourage you from appointing the person of your choice.

The thing to keep in mind is that the Guardian of your choice will take over only if the other parent is deceased or incapacitated. Even if you both die simultaneously, and you each name someone different to serve as Guardian, your choice of Guardian will at least be brought to the attention of the Court.

It is important that the person you choose to serve as Guardian be compatible with the child. If your choice of Guardian is not that of the child's, the child can object to the appointment. If the child is at least 14, the Court will appoint the child's choice of Guardian provided the Court determines that person is qualified to serve and it will be in the best interest of the child (GLM 201:2).

If neither parent has expressed his choice of Guardian, and the child is under 14, the judge will appoint whoever he thinks is best qualified for the job.

As any parent is well aware, it is expensive to raise a child. The person you consider to be the best choice to serve as Guardian might not be able to do so unless you leave sufficient monies to pay for the care of the child. If you have limited finances, consider purchasing a term life insurance policy on your life and/or on the life of the other parent of the child. If you can only afford one policy, insure the life of the parent who contributes most to the support of the child. Term insurance policies are relatively inexpensive if you limit the term to just that period of time until your child becomes an adult.

If you are married, you may want to name your spouse as the beneficiary with the child as an alternate beneficiary or you can name the child as primary beneficiary. Under Massachusetts law, the insurance company may give amounts up to $10,000 to the child by transferring the funds to an adult member of the minor's family.

The company is required to seek Court permission before transferring funds that exceed that amount (GLM 201A:7). If the sum to be transferred is substantial, the Court will require that a Guardian of the property be appointed to protect the funds until the child reaches 18.

AVOIDING AN UNNECESSARY GUARDIANSHIP

We discussed the ways parents can control who is appointed to serve as the Guardian of their minor child should both parents be incapacitated or deceased. Guardianship is a necessity in such cases. But if at least one of the parents is able to care for the person of the child, it may be wise to avoid the need for the Court to appoint a Guardian of the property. If you leave the child a significant amount of money, the Court will appoint a Guardian of that property. Even if the surviving parent is appointed to serve as Guardian, the amount you leave to the child will be reduced by the cost of establishing and maintaining the guardianship.

An attorney must be employed to establish the guardianship. His fee is charged to the child's Estate (GLM 215:39A). Once appointed, the Guardian must prepare an inventory and account each year for monies spent. He may need to employ an accountant to assist with the preparation of the inventory and the annual accounting. The Court may order him to obtain a surety bond for the protection of the property. All these expenses are paid from the money left to the child (GLM 205:1, 206:1).

Whatever is left to the child may be significantly reduced by the cost of caring for the property. This can be avoided by leaving property to the child in such a way, that will make it unnecessary for the Court to appoint a Guardian of the property of the child. One way to do so is to include a Trust for the child as part of your Will. Another is to set up a Revocable Living Trust that includes provisions for the care of your child. If you have limited finances, a good alternative is to appoint someone to serve as Custodian of the gift under the MASSACHUSETTS UNIFORM TRANSFERS TO MINORS ACT.

The ***Massachusetts Uniform Transfers to Minors Act*** is designed to protect gifts made to a minor by appointing someone to be the ***Custodian*** of a gift until the child is an adult. For example, you can make a minor child the beneficiary of your life insurance policy, and name a trusted relative or friend or even a financial institution to be the Custodian of the gift. Should you die while the child is a minor, the insurance company will give the proceeds of the policy to the person you named as Custodian to hold until the child is an adult.

You can make a gift to a minor in your Will. You can appoint your Personal Representative (or anyone else) as Custodian of the gift (GLM 201A:3, 201A:5). For example:

> I give the sum of $100,000 to ______________(name) as custodian for ________________ (name of minor) under the Massachusetts Uniform Transfers to Minors Act.

THE LIFETIME GIFT

You can even use the Massachusetts Uniform Transfers to Minors Law to make a gift during your lifetime of items such as a share in a corporation or a limited partnership interest. You can nominate yourself as Custodian of the gift, or you can name another person to serve as Custodian. Once the lifetime gift is made it becomes irrevocable, so this method is not appropriate unless you are sure that you want the child to have the gift once he/she is an adult (GLM 201A:4, 201A:9).

In general, the Custodian must distribute the gift when the child reaches 18; however, if you make a lifetime gift, or a gift as part of your Will, you can direct the Custodian to distribute the gift when the child reaches 21 (GLM 201A:20).

MANAGING THE PROPERTY

Under Massachusetts law, while the Custodian is in possession of the gift, he can use as much of the gift as he thinks advisable for the benefit of the child. He can pay monies directly to the child, or use the funds for the child's benefit. In making the distribution he is not obliged to take into account that someone else has a duty to support the child — even if the Custodian is the child's parent and it is his own responsibility to support the child (GLM 201A:14).

The Custodian can do the opposite and distribute nothing. He can refuse to use any of the monies for the child and just keep the funds invested until the funds are distributed when the child is an adult. In such case, the child's parent or guardian (or even the child once he is 14) can ask a Court to order that the monies be used for the care of the child. The judge will determine what is in the child's best interest and then rule on the matter (GLM 201A:12).

Hopefully, the Custodian will give a regular accounting to the child's parent or guardian. If not, any member of the child's family, or the child once he/she reaches 14, can ask the Court to order a full accounting of the custodial property (GLM 201A:19).

As with any type of Estate Plan, you need to examine all aspects of the transfer to see if there is anything that may be objectionable to you.

THE CUSTODIAN'S FEE

The law requires the Custodian to invest and manage the property in a responsible, prudent manner. The Custodian is entitled to be paid for his effort. If the gift is sizeable, his fee can be sizeable. Before appointing a person or a financial institution as Custodian, it is best to come to a written agreement about how the property will be managed and the charge for doing so (GLM 201A:15).

NO GROUP GIFT

You cannot make a single gift to more than one child under the Uniform Transfers To Minors Act. For example, if you want to make a single gift of real property to two or more minor children, you need to do so by another method, such as creating a Trust for the children (GLM 201A:10).

THE COST OF PROBATE

As discussed, you can include a gift to a minor in your Will by naming a Custodian for the gift. As with any gift made under a Will, a Probate procedure will be necessary to distribute the gift to the Custodian. If you are trying to avoid Probate, then this may not be the best way to go. If your gift is significant, the better route is to set up a Revocable Living Trust. You can manage the Trust while you are able. Should you become incapacitated or die before the child is grown your Successor Trustee will take over. Unlike the Uniform Gift to Minors, you can direct the Trustee to give the gift to the child at any age you think proper.

Which brings us to another problem, namely, that there is no flexibility as to the final distribution of a gift made under the Uniform Transfers to Minors Act.

MANDATORY DISTRIBUTION

A Custodian appointed under the Uniform Transfers To Minors Act must distribute the gift by the child's 18th birthday (21st if your Will or lifetime gift so directs) (GLM 201A:20).

The gift must be made regardless of whether the child is mature enough to handle the money in a responsible manner. A sizeable gift to an immature beneficiary is not the best Estate Plan.

Perhaps the reason that the story of Cinderella has such universal appeal is that many stepchildren, at one point or another, feel left out. The law seems to reinforce that perception. Unless a married person makes provision otherwise, a spouse has priority over the child in health matters both before and after death. If a married person is too ill to make medical decisions, the doctors will turn to the spouse for directions. Should a married person die, the decedent's spouse and not the child, has the authority to agree to an anatomical gift (GLM 113:8).

If a married couple hold all of their property jointly, that property will go to the surviving spouse and not to the child of the deceased parent. This might not be a problem if the surviving spouse is the natural parent of the child. It could be a major problem if the natural parent dies first. The stepchild of the surviving parent may be left with nothing.

In such situations, the stepparent comes across as villain, but it is the parent, and not the stepparent, who decides whether the child will inherit property belonging to the natural parent. Too often the stepchild is left out by default, i.e., the natural parent doesn't give the matter any thought, or perhaps the natural parent is confident that the stepparent will do "what's right."

That was the case with Walter. He always wanted to be a father, so he was pleased when Todd was born just before the first anniversary of Walter's marriage to Nancy. Twin girls were born just 15 months later. Unfortunately the twins' birth was premature, causing them to have medical and developmental problems. Nancy had her hands full just caring for the three children, so it was up to Walter to support the family.

Walter was up to the job. He was both conscientious and ambitious. He started his own interior decorating business, complete with a retail sales storefront to sell fabrics, and an upholstery shop in the rear of the store. With hard work and long hours, he was able to make a comfortable living. But the strain of raising a family and running a business took its toll, both on him and the marriage. At 40, he felt like an old man.

All that changed when he hired Annie to manage the retail part of his business. Her energy and sunny disposition were just what the business (and Walter) needed.

Walter's divorce from Nancy was amicable. Walter was a loving father who took his responsibilities seriously. He was generous when it came to supporting the children. Walter had only finished high school, and he wanted more for his son. He encouraged Todd to do well in school so that he could go on to college, and maybe become a doctor or lawyer. The twins had developmental problems; but Walter encouraged them to reach their maximum potential. It was his goal to help them become self sufficient.

Annie got along very well with her stepchildren. She had no trouble with Walter's desire to support the children and give them a good start in life. Even though they held all of their money in a joint account, she never questioned any expense made on behalf of the children.

Walter never gave much thought to an Estate Plan. After all, he was healthy, and in the prime of his earning capacity. He often said that he was fortunate to have married two wonderful women. If he had a dark thought, it soon passed, rationalizing that if something happened to him, Annie would take care of the children.

But she didn't.

Walter died in one of those freak accidents. He was trimming the branches from his tree with an electric saw and accidentally touched an overhead wire. All he owned was tied up in the business that he held jointly with Annie. Annie felt that she was a major factor in the success of that business. Why should she share any of her hard earned money with Nancy? As for the children, it was Nancy's job to raise them. After all they were Nancy's children, and not Annie's. If it was a struggle to support the children, that was Nancy's problem!

A better argument (but one she didn't raise) was that Walter really wanted Annie to inherit everything. If he wanted to provide for his children, he could have done so in any number of different ways, beginning with his marriage to Annie:

✍ He could have insisted on a Premarital Agreement that would have provided for certain funds to be kept separate for the benefit of his children.

✍ He could have signed a Partnership Agreement with Annie that would have given his share of the business to his children, in the event of his death.

✍ If he didn't want to negotiate with Annie about a Premarital or Partnership Agreement, he could have had his attorney prepare a Trust that would have cared for the children until they were old enough to be on their own.

✍ If nothing else, he could have purchased a life insurance policy with his children as beneficiaries of the policy.

Walter's situation is not unique. Second marriages are commonplace in America. Many who are widowed or divorced, remarry. If children are involved, the parent may have divided loyalties. The parent may want to provide income to the child until the child completes his education, and then leave whatever is left of his Estate to his surviving spouse. More often it is the other way around. The parent wants to be sure that the surviving spouse has sufficient income to support his/her current life-style, but once the surviving spouse dies, the parent wants all that remains to go to his children. A properly drafted Trust can provide for the care of a spouse and child in whatever way the Settlor of the Trust thinks best.

That was the case with an elderly widower who married a pretty girl less than half his age. Their Premarital Agreement made it clear that all his property would go to his son from his first marriage. Surprisingly, the marriage turned out well. So well that the couple had two daughters. The husband decided to divide his Estate equally between his three children and to provide for the care of his wife until the youngest child was grown.

His attorney suggested a Trust. "You can be Trustee during your lifetime. Once you die, your Successor Trustee can immediately distribute one-third of the Trust to your son who is now 55. No sense to keep him waiting. The rest of your money can remain in your Trust. Income from the Trust can be used to support your wife and children until the youngest is 25. Whatever remains in the Trust can be distributed equally to your daughters."

"Good idea" said the elderly gentlemen, with a smile "Just make sure it is revocable during my lifetime. Who knows what adventures I might be up to in the future?"

It isn't just stepchildren who can be left out if no provision is made. Even a child from a long-standing marriage can be cut off against the wishes of a parent. A parent may assume that all of their children will be treated equally when both parents are gone, but if all their property is held jointly, the last parent to die is the one who gets to decide "who gets what." Too often, the wishes of the deceased parent are ignored.

That was the case with Joan. She was married to Herb for over forty years. He was the breadwinner, but he was content to let Joan handle all of the finances. Joan wanted to be sure that each of their three daughters would always have a decent place to live. They purchased a three story house and each of the daughters moved into a different floor of the home. It was the parent's intent that once they were both gone, the daughters would inherit and occupy the building. The couple owned everything jointly, so when Joan died, all of their property, including the home, was owned by Herb.

The grief suffered by Herbert at his wife's death was more than he could manage. He alternated between sadness, despair and anger.

His middle daughter took the brunt of his anger. Their relationship had always been strained. She felt she could never live up to her father's expectations. She was not the cute baby of the family as was her younger sister. She was not the eldest daughter who always seemed to make her Dad proud. He always made her feel that she was a disappointment to him. Once her mother died, she had no one left to buffer the relationship with her father.

Soon after Joan's death, Herb had an attorney draft a Will leaving all property to his eldest and youngest daughter. None of the children knew what he had done.

Herbert decided to take a trip to Europe to try to escape the pain of his mourning. When he was in France, he suffered a heart attack and died. He died within six months of Joan's death. If he had returned from Europe, he may have reconciled with his daughter, but as it happened, there was no time for them to develop a better relationship.

With both their parents gone, the eldest and youngest daughter decided to sell the home. The youngest sister offered some of the proceeds to the middle daughter. She refused the offer with unkind words. In her mind, being offered less than her one-third share meant that her sisters approved of their father's action. It was as if she were being disinherited all over again.

It was unfortunate that Joan's best plans were thwarted. They didn't have to be. She and Herbert could have kept a Life Estate in the property with the remainder going to all three girls. That would have ensured that each daughter received an equal inheritance. More importantly, the family would not have been torn by the hurt and anger that was more a product of a husband's grief rather than the absence of a father's love.

Still another way to solve the problem is to set up a Family Trust so that the beneficiaries of the Trust cannot be changed unless both parents agree to the change. Family assets are placed in the Trust with the parents as co-Trustees. When one parent dies, the Trust becomes irrevocable. The Trust income goes to the surviving parent. Once the parent dies, whatever remains in the Trust is distributed in the manner as was agreed by both parents.

The caregiver of someone who is incapacitated, or developmentally disabled needs to, as part of his Estate Plan, provide for the care of the incapacitated person as well as himself. Should the caregiver become disabled or die, someone will need to take over and make medical decisions for the incapacitated person and see to it that he is properly housed and fed.

An aging parent of a developmentally disabled child may worry about how the child will manage without the parent to oversee his care. The parent can ask the Court to appoint a Guardian to care for the child. If the child has significant assets, the parent may ask the Court to appoint a Conservator to manage the child's finances (GLM 201:6A, 201:16B).

An aged spouse caring for his incapacitated spouse, may be concerned about who will care for the ill spouse should he die first. Often a family member will agree to take responsibility for the care of an incapacitated person; but perhaps no one wants the job.

If there are large sums of money involved it may be the opposite case, too many people may want to be in control. One family member may want the incapacitated person to remain at home with the assistance of a home health care worker. Another may think the best place is an assisted living facility with 24 hour care. The caregiver may worry about a tug-of-war erupting should he dies. In such case, the caregiver should consult with an attorney to ensure future care for the incapacitated person.

In both cases (i.e., disabled child or spouse), the attorney may suggest that a guardianship be set up with the caregiver and his choice of successor caregiver serving as Co-Guardians. The Co-Guardian can take full responsibility for the job should the caregiver become disabled or die.

Once the guardianship, or conservatorship, is in place, the Court will continue to supervise the care of the incapacitated person until he is restored to capacity or dies (GLM 201:13).

The only problem with setting up a conservatorship or guardianship while the caregiver is able to care for the disabled child or spouse is the legal cost. It may cost hundreds, if not thousands, of dollars to set up and maintain the guardianship. If the incapacitated person is without funds, the caregiver can ask the Legal Services for assistance. See page xii for information about finding the nearest Legal Services office. But those who have adequate funds may hesitate to go through the effort and expense to set up a guardianship if it may not be needed for years to come.

Your attorney may suggest that a Trust be established to provide funds to care for the incapacitated person. The only problem with establishing a Trust is the possible loss of government benefits. To avoid that problem the attorney can draft a SPECIAL NEEDS TRUST.

Government assistance is available to provide medical and custodial care for those who are disabled and without the means to care for themselves. Both state and federal government provide such assistance with programs such as Social Security disability benefits and Medicaid. The family often supplements the government program by providing for the incapacitated person's ***special needs*** or ***supplemental needs*** such as hobbies, special education, outings to a movie or a sports event — things that give the incapacitated person some quality of life.

This is not a problem while family members are alive and able to provide for the incapacitated person. The worry is how to continue that care should the provider die. To be eligible for government assistance programs the incapacitated person must essentially be without funds. Family members fear that leaving money to the incapacitated person in a Will or Trust will disqualify him from receiving government assistance. Parents of a disabled child may decide to solve the problem by leaving the money to a sibling or other family member with verbal instructions to take care of the child once the parent is deceased.

Of course, the problem with that approach is that once the funds are left to the family member, they become his property. Property of the family member is available to his creditors. The funds could be lost in a divorce, or the family member could die and the funds inherited by someone who is not willing to care for the disabled child.

A better solution is to have an experienced Elder Law attorney set up a ***Supplemental Needs Trust.*** The Trust can be funded by the parent during his lifetime, or after his death by making the Trust the beneficiary of his Will or Trust. It can also be funded by a life insurance policy on the life of the parent. The parent can purchase the policy and name the Supplemental Needs Trust as the beneficiary of the insurance funds.

The Trustee of the Supplemental Needs Trust can use the monies in the Trust to provide for the child's supplemental or special needs during his lifetime. The Trust Agreement can provide that upon the death of the incapacitated person, whatever remains in the Trust be distributed to whoever the parent names as the remainder beneficiary of the Trust.

CAUTION NOT RECOMMENDED FOR DISABLED SPOUSE

The Trust we have just described is appropriate for a disabled child, who has no funds of his own. The Trust is funded with monies owned by a parent and not the child. This Trust may not be the way to go if the disabled person is married and the Trust is funded by monies owned by the well spouse. When determining Medicaid eligibility, the federal government considers monies owned by both the husband and wife. If a Trust is set up using money owned by either of them, the government will consider the Trust funds to be available to pay for the care of the disabled spouse (42 U.S.C.1382c(a)(3), 1396p(d)(4)(A)).

In Chapters 9 and 10 we discuss different ways a married couple can arrange their finances to provide for their health care without jeopardizing their right to qualify for medical assistance.

CARING FOR YOUR PET

A woman died at peace,
leaving her fortune
and care of her cat to her niece.
Alas, the fortune and the cat
disappeared soon after that.

You could leave money to someone with the understanding that the person will take care of your pet, but the moral of the above limerick, is that just leaving money will not guarantee care for your pet. The better route is to have your attorney prepare a Will that includes specific instructions and funds to provide for the care of your pet during its lifetime.

Those with a Trust can include a provision for the lifetime care of your pet. The person you name as Trustee of the Pet Trust will be charged with the duty to use Trust funds to pay for the care of those animals who survive you. You will need to name a residuary beneficiary (a person or perhaps a charitable organization) to receive whatever remains in the Trust once all of the animals are deceased. Animal support groups, such as the Humane Society, have people who will care for the pet of a deceased owner. You might consider appointing such group as the remainder beneficiary of the Trust in exchange for checking to see that your pet is cared for in a humane and benevolent manner.

A Trust created for the benefit of a person can be enforced by Massachusetts Court. However, this is not the case with a Trust created for the benefit of an animal. It is important that you choose a Trustee and residuary beneficiary that you feel confident will follow the directions in the Trust, because as of mid 2006, there are no laws in the state of Massachusetts that will enforce the terms of a Trust created for the benefit of a pet.

Still another alternative is to ask a fellow pet lover to care for the animal. If no one among your circle of family and friends is able to do so, then ask your pet's veterinarian to consider starting an "Orphaned Pet Service" to assist in finding new homes for pets who lose their owners. It is good public relations and a potential source of income. If this is agreeable to the Veterinarian, you can make arrangements in your Will to pay the Vet to care for the pet until a suitable family can be found. This is a more humane approach than the, all too common practice of putting a pet "to sleep" rather than have the pet suffer the loss of its master. And in at least one case, that reasoning backfired.

Eleanor always had a pet in the house. After her husband died, her two poodles were her constant companions. When Eleanor became ill with cancer, she worried about what would happen to her "buddies" without her to care for them. She finally decided it best to have her family put them to sleep when she died.

Eleanor endured surgery, chemotherapy, radiation therapy, and even some holistic remedies, but she continued to go downhill. Eleanor's family came in to visit her at the hospital to say their last good-byes. She was so ill, she didn't even recognize them. No one thought she could last the day. Because the family was from out of state, and time short, they decided to put the pets to sleep so that when she died, they need only take care of the funeral arrangements.

To everyone's surprise, Eleanor rallied. She lived two more long, lonely years.

She often said she wished they had put her to sleep instead of her buddies.

THE CHARITABLE TRUST

We explained how a Trust can be set up to care for a pet and whatever is left over (the remainder) given to a charitable organization. There are other kinds of charitable trusts that can be set up to benefit the giver as well as the receiver. For example, suppose you own stock which has appreciated substantially over the years, but pays few dividends. This hasn't been a problem in the past because you earned a good income. But now you wish to retire, and will need additional income. You would like to cash in the stock and invest the funds in something that can supplement your retirement income, but your accountant says that a significant portion of the value of the stock will go to Uncle Sam as payment for the Capital Gains Tax.

By now you know that a clever Estate Planning attorney will have any number of ways to solve the problem. The dialogue with your attorney might go something like this:

ATTORNEY: "Do you have a favorite charity?"

"Yes, why do you ask?"

ATTORNEY: "You can set up a Charitable Remainder Trust and donate the stock to that charity by depositing the stock in the Trust. Charities don't pay taxes, so the stock can be sold and the proceeds invested in property that produces a good income. In return for the donation, you can receive an income for the next 20 years or you can receive a monthly annuity based on your life expectancy."

"What's in it for the charity?"

ATTORNEY: "The charity gets whatever is left after paying you the annuity."

"Yes, but suppose I die next year, and my wife is left without the securities and no income."

ATTORNEY: "No problem. If you decide on a 20 year annuity, you can name your wife or any other beneficiary to receive the balance of the annuity. If you wish, you can have an annuity based on your life expectancy and that of your spouse. If you predecease your spouse, then the income continues until she dies."

"It seems to me that if the annuity is based on my life expectancy AND my wife's life expectancy, there won't be much left for the charity."

ATTORNEY: "How much is left for the charity depends on the value of the gift and the cost of the annuity. The cost of the annuity depends on the combined life expectancy of you and your wife. I think the best way to understand this plan is for you to look at actual numbers. There are any number of ways to set up a Charitable Remainder Trust. I can explain each option to you. For each option, I will give you the cost of setting up the program; the amount of money you will get; and how much money will actually go to your favorite charity. Of course it must be an IRS approved charity. Once you see the numbers you can make an informed decision as to whether you want to sell the stock and pay the Capital Gains Tax, or set up a Charitable Trust and receive an income."

"Good idea."

Historically, Estate Planning for the wealthy was all about the Estate Tax. Estate Planning attorneys would spend their time dreaming up different ways to reduce Estate Taxes for their wealthy clients. The IRS would spend their time examining and challenging any Estate plan that appeared too innovative. It seems likely that by 2010 the federal Estate Tax will be a memory. Is the game over?

Hardly. As explained in Chapter 3, instead of paying an Estate Tax, the child who inherits property that has appreciated more than 1.3 million dollars will pay a Capital Gains Tax on the excess when he sells the property. In a way, that makes sense. A major criticism of the Estate Tax was that it had to be paid within nine months of the date of death. That created a hardship for those inheriting property with a high market value but with no cash to pay taxes on that value.

Critics of the Estate Tax often cited the example of the cash poor farm located on valuable land. Once the owner of the farm died, the family would be forced to sell the farm just to pay Estate Taxes. By substituting the Capital Gains Tax for the Estate Tax, that problem is eliminated. No tax is due until the beneficiary sells the property. Theoretically, the family farm can now be inherited generation to generation without a tax consequence.

But there are few family farms in today's economy. Future heirs are more likely to inherit highly appreciated real property or securities that they will want to sell. And when they do, they may need to pay a significant Capital Gains Tax.

The new game for Estate Planning attorneys will be to devise an Estate Plan that will reduce the Capital Gains Tax. The IRS will, no doubt, enjoy challenging those plans.

One tried (and legal) method of reducing the Capital Gains Tax is the Charitable Remainder Trust as was just discussed. It doesn't take a crystal ball to see that this could well be the basis of future Estate Plans, so we will take a few more pages to describe the pros and cons of the Trust.

THE CHARITABLE REMAINDER ANNUITY TRUST

A ***Charitable Remainder Annuity Trust*** is a Trust that is established according to the Internal Revenue Code (26 U.S.C. 664). Charities do not pay taxes, so property donated to the Trust can be sold by the Trustee free of the Capital Gains Tax. Money from the sale is invested so that it provides an income (an *annuity*) to the beneficiary (the *annuitant*) for a fixed period of time, say 20 years, or for the annuitant's lifetime as computed by actuarial tables (i.e., life expectancy tables). The charity receives whatever is left (the *remainder*) after payment of the annuity. How much income the donor will receive and how much the charity will receive, is agreed upon at the time the Trust is set up.

The Trust can be set up in any number of ways depending on the goal of the *donor* (the person making the gift). In the example just given, the goal of the donor was to convert non-income producing property to income producing property without paying a high Capital Gains Tax. A wealthy donor may be more concerned about his child paying a high Capital Gains Tax should the child inherit highly appreciated property.

For example, suppose you bought acreage in Massachusetts that appreciated significantly over the years and is now worth 1 million dollars. You have been putting off selling the property because of the Capital Gains Tax. But it has been a burden to you. It produces no income and because the property continues to appreciate, each year you are paying more and more in property taxes. You did not mind the sacrifice because you figured that your son would inherit the property at a step-up in basis. But now with the new tax law, by the time you die, the property may be worth three million dollars. He is only allowed a 1.3 million dollar step up in basis, so your son may need to pay a significant Capital Gains Tax when he sells the property.

Setting up a Charitable Remainder Annuity Trust solves the problem of the Capital Gains Tax. The land is transferred to the Charitable Trust. Charities pay no tax, so the Trustee can sell the land and the full market value of the property will be available for investment.

The Trust could be set up with you receiving an income for life, and your son receiving the annuity after your death. The only problem with this arrangement is that your son is significantly younger than you are. There may not be much left to benefit the charity if they must wait for both of you to die. The solution is to have the annuity based on your life only and then use part of the income that you receive to purchase a three million dollar insurance policy on your life with your son as beneficiary. The three million dollars is the estimated value of the land that your son would have inherited at your death. But with this arrangement he will inherit the insurance proceeds free of any Capital Gains Tax.

The astute reader (and probably one with an accounting background) will say "Aha, you may have avoided the Capital Gains Tax, but the Estate Tax Exclusion value does not increase to 3.5 million dollars until the year 2009 — and Massachusetts Estate Taxes are due on anything over a million dollars. The three million dollar life insurance policy counts as part of your taxable Estate, so if you die before 2009, your son will pay an Estate Tax! "

And of course our clever imaginary attorney has a solution in the form of an Irrevocable Insurance Trust. You can set up an Irrevocable Trust so that the Trust owns the insurance policy and not you. The insurance policy is not included in your taxable Estate, so your son pays no Estate Tax. See the end of Chapter 6 for an explanation of how the Irrevocable Insurance Trust works.

As with any Estate Plan you need to consider the down-side, and the Charitable Remainder Annuity Trust is no exception.

⌦ ATTORNEY FEES

It may cost significant attorney fees to set up the Trust. Some charities may offer to have their attorney prepare the Trust at no cost to you, or perhaps they offer a "standard" Trust document that their attorney prepared. But using the charity's Trust document represents a conflict of interest. Their Trust was prepared by an attorney for the greatest benefit to his client (that's the charity, not you).

It is important that you employ your own attorney to represent you. He knows the extent of your Estate and he understands what you wish to accomplish.

☒ THE COMPLEXITY OF THE PLAN

A Charitable Remainder Annuity Trust is a sophisticated Estate Planning tool designed to benefit the well-to-do donor and an IRS approved charity. There are any number of ways to set up the plan. It is important to have an attorney who will take the time to explore different plans until you determine the best plan for you.

☒ THE TRUST IS IRREVOCABLE

Once established, the Trust is not revocable, so it is important to understand all of the aspects of the Trust. In particular, you need to know how much it will cost in attorney's fees to set up the Trust, how much income you will receive, and over what period of time. The income you receive as an annuitant is taxable to you. You need to consider that while taxes may change over the years, the terms of the Trust cannot be changed. Have your attorney, accountant or financial planner give you an educated guess as to what you might expect in terms of future income tax liability.

Although future income tax payments may be uncertain, the power of the Charitable Remainder Trust is the tax benefit to the donor at the time the Trust is set up.

☑ NO CAPITAL GAINS TAX

Had you sold the property and invested the money yourself, you would have paid a Capital Gains Tax. That tax could have been substantial, depending on the tax rate in effect at the time of the transfer. By gifting the property, the full value of the land can be used to produce investment income.

☑ NO PROPERTY TAX

Once your property is transferred into the Trust, you will no longer need to pay annual property taxes.

☑ NO GIFT TAX

The property you transfer into the Trust is a gift to a charity and as such is not included in the sum total of taxable gifts that you give during your lifetime.

☑ INCOME TAX DEDUCTION

Because you are making a charitable donation, you should be able to take a charitable deduction on your income tax return in the year of the donation.

There are other "perks" in addition to the tax benefits:

☑ NO PROBATE EXPENSE

It might take an expensive and time consuming Probate procedure to transfer the property to a beneficiary upon your death. By transferring the property to the Trust during your lifetime, you avoid the need for a Probate procedure to transfer the property after your death.

☑ GIVE WHEN NEEDED INSTEAD OF LATER

A Charitable Remainder Annuity Trust can be set up in any number of different ways to accommodate your Estate Plan. For example, if you are not in need of a present income, but expect that you will spend significant sums on your child's education, you can set up a 20 year annuity with your child as the annuitant. This will get the child through college and probably be a great help should the child decide to start a family. Why have the child inherit property in later, high earning years rather than in the early, high expense/low income years?

☑ CREDITOR PROTECTION

If you keep the land and are sued, you could lose it to pay your creditors. If a beneficiary inherits the land, it could be lost to his creditors. But once the property is transferred to the Trust, the gift is made. Neither your creditors nor your beneficiary's creditors can gain access to the Trust funds. The most a creditor can do is seek payment from the money that is received as an income.

☑ GOOD DEED

If you are concerned that your son will be tagged with a Capital Gains Tax once you die, it means that your property has appreciated more than 1.3 million dollars, and you are fortunate indeed. By setting up a Charitable Trust, you are making a donation to the charity of your choice. You are sharing your good fortune with others. You can consider this as "giving back" to the community, or just plain doing a good deed.

BECOME A PHILANTHROPIST

Instead of giving the property to an established charity, you can become a philanthropist and set up your own Charitable foundation. The foundation can be in the form of an IRS approved Charitable Trust. You can be the Trustee of the Charitable Trust and your child the Successor Trustee. The Trust can be set up according to your specific charitable purposes. You can use the Trust to benefit a single cause or several worthy projects. This can be an exciting adventure for those with ample resources and a community spirit.

An Estate Plan For Your Person 8

The law makes a distinction between your property (what you own) and your person (your body). We have been discussing how to set up an Estate Plan for your property with the goal of maximum control over your Estate during your lifetime, and minimum cost and hassle to your heirs once you die. An Estate Plan for your body is just as important as an Estate Plan for your property. The goals are much the same. Maximum control over your body during your lifetime. Minimum cost and hassle to your family for your final disposition.

You may think it strange to speak of planning for maximum control of your body during your lifetime. After all, it's your body. Who else but you has any right to control what you do with your body? That may be true so long as you have capacity, but should you become seriously ill, you may be unable to express your wishes about the care you wish to receive. If you do not have an Estate Plan in place for your person, then your next of kin, or maybe the state of Massachusetts may make health decisions for you.

The same applies to the final disposition of your body. If you don't make burial and funeral arrangements, then someone will need to make these decisions for you.

As this chapter will show, it is relatively simple and inexpensive to set up an Estate Plan for your Person.

People with a large family often arrange for a family burial site. Over the years deceased family members come to occupy a space in that site, but others may have been buried elsewhere. Surviving family members often lose track of the number of spaces left. If this is the case with your family, you need to take inventory of the number of spaces available and who in the family expects to use those spaces.

It is important to keep in touch with the cemetery and let them know if there is a change in the expected occupant of the burial site.

OUT OF STATE BURIAL SITE

It may be that the family burial site is not in the state of Massachusetts. In such case, it is important to consider the cost of transporting the body from Massachusetts to the out-of-state cemetery. That cost can be substantial, in some cases doubling the cost of the burial. If there is no emotional attachment to the out-of-state burial site, you may want to consider assigning the burial site to a family member who lives closer to the site and making your own burial arrangements here in Massachusetts.

Even if you don't care where you are buried, it may be very important to your family. That is often the case in second marriages. If you have children from a first marriage, they may want their parents to be "reunited in death." Your current spouse may not take kindly to having you buried with your former spouse. This might result in hard feelings, if not an out-and-out battle.

Increasingly people are opting for cremation. The reasons for choosing cremation are varied, but for many, it is a matter of finances. The cost of cremation is approximately one-sixth that of an ordinary funeral and burial. A major saving is the cost of the casket. A casket is not necessary for the cremation. An alternate container of fiberboard or similar materials, can be used to transport the body. Embalming is not necessary either, unless there is to be a funeral with a viewing. Federal law prohibits a funeral director from saying that a casket or embalming is necessary for a direct (immediate) cremation (16 Code of Federal Regulations ("CFR") 453.3 (b)(1)(ii)).

For those who are considering cremation, there are a few things to consider.

THE PACEMAKER

Cremating a body with a pacemaker or any radiation producing device can cause damage to the cremation chamber and/or to the person performing the cremation. If you have such an electronic aid, it will need to be removed prior to the cremation. You might check with the cremation service to determine the cost of having the pacemaker removed.

A pacemaker can be donated for use in animals with a medical need for the device. If you are interested in making such donation, you can ask your local veterinarian to refer you to an animal clinic that performs the procedure, and then arrange to have it removed prior to your burial or cremation.

THE OVERWEIGHT

Cremation technology has kept up with the expanding waist line of our population. Most Cremation Services can accommodate a body weighing up to 400 pounds. But if you are extremely obese, you need to ask the cremation service whether their facility is large enough. If you cannot locate a crematory that can accommodate your weight, you will need to make burial arrangements.

WHAT TO DO WITH THE ASHES

In addition to planning for the procedure, you need to give your family some guidance as to where to place the ashes. Some cemeteries allow an urn containing the cremated remains of a family member to be placed in an occupied family plot. Similarly, some cemeteries will allow the cremated remains to be placed in the space in a mausoleum that is currently occupied by a member of the decedent's family. If you intend to be cremated and all your family spaces are occupied, you may want to call the cemetery and ask them to explain their policy as it relates to the burial of urns in occupied sites.

If burial in the family site is not an option, you will need to arrange for a separate burial space. Many cemeteries have a separate building called a *columbarium*, which is especially designed to store urns. You can purchase a storage place for the urn in the same manner as the purchase of a burial space in a cemetery.

If you wish to have your cremated remains scattered, you need to let your next of kin know where and how this is to be done. If you want your ashes spread out to sea, your family will need to arrange to have a boat go out at least three nautical miles, because federal law prohibits ashes from being scattered any closer than that distance from land (40 CFR 229.1).

THE MILITARY BURIAL

If you are an honorably discharged veteran or the spouse of such veteran, you have the right to be buried in a Veterans National Cemetery. If your Veteran spouse was buried in a Veterans National Cemetery, you have the right to be buried in that same grave site unless soil conditions require a separate burial site.

You can get information about burial at a Veterans National Cemetery by calling the Veteran's Administration at (800) 827-1000, or visiting their Web site.

VA CEMETERY WEB SITE
http://www.cem.va.gov

The site has information on the following topics:

- National and Military Cemeteries
- Burial, Headstones and Markers
- State Cemetery Grants Program

You cannot reserve a grave site in advance, so your family will need to make arrangements and establish your eligibility to be buried in a Veterans National Cemetery. At that time, they will need to provide the following information:

- your rank, serial, social security and VA claim numbers
- the branch of service in which you served, the date and place of your entry into and separation from the service
- a copy of your official military discharge document bearing an official seal or a DD 214 form.

If you wish to be buried in a national cemetery, you need to make all of these items readily accessible to your family.

In addition to making arrangements for a burial space or for a cremation, consider purchasing a Pre-need Funeral Plan. It will be easier on your family emotionally and financially if you make your own funeral arrangements.

Federal law requires that you receive a general price list at the beginning of any discussion for the purchase of funeral services (16 CFR 453.2). In addition to federal law, the sale of Pre-Need Funeral Contracts is regulated by Chapter 239 of the Code of Massachusetts Regulations ("CMR"). Section 4.04 of the Code requires the funeral director to give you a copy of a "Buyer's Guide To Pre-Need Funeral Arrangements (239 CMR 4.04). It is a good idea to take the time to read the Guide before signing your contract.

Once you decide upon a plan, the seller should give you a contract that states the prices charged for *services* (embalming, viewing, transportation, etc.) and *merchandise purchased* (casket, urn, acknowledgment cards, register books, clothing, etc.) and *cash advance items*, i.e., things paid for by the funeral director and then reimbursed back to him. This includes paying for death certificates, arranging to have the obituary printed, payment for religious services, etc. (16 CFR 453.5, 239 CMR 4.01).

Even though the seller gives you a "standard" contract that is prepared according to Massachusetts law, it does not mean that it cannot be changed. If you are not satisfied with the way a certain section of the contract reads, attach an addendum to the contract that explains, in plain English, your understanding of that passage. If you are concerned about something not mentioned in the contract, insist that the contract be amended to include that item.

In particular, check to see whether the contract answers the following questions:

Does the contract cover all costs?

The contract should contain an itemized list stating exactly what goods and services are included in the sales price. Your contract may include an allowance towards cash advance items such as the printing of the obituary or payment to the clergy, or your contract may provide that payment be made at the time of the funeral. Your contract should state that the amount charged by the funeral director for a cash advance item be no more than the amount paid by the director for that item.

Is the contract cost-protected?

Some Pre-need Funeral Plans have a fixed price for the goods and services you choose, meaning that the funeral director will provide the goods and services at the same price as agreed at the time of the contract (239 CMR 4.05). It is important that your *Cost-Protected Funeral Contract* state that the person or company who is selling you the Funeral Plan is the same person or company who will actually provide those goods and services. If not, you need to have the provider of the goods and services sign the contract saying that he agrees to be bound by the terms of your agreement. If the seller says that it is not necessary for the provider to sign your contract because he and the provider have a separate written agreement, have that agreement attached to your contract.

If you opt for a Pre-need Funeral Contract that is not cost-protected, the company can charge additional monies for the plan upon your death. In these days of an ever increasing life expectancy, it is important that such a contract clearly state how the price will be determined when the contract is finally put into effect.

How are your contract funds protected?
You can fund your Pre-need Funeral Plan by purchasing a life insurance policy and assigning the proceeds of the policy to the seller to pay for the goods and services under your Pre-need Funeral contract. In such case, your Pre-need contract and the assignment should identify the insurance company and the policy that is being assigned.

TRUST ACCOUNT
You may decide to pay cash for your Pre-need Funeral Plan. Under Massachusetts law, within 15 days of the day you sign the contract, at least 90% of what you paid must be deposited into a Funeral Trust Fund bank account. The Trustee of the account can be the funeral firm or the Trust department of the bank (239 CMR 4.09). You may want to have your contract state that you will be given proof of deposit. Your contract should also state that you will receive an annual statement of the amount on deposit and that you will receive written notice in the event that the Trust funds are moved to a different bank or Trust company.

The monies in the account will belong to you during your lifetime, and will be paid to the funeral firm upon your death and completion of the contract. But there are downsides to such a plan.

INTEREST IS INCOME TO YOU
Because you own the account, interest on that account will be included as taxable income to you.

SERVICE FEE
The funeral firm may charge a service fee that will be deducted from the interest earned on that account. Your contract will probably state that you will forfeit the service fee should you decide to cancel the contract.

Is the funeral firm reputable?

All these protections don't do much good if you are not dealing with a reputable company. It is important to take the time to check up on whoever is selling you the contract. In Massachusetts, anyone who offers Pre-need Funeral contracts to the public must be licensed to do so (239 CMR 4.02). You can check to see if the seller is licensed by calling the MASSACHUSETTS BOARD OF REGISTRATION OF EMBALMERS AND FUNERAL DIRECTORS at (617) 727-1718. You may want to ask how long the firm has been in business and whether any complaint has been filed against them.

Can you cancel the contract?

Massachusetts law gives you the right to cancel your Pre-need Funeral Contract within ten days of signing the contract and receive all of your money back. After ten days, the amount returned depends on the terms of your contract. Massachusetts law requires that you give written notice of the cancellation to the funeral director. The director will forward the notice to the Trustee of the funeral Trust Account. The Trustee must return all of the money in the account to you within ten days of receiving notice (239 CMR 4.07). But only 90% of your money may be deposited in the account. Depending on the terms of your agreement, you may be charged up to 10% for work performed by the funeral director and Trustee in setting up the Trust account.

If you use an insurance policy to fund the plan, you can receive your full premium if you cancel within ten days. After that you will receive the cash surrender value of the policy (239 CMR 4.10). That value should be printed on the policy. If you pay for your plan by installments, you need to know how much of the money you paid will be returned in the event you default on a payment.

FUNERAL PLANS FOR THOSE ON PUBLIC ASSISTANCE

People who are applying for, or receiving, Medicaid, Supplemental Security Income ("SSI") and other public assistance programs have limits on the amount of assets that they own. If someone purchases a Pre-need Funeral Plan, the monies paid into the plan count as an asset because the purchaser of the plan can revoke the contract and get his money back. Understanding the problem, the Massachusetts legislature included a provision in the law that a burial contract does not count as an asset for purposes of qualifying for Medical Assistance provided the contract is irrevocable. (GLM 118E:25(5)).

If you are in the process of applying for a public assistance program, before finalizing your funeral plan, it is prudent to check with your local Division of Medical Assistance to be sure that your plan will not affect your ability to qualify for Medicaid, which in Massachusetts is referred to as *MassHealth*.

Even if you are in good health at this time, it is a good idea to have your contract provide that you can change your plan to conform to state and federal law, if at any time you need to apply for a public assistance program.

Suppose you die in another state or country?

Your contract should spell out what provision will be made in the event that you move to another state or die in another state or country. Many funeral firms are part of a national funeral service corporation with funeral firms located throughout the United States. You may be able to have the contract provide that there will be no additional charge if the contract is performed by one of the funeral firms owned by the parent company.

If your funeral firm is not part of a national organizaton and you happen to die in another state, Massachusetts law requires the transfer or assignment of the Pre-need Funeral Contract to another licensed funeral establishment provided your legal representative gives written authorization for the transfer and the new firm agrees, in writing, to honor your Massachusetts contract (239 CMR 4.06). The only problem with the transfer of the contract is that it may take a Probate procedure to appoint someone as your legal representative. To avoid taking the time to appoint a Personal Represntative, have your contract provide that a family member of your choice has the right and authority to assign the contract to another funeral firm upon your death.

Can the plan be changed after your death?

It may happen that your heirs need to cancel the plan after your death because:

- ➢ your body is missing or cannot be recovered, or
- ➢ you were buried by another facility because no one knew that you had a Pre-need contract, or
- ➢ you died in another country and were buried there.

Your contract should address these potential problems, and spell out how much money will be refunded and who is to receive the refund.

You may also want to specify whether your heirs have the right to alter your funeral plans. In the absence of such a provision in the contract, funeral firms usually allow the family to arrange for a more expensive plan, provided they agree to pay the difference.

You may wonder why anyone would think of changing the decedent's funeral plan, but consider that in today's market, it is not uncommon for a Pre-need Funeral Plan to cost several thousand dollars. A top end funeral complete with solid bronze casket can cost upwards of $30,000. Some heirs might be motivated to save money by changing the plan to one of a lesser value.

That was the case with Lester. His mother, Mona, was a difficult woman with a personality that can only be described as "sour." Her husband deserted her after four years of marriage leaving her to raise Lester by herself. Once Lester was grown, Mona made it clear to him that she had done her job and now he was on his own. Lester could have used some help. He married and had three children. One of his children suffered with asthma and it was a constant struggle to keep up with the medical bills.

Mona believed in being good to herself. She did not intend to, nor did she, leave much money when she died. She knew that Lester would not be able to afford a "proper" burial for her, so she purchased a funeral plan and paid close to $18,000 for it. She was pleased when the funeral director told her that the monies would be kept safely in a Trust account until the time they were needed.

Lester was not familiar with Massachusetts law, so when his mother died he asked an attorney at the Legal Aid office to determine whether the Pre-need Funeral contract was revocable.

It was.

You know the ending to this story.

The reader might be thinking "Revocable. Irrevocable. All this contract stuff is giving me a headache. Why can't I just set aside some money and let my kids figure it out?"

The problem with that approach is that the cost of your final illness may leave you with little or no funds for your burial. To avoid the problem, you could purchase a life insurance policy to fund your funeral and burial, naming one or two trusted family members as the beneficiary of the policy. It is important that the person who is to receive the insurance funds clearly understands why he is named as beneficiary of the policy. It is equally important that the beneficiary agrees to use the monies for the intended purpose.

It isn't so much that a family member is not trustworthy as it is that they may not understand what you intended — especially in those cases where other funds are available to pay for the funeral. Too often insurance funds are left to a child who refuses to contribute to the cost of the funeral saying "Dad wanted me to have this money. That's why he left it to me."

To avoid a misunderstanding, put it in writing. It need not be a formal contract. It could be something as simple as a letter to the insurance beneficiary, with copies to your next of kin.

See the next page for an example of such letter.

Dear Paul,

I purchased a $20,000 insurance policy today naming you as beneficiary of the policy. As we discussed this money is to be used to pay for the following:

- *my funeral, grave site and headstone*
- *perpetual care for my grave*
- *airfare for each of my grandchildren to attend the funeral*
- *dinner for the family after the wake*
- *lunch for the family after the funeral*

If there is any money left over, please accept it as my thanks for all the effort spent on my behalf.

Love,

Dad

P.S. I am sending a copy of this letter to your sister so that she will know that all arrangements have been made.

Whether or not you arrange to pay for your burial or funeral, you need to let your next of kin know your feelings about the burial procedure. If you wish to have a religious service, let your family know the type of service and where it is to be held. Tell your family where you wish to be buried, or if you intend to be cremated, then where to place the ashes.

THE ANATOMICAL GIFT

If you want to make an anatomical gift to take effect upon your death, you can make the gift as part of your Will; but it may be some time before your Will is located (GLM 113:10). The better route is to make the donation by a separate writing. You can complete a organ donor card when you apply for your Massachusetts driver's license or Massachusetts Photo Identification Card. If you do not want the fact that you are an organ donor indicated on your driver's license or Photo ID, you can sign a separate organ donor card. You can get a copy of an organ donor card and information about the Organ Donor Program by calling the New England Organ Bank at (800) 446-6362 or by visiting the Massachusetts Registry of Motor Vehicle Web site.

REGISTRY ORGAN DONOR PROGRAM
http://www.massrmv.com

FACE TRANSPLANT

The Organ Donor Card allows you to give specific instructions about parts of the body that you do (or do not) wish to donate. In 2005, the first partial face transplant was performed in France. It was accompanied by a flurry of controversy regarding the use of the face of a donor without her prior written permission. It is important that you indicate on your Organ Donor Card whether you do (or do not) wish to donate of all, or part, of your face.

GIFT FOR EDUCATION AND RESEARCH

There is no age limit on organ and tissue donations, however doctors will probably not consider your body suitable for transplantation if you are of advanced age and in poor health. You can still donate your body to a school of medicine or dentistry for education and research.

You can make a donation for education and research to a medical or dental school, such as:

University of Massachusetts
Anatomical Gifts Program
55 Lake Avenue North
Worcester, MA 01605
(508) 856-2460

Harvard Medical School
Anatomical Gifts Program
260 Longwood Avenue
Boston, MA 02115
(617) 432-1735

Tufts University
School of Medicine
Anatomical Gifts Program
136 Harrison Avenue
Boston, MA 02111
(617) 956-6685

Boston Univ. School of Medicine
Anatomical Gifts Program
80 East Concord Street
Boston, MA 02118
(617) 638-4245

You can call the school for information about the program, or you can write and ask them to send you information and preregistration forms.

If you do not wish to make an anatomical gift, let your family know how you feel. If you do not make provision for a gift, and do not tell anyone how you feel about donating any or all of your body, the decision will be up to your family. Massachusetts law establishes an order of priority to authorize the donation:

1st spouse
2nd an adult son or daughter
3rd either parent
4th an adult brother or sister
5th decedent's court appointed guardian (if any)
6th anyone else who is authorized to dispose of the body

(GLM 113:8).

The law requires that every effort be made to contact those people with highest priority. If someone agrees to the gift and someone with higher priority objects, then no gift can be made. And no gift can be made if, prior to death, you expressed an objection to making a donation.

AUTOPSIES

An autopsy is one of those things that most of us do not think about; reasoning that if it is needed, it will be carried out and, being dead, you will have no choice in the matter. But there are many times when an autopsy is optional. Sometimes a doctor is not sure of the cause of death, and asks the family to allow an autopsy. It may be in the family's best interest to consent to the autopsy.

The examination might reveal a genetic disorder, that could be treated if it later appears in another family member. Death from a car "accident" could have been a heart attack at the wheel. Perhaps the patient who died suddenly in a hospital was misdiagnosed. The nursing home resident could have died from negligence and not old age. Even if none of these are found, knowing the cause of death with certainty is better than not knowing.

Whoever takes custody of the body for burial may authorize the autopsy. The person giving authorization for an optional autopsy must agree to pay for the autopsy because the cost is not covered under most health insurance plans. An autopsy can cost anywhere from several hundred to several thousand dollars.

Still another reason people hesitate to order an autopsy is because they do not know whether the decedent would have wanted a postmortem examination.

If you have strong feelings one way or another, let your family know how you feel about an optional autopsy.

Of course, there are problems with just telling someone how you feel about your burial arrangements, autopsies, and anatomical gifts:

YOU TELL THE WRONG PERSON

You may tell someone who does not have authority to carry out your wishes. That was the case with James. When his wife died, he moved to a retirement community where he lived for several years until his death. James had two sons who lived in different states. Although he loved his sons, he had difficulty talking to either of them about serious matters. It was easier for him to talk with his friends in the retirement community. They often spoke about dying and how they felt about different burial arrangements. James would reminisce about his youth and growing up in a farming community in the plains state of Kansas.

"I was happy and free. Out there you had room to breathe. It would be nice to be buried there — peaceful and spacious."

When he died, his friends told his sons about their father's desire to be buried in Kansas. They met the suggestion with scepticism and pragmatism:

"Dad didn't say anything like that to me."

"It would cost us double, if we had to arrange for burial in another state. I'm sure he didn't have that kind of expense in mind."

THE PERSON DOES NOT CARRY OUT YOUR WISHES

Sometimes the person you tell about the disposition of your body may not understand what you said or perhaps they hear only what they want to hear. Whether they follow your burial instructions or authorize an anatomical gift or an autopsy may depend more on what costs are involved, and their own feelings, rather than what you may have wanted.

Even if you tell someone and trust that person to carry out your wishes, it could be that the person you confide in cannot carry out your instructions. For example, if you tell your spouse what arrangements to make, he/she may become incapacitated or die before you do; or perhaps you both die together in a natural disaster or in a plane crash.

WHO WANTS TO TALK ABOUT IT?

For many people the main problem with telling someone what to do when you die is talking about your death. It may be an uncomfortable, if not unpleasant, subject for you to bring up, and for your family to discuss. If this is the case, consider putting the information in writing and give the instructions to the person who will have the job of carrying out your wishes.

Making provision for the disposition of your body is important, but it is more important to make sure that you are in control of the health care you receive should you become seriously ill. This is not a problem when you are well enough to make your own medical decisions; however it could happen that you are too ill to let people know what you want. The solution to the problem is appoint someone to serve as your HEALTH CARE AGENT.

You can legally appoint someone, a ***Health Care Agent*** to make your medical decisions in the event that you are too ill to do so yourself. Your attorney can prepare a ***Health Care Proxy*** appointing the person of your choice to serve as your Health Care Agent. You can name an Alternate Health Care Agent in the event your Health Care Agent is not available or willing or competent to make your medical decisions.

You will need to sign the Health Care Proxy in the presence of two witnesses, neither of whom is your choice of Health Care Agent. If you are a patient in a health care facility, you may not appoint an administrator, operator or employee of that facility as your Health Care Agent unless that person is related to you through blood, marriage or adoption (GLM 201D:2, 201D:3).

It is important to give your Health Care Agent specific directions about whether you do, or do not, want life support systems to be used in the event that you are dying and there is no hope for your recovery. If you do not give specific instructions, it will be up to your Health Care Agent to decide whether or not to use life sustaining treatments, such as a ventilator or a feeding tube (GLM 201D:5).

USE THE PROXY FOR ANATOMICAL GIFTS

If you want to make an anatomical gift, you can include an organ donor card and give your Health Care Agent authority to carry out your wishes. If you do not wish to make an anatomical gift, you can direct your Health Care Agent to not allow the procedure.

USE THE DIRECTIVE TO AUTHORIZE AN AUTOPSY

You can use your Health Care Proxy to authorize an autopsy, or you can withhold your consent for the performance of an optional autopsy, or you can leave the decision in the hands of your Health Care Agent.

USE THE PROXY FOR FINAL DISPOSITION

If you have not made Pre-need arrangements you can authorize your Health Care Proxy to arrange for your final disposition in the manner described in your Proxy.

Some readers may be thinking "My family will surely respect my wishes as to my final disposition. Why bother with a Health Care Proxy? I probably will never need anyone to make my health care decisions. And even if I did, my family will tell the doctor what I want."

Those were George's thoughts exactly, even though his attorney advised him differently. George was a wealthy man. He was meticulous when it came to his business affairs, but not about his health care. His attorney said "You made good provision for the care of your property in the event that you become disabled or die, but you have not provided for your health care. You can sign a Health Care Power of Attorney and appoint a Health Care Agent to make your medical decisions in the event that you are too sick to make them yourself. Your wife Loretta is a lovely lady, but she and your son from your first marriage are always at odds. You should give one of them the authority to serve as your Health Care Agent. Whoever you choose will have the right to make your health care decisions in the event that you can't."

George refused "No, if I make one my Health Care Agent, the other will be hurt."

The attorney suggested "If you don't want to appoint a Health Care Agent, under Massachusetts law, any responsible party can make decisions on your behalf (GLM 201D:16). Most physicians will look to your wife to direct your treatment. You should at least give her some instruction about the kind of medical treatment you do, or do not, want to receive in the event in that you are terminally ill and with no hope of recovery."

"You mean sign a Living Will?"

"Well actually a Living Will is not recognized in Massachusetts, but you can appoint someone to make your health care decisions and give them directions about the use of artificial life support systems in the event you can't speak for yourself and there is no hope for recovery."

George said he would think about it. But he didn't.

The attorney's advice turned out to be prophetic. George suffered a stroke while driving. His injuries from the accident combined with the severity of the stroke made for a bleak prognosis. The doctors said George would die unless they put him on a ventilator and inserted a feeding tube. Even with life support systems, it was not expected that he would ever come out of the coma.

Loretta told the doctors "Let's try everything to keep him alive."

George's son did not see it that way.
"Why torture him with needles and tubes? Let him pass on peacefully."

Because George refused to appoint a Health Care Agent, the doctors didn't know who George wanted to make his medical decisions. Fearing that no matter what they did, one family member might be angry enough to file a law suit, the doctors requested that the matter be brought before the court, to let the judge decide the matter.

The judge decided that someone needed to be appointed as George's Guardian to make his medical decisions.

Loretta petitioned the court to be appointed as George's Guardian. So did his son. The court battle over who was to be George's Guardian was bitter (and expensive).

Before Loretta and George married they signed a prenuptial agreement. The agreement provided for each to give up all rights to inherit property from the other. Loretta had little money of her own. The son accused Loretta of thinking of her own best interest and not that of his father. If George were to die, Loretta would be on her own.

George was a wealthy man, but he was not overly generous with his son. His son was married and raising his own family. Without any help from his father, he struggled to support his family. Loretta accused the son of being anxious to get his substantial inheritance.

The judge ruled that each of the parties had a conflict of interest and could be prejudiced by his/her own circumstances. He appointed a professional, independent, Guardian to make medical decisions for George. The Guardian conferred with the doctors and determined that it was futile to continue life support systems.

George died.

A Health Care Estate Plan 9

We discussed an Estate Plan as it relates to the distribution or management of your Estate once you are deceased. In this age of extended life expectancy, a more pressing concern is how to manage and preserve your Estate in the event of a debilitating illness. As life expectancy increases, so does the percentage of the population who suffer incapacitating strokes, Alzheimer's disease or Parkinson's disease. It is estimated that more than half of the population who are 85 or older, have some degree of dementia. Your best Estate Plan could be sabotaged by a lengthy illness. In this chapter we will explore ways to pay for the health care that you may require as you age.

In addition to paying for your health care, you need to consider who will care for your finances and everyday physical needs in the event that you are too ill to do so yourself. A ***Health Care Estate Plan*** is a plan designed to care for your person and property in the event of an incapacitating illness. In the last chapter, we discussed how you can appoint a Health Care Agent to care for your person in the event of your incapacity.

But there is still the problem of who will care for your property. In this chapter we will discuss how you can appoint someone to care for your property and manage your finances in the event of your incapacity.

The optimum way to provide for the care of your property in the event of your incapacity is to set up a Trust appointing a Successor Trustee to care for your property according to the directions given in your Trust. You can be Trustee of the funds while you have capacity. Should you become incapacitated, then the person you name as Successor Trustee will take over. But if you do not have sufficient assets to justify the cost of employing an attorney to draft a Trust, there are other strategies you can use to solve the problem.

THE JOINT ACCOUNT

You can set up a joint checking account so that a trusted family member can write checks on the account. Of course there are all the inherent problems of a joint account that we discussed in Chapter 2. You can avoid many of those problems by limiting the amount of money that can be accessed by the family member. For example, you can arrange your finances so that all of your bills are paid from a single checking account and your family member can access that account, only.

THE LIMITED ACCESS ACCOUNT

If you set up a joint account, your family member will own whatever is in the account should your die. If this is not as you wish, you can set up a ***Limited Access Deposit Account*** giving your family member the ability to write checks on your account during your lifetime. Your agreement with the bank will state that should you die, your family member may no longer access your account. But ultimately your relative must be trustworthy because the bank is under no duty to stop him from writing checks on your account until the bank learns of your death (GLM 167D:5A).

A better solution may be to set up an account in the name of a family member as your STATUTORY CUSTODIANSHIP TRUSTEE.

You can transfer your money or property to a trusted friend or relative to manage in the event you are ill or aged and are having difficulty managing your property. You do not need a separate Trust Agreement because anything you transfer to your ***Statutory Custodianship Trustee*** must be managed according to Massachusetts law. For example, if you open an account in the name of a family member as your Statutory Custodianship Trustee, then under Massachusetts law:

- ➪ Any money you place in the account must be used by the Custodianship Trustee for your benefit.
- ➪ Each year the Custodianship Trustee must give an accounting of monies spent.
- ➪ You can revoke the appointment at any time and take your money back.
- ➪ Should you die, all the money in the account becomes part of your Estate.

Your Custodianship Trustee is not required to obtain a bond unless you require him to do so, or unless someone who stands to inherit your Estate goes to the Probate Court and asks the judge to order that he do so (GLM 201C:1, 201C:2, 201C:3).

One potential problem is that upon your death, property transferred to your Custodianship Trustee becomes part of your Probate Estate. If you are trying to avoid Probate, and you have sufficient assets, the better route is to set up a Revocable Living Trust.

The joint or Limited Access account solves the problem of how to pay your bills in the event you are temporarily ill. It does not solve the problem of how to manage your business affairs in the event of an extended illness. You could appoint someone as your Statutory Custodianship Trustee. However, your Trustee can only manage property you place in the Trust. It could happen that you take suddenly ill and can no longer be cared for at home. Should it be necessary for you to sell your home and move to an assisted living facility, no one may have the authority to sell the house for you. In such case, your friends or family members may be forced to ask the Court to appoint a Guardian to manage your finances, and if you did not appoint a Health Care Agent, to care for your person and make your medical decisions.

Before doing so, the judge will need to be convinced that you are unable to care for yourself. He will set a time for a hearing on the matter. Those who stand to inherit your property will be given notice of the hearing (GLM 201:7, 201:17). Evidence will need to be presented to the Court that you are incapacitated. Determining whether you have capacity to take care of yourself can be an embarrassing, and demeaning experience, if you are sufficiently aware of the proceedings. You may even want to employ an attorney to fight the matter.

If the judge decides that you are incapacitated, he will appoint a Guardian with authority to care for your person or property. If you have significant assets, he may decide to appoint a Conservator to care for your property (GLM 201:6B, 201:16).

If a Guardian of your person is appointed, he will see to your health care. The Court may require him to file a report each year regarding your well-being. If a Guardian of your property is appointed, he will take possession of all that you own and file an inventory with the Court. The Court may order that your property be appraised. If you have substantial assets, the Court may require a surety bond for the protection of your property. Each year the Guardian will account to the Court for monies spent. He may need to employ an accountant to help prepare the inventory and annual accounting (GLM 201:19, 201:46).

Whoever wishes to serve as your Guardian will need to employ an attorney to establish the Guardianship and to see that reports are properly and timely filed. The Guardian and his attorney are entitled to be paid for their services. Their fees must be approved by the Court, but in general, the amount paid is comparable to fees paid to fiduciaries such as a Trustee or a Personal Representative, and to their attorneys.

Court filing fees, the competency examination fee, the cost of a bond, accounting fees, appraisal fees, the Guardian's fee, the Conservator's fee, your attorney's fee and the Guardian's attorney fees, the Conservator's attorney fees, are all charged to you.

Strange that so many people worry about avoiding Probate, when the larger concern should be how to avoid guardianship. It is not all that hard to arrange your finances so that no Probate is necessary. The cost to transfer your property to your beneficiaries should be minimal. Even with a full Probate procedure, whatever it costs to Probate your Estate is a one-time expense. And Probate is a one-time procedure. Once monies are distributed to your beneficiaries, it is over.

Not so if you become incapacitated. It may cost thousands of dollars to set up the guardianship; and significant sums to care for you and your property each year. This expense goes on, year after year, until you are returned to capacity, or die (GLM 201:13, 201:13A).

As with Probate it is not all that hard to avoid these unnecessary charges to your Estate. To avoid the need for a Guardian of your person, you can appoint a Health Care Agent to make your medical decisions should you be too ill to do so yourself. To avoid the need for a Guardian of your property, you place all of your property in a Revocable Living Trust. Should you become incapacitated, your Successor Trustee will care for your property.

For those of limited means, a DURABLE POWER OF ATTORNEY may be the next best Estate plan.

A POWER OF ATTORNEY FOR FINANCES

A ***Power of Attorney*** is a legal document by which someone (the *Principal*) gives another (his *Agent* or *Attorney-In-Fact*) authority to do certain acts on behalf of the Principal. If you wish to have someone to be able to conduct business on your behalf in the event of your incapacity, you can make the Power of Attorney *durable* by including the phrase

> This power of attorney shall not be affected by the subsequent disability or incapacity of the principal (GLM 201B:1).

You can give your Attorney-In-Fact general powers to manage your finances and do much the same with your property as you can do yourself, such as:

- ⇨ buy or sell real property on your behalf;
- ⇨ buy or sell personal property for you;
- ⇨ trade in securities (stocks, bonds, etc.)
- ⇨ pay your bills and/or taxes;
- ⇨ operate your business;
- ⇨ have access to your safe deposit box;
- ⇨ borrow money on your behalf;
- ⇨ purchase insurance policies and name beneficiaries;
- ⇨ sue or defend a law suit on your behalf;
- ⇨ apply for government benefits on your behalf;
- ⇨ have access to your business and personal records.

You can give your Attorney-In-Fact power to make gifts of your property in accordance with your Estate Plan. For example, you can direct him to give certain family members up to the federal Gift Tax Exclusion Amount. As explained in Chapter 3, the Exclusion Amount for the year 2006 is $12,000.

Notice that there are many things that your Attorney-In-Fact can do for you personally, such as defending a law suit or suing on your behalf or applying for government benefits. Even if you have a Trust, it is important to appoint an Attorney-In-Fact to do these important, personal, things for you, in the event you can't.

Your Trust can only authorize your Successor Trustee to manage property that is placed in your Trust. Your Successor Trustee has no authority over you, personally. But you can give him (or anyone else) that authority by making him your Attorney-In-Fact under a Durable Power of Attorney.

GENERAL VS. LIMITED POWER OF ATTORNEY

You can sign a Power of Attorney giving your Attorney-In-Fact broad general powers. With these powers your Attorney-In-Fact can do much the same with your property as you can. If this is of concern to you, instead of giving a General Power of Attorney, you can give a ***Limited Power of Attorney*** and restrict the things your Attorney-In-Fact can do to just those things authorized in the document.

One power that should be specifically granted in your Power of Attorney, is the power to apply for medical assistance benefits in the event of your incapacity. In the next chapter we will be discussing the many things you can do to qualify for Medicaid. You need to give someone authority to take the necessary steps for you to become eligible for government benefits, in the event you are too ill to do so yourself. Even if you do not wish to give someone control over your finances at this time, you should give someone a Limited Power of Attorney for the purpose of qualifying for Medicaid.

Limited or General, the operative word in any Power of Attorney is POWER. Once your Attorney-In-Fact has authority to act, he essentially steps into your shoes and can do whatever you gave him authority to do. Your primary consideration in choosing an Agent is trustworthiness. You need to choose someone who will follow your instructions and put the Power of Attorney to the use you intended. You need to choose someone, who, when using your Power of Attorney, will always put your interests ahead of his.

You may be less concerned with trustworthiness than the loss of independence. But the thing to keep in mind is that you still have the power to do all of the things you gave your Attorney-In-Fact authority to do. The only difference is that now, you both have the power to conduct your business transactions. Of course, shared authority is still less independent than sole authority; so you may hesitate to give someone a Power of Attorney until it is needed. But if you wait until it is needed, you may be too sick to sign the document. There are two simple solutions to this dilemma — keep it in your possession, or make it effective only upon your incapacity.

USING THE POWER OF ATTORNEY

An Attorney-In-Fact under a Power of Attorney cannot operate on behalf of the Principal, unless the Attorney-In-Fact has possession of the original Power of Attorney and presents it to whomever he wants to rely on that document. For example, if your Attorney-In-Fact wants to use the Power of Attorney to sell one of your securities, he will need to produce the original document and perhaps sign an Affidavit (a written statement sworn to before a Notary Public) saying that the Power of Attorney is still in effect and that you did not revoke that Power of Attorney.

KEEP THE DOCUMENT IN YOUR POSSESSION

Before anyone (a bank, stockbroker, closing agent, etc.) will accept the Power of Attorney they will want to see the original document so that they are assured that your Attorney-In-Fact has authority to transact business on your behalf. If you keep the original document in your possession and do not give anyone a copy, your Attorney-In-Fact will not be able to act for you.

The only problem with this arrangement is that you need to arrange to make the document accessible to your Attorney-In-Fact in the event of your incapacity. If your Attorney-In-Fact is a trusted family member, you can give him the location of the document with instructions to take possession of the Durable Power of Attorney in the event of your incapacity.

THE SPRINGING POWER OF ATTORNEY

A better solution may be to have your attorney draft a "springing" Durable Power of Attorney that is not operational until your family doctor and/or independent physician says that you are incapacitated and unable to manage your financial affairs.

Your Attorney-In-Fact can hold the original document, but cannot use it until it "springs to life" when a doctor determines that you are too ill to care for your property. You can create a Springing Durable Power of Attorney by adding the following provision to the document.

> This Durable Power of Attorney shall become effective upon the disability or incapacity of the principal as determined by the principal's regularly attending physician (GLM 201B:1).

Your attorney can design a Durable Power of Attorney, to meet your special needs. He can even include powers that relate to your health care (GLM 201D:16). But as a practical matter, it may be better to have a separate Health Care Proxy. As explained in the previous chapter, the Health Care Proxy can be used to appoint a Health Care Agent and to give your Agent directions about the care you wish to receive in the event you are too ill to direct your medical treatment. There are at least two reasons to have a separate Health Care Proxy.

DIFFERENT PEOPLE CAN SERVE

You may want one person to serve as your Health Care Agent and another to serve as your Attorney-In-Fact. One family member may be an excellent choice to make your health care decisions, yet that person may not be the best person to make financial decisions on your behalf.

PRIVACY

Even if you want the same person to serve as your Health Care Agent and Attorney-In-Fact, there is still the matter of privacy. Your Health Care Agent will give a copy of your Health Care Advance Directive to your physician to be placed in your medical file. Your doctors have no need to know of your business dealings; and vice versa. To conduct business on your behalf your Attorney-In-Fact will need to give a copy of the Power of Attorney to your business associates (banks, stockbrokers, etc.). Your business associates have no need to know of your medical decisions.

For privacy, and perhaps security reasons, consider having a separate Health Care Proxy and Power of Attorney, rather than try to get it all into a single multi purpose document.

As explained, it is relatively simple and inexpensive to head off a guardianship. All you need to do is appoint an Attorney-In-Fact under a Durable Power of Attorney to manage your finances, and a Health Care Agent under a Health Care Proxy to make your medical care decisions. These documents authorize people of your choice to care for you and your property in the event of your incapacity. But, despite your best plans, something unusual could happen causing a Court to decide that you need a Guardian. For example, suppose you develop an addiction or a mental illness causing self-destructive behavior.

A Guardian may be appointed for someone who just wastes his money. Under Massachusetts law, "a person who by excessive drinking, gaming, idleness, or debauchery of any kind, so spends, wastes or lessens his estate as to expose himself or his family to want or suffering, . . ." or to cause his family to go on welfare, is considered to be a ***spendthrift***. The Department of Public Welfare, or any member of his family can ask the Court to appoint a Guardian or Conservator who can use the spendthrift's money for his maintenance and that of his spouse and children (GLM 201:8, 201:11, 201:16).

Although it may not be possible to avoid all guardianship and conservatorship procedures, you can have a measure of control over your fate. Massachusetts statute gives you the right to name the person of your choice to serve as your Guardian. You can use your Durable Power of Attorney to name someone to be Guardian of your person, or property or both (GLM 201B:3).

If you do not express your choice of Guardian, and two people want the job, both equally qualified, it will be up to the judge to decide who should be appointed. In making the selection, he will be guided by your best interests; meaning that he will choose the person he thinks will do the best job in caring for you.

However, some people look good on paper, but in fact may be a poor choice. For example, suppose the Court finds that a woman is not capable of handling her finances and is in need of a Guardian of her property. If her son and daughter both want the job, the Court will consider their backgrounds and current commitments. Suppose the son is a college graduate with a degree in business administration, and the daughter a homemaker with three small children, the judge might think the son a better choice.

But it could be that the mother would never have chosen her son because of all the many times she had to bail him out of debt.

Again, it is a matter of planning ahead, and being in charge of your own destiny, rather than leaving the choice up to a judge to decide.

The good news: You are going to live longer.
The bad news: It's going to cost you.
Scientists are doing a great job of prolonging life, but unless they find Ponce De Leon's fountain, the general population will continue to age. Along with age comes infirmities. Eyes fail. Hearing diminishes. Mobility declines. Digestive systems either speed up or slow down, all to the discomfort of the unhappy occupant of the body. It's all part of the "golden" years.

The pharmacology industry is well motivated to produce drugs that manage the ills associated with aging. Their research has led to a wealth of pharmaceutical products that do not cure, but do allow people to live in relative comfort into advanced age. The only problem is the cost of these drugs. Medicare covers the treatment of life-threatening brushes with heart disease, stroke, cancer and diabetes, but paying for maintenance medication is up to you. Even if you belong to a Medicare Prescription Drug Plan or have some other prescription insurance, you will need to contribute to the payment of your medication.

Medicare is also limited in long term nursing care coverage. The structure of Medicare has changed giving people the option of staying with the ***Original Medicare Plan*** or choosing a ***Medicare Advantage Plan*** such as a Medicare Health Maintenance Organization ("HMO"), or other Medicare Health Plans. Coverage depends on which plan is chosen. If you remain with the Original Medicare Plan you do not pay for the first 20 days of a stay in a skilled nursing facility (i.e., a nursing home). You pay up to $119** per day for days 21 through 100.

**This is the value for the year 2006. The federal government adjusts the amount each year.

Unless you have Medicare Supplemental Insurance coverage, it will cost you up to $9,520 for the next 80 days. After 100 days, you are on your own. A nursing home stay of one or two years can wipe out the life savings of most working people. Once savings are gone, the government provides care in the form of Medicaid coverage. If you have no assets to speak of, and a relatively low income, the cost of long-term nursing care is the least of your worries. Medicaid is available to take care of your medical and nursing care needs. And no need to worry if you are wealthy. You have enough money to pay for the care you might need. The rest of us need to think about ways to provide for long-term health care.

For those concerned about the loss of life savings because of illness, there is supplemental and/or long-term health care insurance. There are many different insurance plans available. You can call the National Association of Insurance Commissioners at (816) 783-8300 for information about long-term health care insurance. You can also find information about long-term health care insurance at the Massachusetts Division of Insurance Web site.

MASSACHUSETTS DIVISION OF INSURANCE
http://www.mass.gov/doi

LONG TERM INSURANCE FOR FEDERAL EMPLOYEES

The Long Term Care Security Act is designed to make long term care insurance available to federal employees, including postal workers, members of the uniformed services, civilian and military retirees, and their qualified relatives. You can call the Office of Personnel Management at (800) 582-3337 for information about the federal long term care insurance program or you can visit their Web site.

OFFICE OF PERSONNEL MANAGEMENT
http://www.opm.gov/insure/ltc

The National Association Of Retired Federal Employees ("NARFE") was actively involved in developing the federal long term care insurance program. You can get information about the program by calling the NARFE Legislative Hot-line toll-free (877) 217-8234 or by visiting their Web site.

NATIONAL ASSOC. OF RETIRED FEDERAL EMPLOYEES
http://www.narfe.org

THE PROBLEM OF COST AND ELIGIBILITY

Long term care insurance sounds like the perfect solution, until you start examining the cost. The cost isn't too bad if you are comparatively young, say in your 50s. But can you imagine paying that premium each month until you are in your 80s and never needing nursing care?

Many decide to wait till they are old and going downhill. But that just brings other problems. The older you are, the greater the cost of insurance. And there is the risk that you will be refused coverage because of a "pre-existing" condition, i.e., the insurance company may consider you to be too great a risk for them to insure.

Different insurance companies have come up with insurance plans that may provide a solution for the person who is relatively young and in good health. Some companies offer long-term care insurance that is paid-up within a fixed period of time. Once payments are made for a certain number of years, the person is insured for long-term care without further payment. Other companies combine long-term care insurance with a life insurance policy. They offer long-term care insurance that converts to a life insurance policy, if it happens that the insured person dies before needing long-term care. When shopping for a long-term care policy, consider including different insurance alternatives in your investigation.

WHEN INSURANCE IS NOT AN OPTION

For some people long term care insurance is not an option. An elderly person living on a low fixed income may not have enough money to pay the monthly premium for a long term care insurance policy. And long term care insurance is not an option for the person who has been diagnosed with a chronic, debilitating disease.

People in such a position worry that they may need to deplete their life savings, just to pay for a year or two of nursing care.

Both of these problems can be solved by using current law to become qualified for Medicaid. Medicaid is a public assistance program that is funded jointly by the federal and state government. There are state and federal laws governing who may become eligible for the program.

A ***Medicaid Qualifying Plan*** is a plan that takes both state and federal laws into consideration. Operating within the boundaries of these laws, those who are concerned about becoming impoverished in order to pay for long-term care, seek to preserve and protect their Estate by implementing a Medicaid Qualifying Plan.

There has been controversy about plans designed to qualify a person for Medicaid. Some think that to intentionally arrange finances to qualify for Medicaid is immoral — a legal method of working the system.

Those people may argue: "Why are such things allowed? After all, wasn't Medicaid designed to help poor people? Why should people be allowed to make themselves poor to get on the public dole???

Those who feel they need to qualify for Medicaid have a different point of view. They may argue:

"I worked all my life and hoped to leave a few pennies for the kids. Why did I work so hard? To give it all to a nursing home? I paid my taxes just like everyone else. The government pays hundreds of thousands of dollars for people on Medicare to have open heart surgery, and they pay for lengthy and expensive cancer treatments. Why should those who have Alzheimer's or Parkinson's or those who suffer a debilitating stroke, not be entitled to receive equal benefits?"

Although we can understand and appreciate both points of view, our job, as we see it, is to just explain the law as it is at the time of publication. We think it is important to do so because many people take a position (pro or con) based on what they perceive the law to be, and not based upon the law as it actually is.

Once the reader understands what it takes to qualify for Medicaid in the state of Massachusetts, he can decide for himself whether the law is basically fair to the people who need to qualify, or whether it is flawed (either too restrictive or too liberal) and needs to be changed.

Hopefully, those with a strong opinion will share those views with their legislators.

A Medicaid Qualifying Plan 10

A better name for this chapter might be "A Health Care Contingency Plan." A lengthy stay in a nursing home is something most of us do not want to even think about, much less prepare for. Why prepare for something that may never happen? Yet as we age, there is that nagging "What if?" "What if I need long term nursing care? How will I pay for it?"

An effective way to put this anxiety at rest is to have a contingency plan. To form a contingency plan, you need to know your options. In this case, your options are directly related to your ability to pay for that care. But it is hard to predict future fortunes. People win the lottery. Those with a large portfolio may have their fortunes disappear in a market melt-down. There is no need for concern if it turns out that you can afford to pay for your own nursing care; and there is no concern should you become impoverished because there are government programs that provide for your health care. The worst case scenario is that you will be able to afford long-term care, but at the cost of your life savings.

In this chapter, we will discuss options available to you under that worst case scenario. We will explain current state and federal law as it relates to qualifying for medical assistance programs.

MEDICAID — A STATE OF LIMBO

On February 8, 2006, President Bush signed the Deficit Reduction Act of 2005. The Act reduces spending on Medicare, Medicaid and other domestic programs. The Act gives states certain options, such as disqualifying an Applicant for Medicaid if the equity in his home exceeds $500,000 or $750,000. Each state must pass new regulations to conform to the new law, including choosing an option for the $500,000 limit, or for the $750,000 limit. Beginning in 2011, the law requires that the above dollar amounts be increased by the cost of living rounded to the nearest $1,000 (42 U.S.C. 1396p(f)).

As we went to print in mid 2006, Massachusetts has not adopted new Medicaid regulations. That is not the only impediment to putting the new law into effect in this state. The Deficit Reduction Act is being challenged on Constitutional grounds. Before the President can sign a bill into law, both the House of Representatives and the Senate must adopt identical measures. However, the House version and the Senate version of the Deficit Reduction Act differ on Medicare payments for administering oxygen. There is no telling what action the Court will require. A judge might order the Congress to start all over again and send a corrected Deficient Reduction Act to the President, or he might rule that the law is constitutional, but not as it applies to payments for administering oxygen.

The new law relates to transfers to qualify for Medicaid made after the "date of enactment," so theoretically, whenever the state and federal government settle on the details, the new law can be applied retroactively back to February 8, 2006. We are of the opinion that within the next year or so, the new law will be implemented in Massachusetts, so the discussion that follows in this chapter will be based on that assumption.

WHO IS ENTITLED TO MEDICAID?

Medicaid is a program that provides medical and long term nursing care for people with limited resources. Medicaid is an entitlement program, meaning that whoever qualifies for the program is entitled to receive benefits under that program. Those who do not qualify are not entitled to any Medicaid benefits.

The Medicaid program is funded and regulated by both federal and state government. The governing agency for the federal government is the *Centers for Medicare and Medicaid Services*. The Massachusetts office of HEALTH AND HUMAN SERVICES is responsible for the administration of the Medicaid Program within the Commonwealth. In Massachusetts, the Medicaid program is referred to as ***MassHealth*** (651 Code of Massachusetts Regulations ("CMR") 14.01). We will use the terms "MassHealth," "Medical Assistance Program," and "Medicaid" interchangeably.

There are many benefits offered under Masshealth, from health care for mothers and children; to community based services for those who need some assistance with their health care; to full nursing care for those who need assistance with dressing, bathing, eating, walking and toileting. We will limit our discussion of Medicaid to aged persons in need of institutional nursing care. You can get information about other Medical Assistance programs by calling your local MassHealth Enrollment Center. You can also get information by calling Health and Human Services at (800) 841-2900 or visit go to the Health and Human Services section of the Massachusetts Web site.

http://www.mass.gov

To apply for long-term-care services, an application must be completed and submitted to the Massachusetts Health and Human Services ("HHS"). You can get an application by calling the MassHealth Enrollment Center at (888) 665-9997 or you can download the form from the HHS Web.

Persons who are receiving Supplemental Security Income ("SSI") may be eligible to receive Medicaid benefits in Massachusetts because the requirements for these programs are much the same. A person who is not receiving SSI, may be eligible for Medicaid if he is 65 or older, or blind, or disabled (GLM 118E:9).

When a person applies for Medicaid (the "Applicant"**) the HHS will investigate his medical condition, income, and assets. If the Applicant is too ill to apply for himself, someone may do so for him, The Applicant's spouse, Health Care Agent, relative, guardian or friend may serve as his *Eligibility Representative*, to apply on his behalf, provided that person is sufficiently aware of the Applicant's circumstances to assume responsibility for the accuracy of statements made during the eligibility process (42 US Code of Federal Regulations ("CFR") 435.908, 130 CMR 515.001).

CITIZENSHIP ELIGIBILITY

To be eligible for Medicaid, the Applicant must be a resident of the United States, and either a U.S. citizen or an alien who is lawfully admitted for permanent residence (GLM 118E:16D).

** For simplicity, we will use the male gender for the Applicant and the female gender for his spouse.

MEDICAL ELIGIBILITY

Generally an Applicant who is currently receiving institutional care is medically eligible for Medicaid. A clinical assessment is done by the Aging Services Access Points ("ASAP"), non-profit agencies under contract with Elder Affairs to do the necessary clinical screening. A registered nurse will determine whether the Applicant is medically eligible based on his medical records (42 CFR 435.541, 651 CMR 14.01).

INCOME ELIGIBILITY

In Massachusetts, there is no limit on the amount of income earned by the Applicant each month, provided his net income does not exceed the private-pay rate of the long term care facility (130 CMR 520.028).

THE PERSONAL NEEDS ALLOWANCE

Once the Applicant is approved and becomes a recipient of Medicaid benefits, he is referred to as a ***Member*** of MassHealth (130 CMR 456.402). He will be allowed to keep a certain amount of his income each month (currently $60***) for his personal needs, such as clothing or hair cuts (130 CMR 520.025, 520.026).

The rest of his income, after all other deductions authorized by HHS, will be used to supplement the cost of his nursing care.

*** The figures used in this Chapter are for the year 2006. The federal and state government adjust these values on a regular basis. Check the UPDATE section of the EAGLE PUBLISHING COMPANY Web site for later values.
http://www.eaglepublishing.com

ASSET ELIGIBILITY

There is a limit on the amount of ***Countable Assets*** that an Applicant may own and still qualify for MassHealth. Currently, the maximum dollar value that can be owned by, or available to, the Applicant is $2,000. The Applicant's assets are counted as of the first day of the month that the Applicant enters the long-term care facility and applies for MassHealth. An Applicant who is over the ***Asset Limit*** needs to "spend down" to $2,000. Medical assistance can be retroactive to the first day of the third month before the month he applies, provided he received medical services during that time and he was eligible for MassHealth during that period of time (130 CMR 515.001, 516.004, GLM 118E:30).

THE COMMUNITY SPOUSE

If the Applicant is married, he can transfer all of his assets that exceed $2,000 to his spouse, but there are limits to his spouse's assets as well. If his spouse lives in their home or elsewhere in the community (i.e., not in a nursing home) she is referred to as the ***Community Spouse***.

NOTE ⇨ As discussed earlier, Medicaid is both a state and federal program. The federal government passed the Defense of Marriage Act recognizing a marriage only if it is between one man and one woman. So far as the federal government is concerned, a same-sex marriage partner has the legal status of a friend. The federal laws relating to a Community Spouse apply only if the Applicant is legally married to a person of the opposite sex.

Prior to 1988, the Community Spouse was required to use whatever assets she had to pay for the nursing care of her spouse. The Applicant could not quality for Medicaid until they both were virtually impoverished.

In addition to being unfair to the Community Spouse, this was not good government policy because it often resulted in the impoverished spouse turning to local government social service programs for support. The Medicaid provisions of the Medicare Catastrophic Coverage Act of 1988 remedied the situation by considering the assets of the couple as being part of a common pot and allowing the Community Spouse to keep her own share of that pot. The amount allowed has been increased over the years. In 2006, the federal government allows the Community Spouse to keep up to $99,540 of their combined countable assets.

The federal government also considers that the Community Spouse needs money each month for her maintenance. If her income is not sufficient to support her, the income of the Medicaid Member will be used to supplement the income of the Community Spouse up to a maximum of $2,488.50 per month. Each year, the federal government adjusts the spouse's asset allowance and monthly maintenance allowance for cost of living increases (42 U.S.C. 1382b).

Notice that $99,540 and $2,488.50 are the maximum values set by the federal government. States have the right to administer the Medicaid program according to their state law, provided their state law is within federal guidelines and does not exceed the maximum values set by the federal government. The actual amount allowed to the Community spouse can vary significantly state to state.

THE SPOUSE'S INCOME

The current value set by the state of Massachusetts as the Community Spouse's ***Minimum Monthly Maintenance Needs Allowance*** is $1,604. The HHS considers $481 of this value to be used for shelter (condo maintenance fees, rent, mortgage, property taxes, etc.) (130 CMR 520.026).

If the spouse's shelter costs are greater than $481, the spouse is allowed an ***excess shelter allowance***, provided the total value allowed as her monthly Income Allowance does not exceed the federal value of $2,488.50.

None of the Member's income is available to his spouse, if the Community Spouse has an income that is greater than the amount determined by HHS as her Minimum Monthly Maintenance Needs Allowance. But if her income is less than her Allowance, the Member's income can be used to supplement her income. For example, suppose the Community Spouse has a monthly income of $2,000 and HHS finds that she needs the current maximum value of $2,488.50 a month for her maintenance. In such case, she will be allowed to keep $488.50 of the Recipient's income each month. If for some reason (high medical bills, the need for special care, etc.) she needs more than $488.50 a month, she can appeal to have that value increased (130 CMR 520.017). See the next chapter for a discussion of the appeal process.

THE SPOUSE'S RESOURCE ALLOWANCE

Property owned by the Applicant, or his Community Spouse, that can be converted to cash and used for their support, are considered to be a *Resource*. This includes bank accounts, property in a Revocable Living Trust, stocks, bonds, and so on. Under federal law, the spouse is entitled to keep a share of the couple's Resources up to the current maximum of $99,540. That share is called the ***Community Spouse Resource Allowance*** (42 U.S.C. 1396r-5(c)(2), 1396r-5f, 130 CMR 520.007, 130 CMR 520.023).

NONCOUNTABLE ASSETS

Suppose a couple have $200,000 worth of Resources between them. The Community spouse can keep her Resource Allowance of $99,540. The Applicant can keep his allowance of $2,000, but that leaves them with $98,460 above their limit. The first question to ask in such a situation is whether all of their Resources are *Countable Assets* for the purpose of qualifying for MassHealth.

Some items owned by the Applicant, or his spouse, can be converted to cash, but are not counted as an asset. Such items are considered to be "Excluded Resources" or "Exempt Assets." We will refer to them as ***Noncountable Assets*** (42 U.S.C. 1382b, 130 CMR 520.007). The following items are Noncountable Assets and are not counted for purposes of determining eligibility for MassHealth.

AUTOMOBILE

⇨ A car that is being used by the Community Spouse does not count as an Asset, regardless of its value.

The car of a single Applicant who is in a nursing home, does not count, provided:

⇨ he needs it to travel to receive medical treatment for a specific and regular medical problem, such as kidney dialysis - or -

⇨ it is modified for the transportation of a handicapped person - or -

⇨ its equity value (market value less monies owed) does not exceed $4,500. Anything over $4,500 counts as an Asset.

The full equity value of a second automobile is a Countable Asset (130 CMR 520.007(F).

LIFE INSURANCE

- ➪ Life insurance policies owned by the Applicant or his spouse are Noncountable Assets provided the sum total of all of the face values (the amount paid at death) does not exceed $1,500 and the policies are to be used exclusively for funeral and burial expenses (130 CMR 520.008 (E)). If the sum of the face values of the policies exceeds $1,500, the *Cash Surrender Value* of the policy counts as an asset.

- ➪ A term life insurance policy has no cash-surrender value, so it does not count as an asset , regardless of its face value (130 CMR 520.006 (B)(2)).

BURIAL ARRANGEMENTS

- ➪ Burial funds of up to $1,500 for the Applicant and/or his Community Spouse are Noncountable Assets provided they are held in a separate account which is clearly identified as a burial account.

- ➪ Burial spaces for the Applicant or his family (spouse, child, parent, sibling and the spouse of a family member) are Noncountable Assets. This includes prepaid burial space items such as grave sites, mausoleums, urns, niches, etc. Opening and closing the grave, headstones, and headstone engravings are also considered burial space items.

- ➪ An Irrevocable Pre-Need Funeral Agreement for the Applicant or his spouse as described in Chapter 8 is a Noncountable Assets (130 CMR 520.023).

PERSONAL PROPERTY

Personal property being used by the Applicant or his spouse are Noncountable Assets. They include:

- ➪ wedding and engagement rings, regardless of their value;
- ➪ home furnishings and appliances, books, household tools

The HHS considers heirlooms, coin or stamp collections as personal property, provided they are not worth very much. Household items that are worth a significant amount of money, such as an expensive painting or a valuable antique, can be counted by the HHS as an Asset (42 U.S.C. 1382b(a)2(A)).

BUSINESS PROPERTY

➪ Business property that is essential to the self support of the Applicant or to his Community Spouse are Noncountable Assets. This includes rental properties and other income-producing property such as business equipment (computers, copiers, etc.), farm animals and livestock, special tools and work vehicles (trucks, tractors, etc.) (42 U.S.C.1382B(a)(3), 130 CMR 520.008(D)).

PENSION FUND

➪ Pension funds that are being set aside by a <u>current</u> employer do not count as an Asset; however the cash value of a pension plan from a <u>former</u> employer does count. The cash value of the pension plan, less any penalties for early withdrawal is considered as a countable Asset. This also applies to IRA accounts and Keogh Plans; i.e., the cash value, less penalties for early withdrawal, count as an asset (130 CMR 520.007 (C)).

THE HOMESTEAD — EXEMPT MAYBE

It used to be that the primary residence (home, condominium, cooperative apartment, or mobile home) occupied by the Applicant was an Noncountable Asset for purposes of qualifying for Medicaid. The Applicant could not be denied Medical Assistance because he owned a home — regardless of his *equity* in the home (the current market value less mortgages and liens on the property).

The recent spiral of residential property values has not gone unnoticed by the government. A home purchased years ago is now worth a substantial amount of money. Congress decided that a person whose equity in his home is $500,000 or more should not be able to qualify for Medicaid. As explained, Massachusetts legislators may decide to opt for the higher value of $750,000. The equity limit does not apply if the Applicant's spouse or his minor or disabled child is living in the home. Specifically, the home is a Noncountable Asset regardless of its value if the Community Spouse, or the Applicant's minor or disabled child lives in his home (42 U.S.C. 1396p(f)(2)).

If the Applicant is in a nursing home, and no family member lives in the home, it remains exempt, provided the Applicant has indicated that he intends to return home and his equity in the home does not exceed $500,000 (or $750,000) (42 U.S.C. 1382b). If the Applicant is too ill to indicate that he intends to return home, his home becomes a countable asset. HHS allows the value of the home to remain exempt for nine months provided the Applicant, or someone with legal authority to act on his behalf, signs an agreement with HHS promising to dispose of the property for its fair market value. Once the property is sold, the Member will be disqualified from receiving further MassHealth benefits until he spends down to $2,000 (130 CMR 520.007).

INACCESSIBLE ASSETS

⇨ Property owned by the Applicant or his spouse must be able to be convertible to cash in order to be considered as a Countable Asset. Shares held in a close corporation (i.e. a small private corporation whose shares have no market value), Life Estate interests, certain irrevocable annuities, and other non-saleable items can be considered as Noncountable Assets, subject to the approval of the HHS (130 CMR 520.006).

JOINTLY OWNED ASSETS

The HHS considers the full value of a jointly owned bank account to be available to the Applicant, or his Community Spouse, unless it can be proven that the other owner contributed toward the property. For example, if the Applicant owns a joint account with his son, the entire balance counts unless the son can prove that he contributed his own money to that account. The son's *net contribution* (how much he contributed less how much he withdrew) does not count as an asset.

OTHER NONCOUNTABLE ASSETS

We listed many of the more common items that the HHS considers to be Noncountable Assets. But this is not a complete list. You can find other Noncountable items included as part of the Code of Massachusetts Regulations (130 CMR 520.006 through 520.008) at the Health and Human Services section of the Massachusetts Web site.

http://www.mass.gov/

To find the legal references go to the SITE MAP and then to MEMBER ELIGIBILITY REGULATIONS.

But even reading 520.006-520.008 will not give you the complete list because Section K of 520.008 states "Any other assets considered noncountable for Title XIX eligibility purposes is considered a noncountable asset." In other words, items that the federal government considers to be an Excluded Resource for purposes of determining Medicaid eligibility do not count as an asset in Massachusetts.

To get that complete list you will need to look up 42 U.S.C. 1382b. Better yet, consult with an experienced Elder Law attorney. He will be able to explain to you which of your assets count for purposes of applying for MassHealth.

THE SPEND-DOWN OPTION

Now that we know what does (and does not) count as a Resource, the next question is what options are available to our couple who are over the Asset Limit by $98,460. Those with no knowledge of the law, might think the only option available to this couple is to pay for his nursing care until the $98,460 runs out. Those who carefully read the previous pages, might suggest that the couple check to see whether they can use the money to purchase Noncountable Assets.

Both state and federal law allow the Applicant and his Community Spouse to use their excess resources to purchase Noncountable Assets, without losing the right to receive Medicaid benefits, provided they pay a fair market value for the item. This being the case, the couple can make funeral or burial arrangements, if they have not already done so. They can purchase household items such as furniture, a television set, a new refrigerator or stove, etc.

REPAIRING NONCOUNTABLE ITEMS

Paying money to repair a Noncountable Asset is a good spend-down strategy. Perhaps the family car needs new brakes, or tires. The Community Spouse may decide to replace her car with a new model.

If the house is in need of repair or improvement, then this is the time to fix it up. A new heating, plumbing or electrical system can use up funds quickly. If the couple does not own their own home, the Community Spouse might consider using the excess cash as a down-payment on a home.

SPEND-DOWN BY TRANSFER TO DISABLED CHILD

As explained in Chapter 7, if a disabled child is receiving Social Security disability benefits, the parent can transfer money to a Supplemental Needs Trust for the child. This transfer will not disqualify the child, or the parent, from receiving government benefits, provided the Trust is drafted according to state and federal law (130 CMR 520.019).

SPEND-DOWN BY PAYING DEBTS

Some sceptics might think $98,460 is a lot of money to spend down. Maybe the couple previously made all funeral arrangements. Perhaps they really don't need (or want) new furniture or appliances. In such case, the solution may be to pay off all of their outstanding debts. If the couple have a credit card balance, they can reduce the balance to $0. Paying off loans is a valid spend-down strategy because it is just a return of monies given to the Applicant by the lender for the purchase of a Noncountable Asset (car, house, clothing, household items). The couple will need to prove to the HHS, that the monies spent were used to pay off a valid debt.

Paying off their mortgage is a good spend-down strategy. If the mortgage is paid in full, the HHS will want to see the original promissory note (marked "PAID"), as well as a recorded satisfaction of mortgage.

If their car is a Noncountable Asset, they can pay off any money they may owe on the car. But paying off a car loan may not be a good strategy for a single Applicant because only $4,500 of the value of his car is Noncountable. For example, suppose he owes $10,000 on a car that is worth $14,000. The car does not count as an Asset because his equity in the car is less than $4,500. Paying off the $10,000 will change it to a countable asset and that alone may disqualify him from receiving Medicaid benefits.

MAYBE SPEND-DOWN IS NOT NECESSARY

Suppose the couple with too much assets has too little income. For example, suppose it is determined that the Community Spouse needs at least $2,488.50 per month, but the couple's combined income is only $1,500. In such case, she can ask the HHS to allow her to keep as much of couple's excess assets as is necessary to give her this minimum income. In effect, she needs to ask "May I keep more than my Asset Limit so that the income from this property will help to get me to my Minimum Monthly Maintenance Needs Allowance?"

It is the legal right of the Community Spouse to receive the Minimum amount allowed by both state and federal government. Both federal and state law allow her keep as much of the couple's assets as necessary to achieve that income, even if it means keeping more than allowed as a Countable Asset. But it may take the assistance of an experienced Elder Law attorney to convince the HHS to that allowing her to keep more assets is a proper thing to do.

If the HHS denies the request, it will be necessary to go through an Appeals process to decide the issue (130 CMR 520.017, GLM 118E:21A). As we will see in Chapter 11, the administrative hearing is a complex legal procedure requiring the assistance of an experienced Elder Law attorney. The appeal can drag on for months.

Meanwhile, the status of the Applicant remains in limbo.

Because of the legal cost of the appeal and the uncertainty of whether the hearing officer will agree that additional assets are necessary for the support of the Community Spouse, it may be better to use a spend-down strategy that enables the spouse to obtain additional income. One such strategy is the MEDICAID ANNUITY. The Community Spouse uses the excess assets to buy an Annuity that will give her additional income. This spend-down strategy is allowed provided it conforms to state and federal law.

A spend-down strategy that is currently allowed by both federal and state law is the purchase of an *Immediate Pay Annuity*; i.e., an annuity whose payments begin the month after the purchase and continues for a fixed period of time. For purposes of Medicaid eligibility, that fixed period of time must be less than, or equal to, the life expectancy of the Annuitant (in this case, the Community Spouse). She can name a Successor Annuitant to receive the payments in the event she dies earlier than her life expectancy.

The life expectancy of the Annuitant is determined by referring to the actuarial table as published by the Centers for Medicare and Medicaid Services; State Medicaid Manual, Part 3 (SM3 3259.1) "Life Expectancy Tables—Males and Life Expectancy Tables—Females." You can find excerpts from that table at Public Service Information section of the Eagle Publishing Company Web site.

http://www.eaglepublishing.com

By purchasing an Immediate Pay Annuity, the excess Resources are converted to a monthly income that continues for the term of the policy.

In order to qualify as a permissible spend-down strategy, the annuity must meet both state and federal criteria, specifically:

IMMEDIATE PAY

The annuity contract must provide for equal payments that begin no later than 60 days after the purchase of the annuity (130 CMR 520.007(C)(4)).

ACTUARIALLY SOUND

The Annuity contract must be ***actuarially sound,*** meaning that the money invested in the Annuity (plus a reasonable rate of interest) must be returned to the Annuitant during his life expectancy as printed in the State Medicaid Manual (SM3 3258.9(B), 3259.1).

There is no rounding "up." For example, according to the State Medicaid Manual a 65 year old man has a life expectancy of 14.96 years. An Annuity that makes regular payments to the Annuitant for 14 years is actuarially sound, but an Annuity that makes payments for 15 years is not.

NO CASH VALUE/EQUAL PAYMENTS

The Annuity contract must have no value other than the monthly payments to the Annuitant. The monthly payments must be of equal value, with no deferred payment and no balloon payment (42 U.S.C. 1396p(c)(1)(G)).

UNASSIGNABLE AND IRREVOCABLE

The Annuity contract cannot be transferred, sold or assigned. It must be irrevocable. In other words, nothing can be changed; not the monthly payment, nor the number of payments, nor the identity of the Annuitant.

THE STATE IS THE RESIDUARY BENEFICIARY

The Deficit Reduction Act requires that the state be the Residuary Beneficiary of the Annuity up to the amount paid by the state for his care. If the Applicant is married, his Community Spouse or minor/disabled child may be in first position as beneficiary, provided the state is in second place (42 U.S.C. 1396p(c)(1)(G)). It may be that this requirement does apply to an Annuity purchased by the Community Spouse for her own benefit. However, as of April, 2006, no regulation has been adopted on the matter.

We will refer to an Annuity that meets all of these criteria (immediate pay, no cash value, unassignable, irrevocable, actuarially sound) as a ***Medicaid Annuity***.

CAUTION VERIFY THAT THE ANNUITY MEETS HHS CRITERIA PRIOR TO PURCHASE

Once the Annuity is purchased it is irrevocable, so before you buy it, have your Elder Law attorney, or the agent who is selling the Annuity, check with HHS to be sure the Annuity meets state and federal requirements. If you purchase the Annuity and for some reason the HHS decides that it does not meet state and federal criteria, the entire value of the Annuity might count as an impermissible transfer of assets. In such case, a PENALTY PERIOD of ineligibility will be imposed, i.e., a period of time that the Applicant is disqualified from receiving Medicaid benefits. The Penalty Period is discussed later in this Chapter.

USING THE ANNUITY TO GENERATE INCOME

Purchasing a Medicaid Annuity could solve the problem for the Community Spouse who has too little income and too much in Resources. She can use her excess Resources to buy the Annuity. She will keep the income from that investment, just as she would if she had invested in a stock, bond or Certificate of Deposit. Unlike these investments, part of the money she paid for the Annuity is returned to her each month along with interest. Most importantly, the Annuity is a Noncountable Asset.

This spend-down strategy can be used by the Community Spouse even when her income is not a problem. But it may not make economic sense if the sum of her monthly income, including the income from the annuity, exceeds the value set by the HHS as her Minimum Monthly Maintenance Needs Allowance.

For example, suppose the HHS determines she needs $2,000 per month and her only income is $1,000 from Social Security. The HHS will allow her to keep $1,000 of her husband's income. If the Annuity pays $1,000 a month (or more), she may keep none of her husband's income. All of his income will be used for his nursing care. In other words, purchasing the Medicaid Annuity may enable the Applicant to qualify for Medicaid, but it may not result in extra income for the Community Spouse.

And there are other things to consider.

➪ RISK OF LOSS

By purchasing an Annuity, the Community Spouse is giving her money to a company in exchange for the company's promise to pay interest and return part of the principal each month. The company promises to make these payments every month for a certain number of years. Should the company become bankrupt during that period of time, the monies invested might be lost.

➪ THE COMMUNITY SPOUSE MAY DIE OR NEED NURSING CARE

Buying a Medicaid Annuity for a Community Spouse who is herself aged or in frail health may not be the best option. If she dies before all of the payments are made, whatever remains will go first to the state of Massachusetts as reimbursement for her spouse's nursing care.

It could happen that she lives her full life expectancy, but needs long-term nursing care and will need to apply for Medicaid. If she purchases an Annuity and later becomes a Medicaid Member, that extra income will be used as her contribution to her nursing care.

➪ LOSS OF LIQUIDITY

Should the Applicant die shortly after his Community Spouse buys the Annuity, she cannot cash it in. She must keep the investment for the full term.

➪ RISK OF LOSS

By purchasing an Annuity, the Community Spouse is giving her money to a company in exchange for the company's promise to return part of the principal each month, together with interest. The company promises to make these payments every month for a certain number of years. Should the company become bankrupt during that period of time, the monies invested might be lost.

➪ FIXED RETURN ON INVESTMENT

Annuities offer a fixed rate of return on the money invested and there is no way to adjust that rate for periods of inflation. The rate of return on the Annuity is set at the time of purchase. We are currently in a period of low interest rates, but there are inflationary pressures at work that can operate to quickly increase interest rates. Should interest rates go into the double digit range, the Annuity will still yield the same single digit rate of return as when it was purchased.

All these concerns need to be addressed before investing in a Medicaid Annuity. Consultation with an Elder Law attorney prior to purchase is a must.

NOT THE BEST OPTION FOR THE SINGLE APPLICANT

Although purchasing a Medicaid Annuity may work for a healthy Community Spouse with a low fixed income, it may not be the best strategy for the single Applicant, because any income he receives from the Annuity will be used for his nursing care. He could live in the nursing home longer than his life expectancy and all the money invested in the Annuity would be used for his care.

One exception may be the single Applicant who intends to return home after a few months. For example, suppose an elderly man with $100,000 needs extensive nursing care because of a car accident. If doctors expect he will be able to return home after several months of therapy and nursing care, he might consider purchasing a Medicaid Annuity for $98,000.

Once he makes the purchase, he can immediately apply for Medicaid. He will of course report the purchase to the HHS. The HHS will examine the terms of the Annuity to be sure they satisfy current regulations. If they do and he meets all other requirements, he should qualify for Medicaid.

He's happy because he did not need to spend down his $98,000 in nursing home bills. He's hoping that his condition improves enough so that he can return home. In such case, his nursing care will be paid by Medicaid, and he will continue to receive the income from the Annuity when he returns home.

The HHS is happy because any income he receives while in the facility will go toward payment of his nursing home bill; leaving that much less for the HHS to contribute to his care.

By purchasing a Medicaid Annuity, he is betting that he will not need nursing care for the rest of his life expectancy. If he loses his bet, none of his assets are protected. All his money will be used to pay for his nursing care. In such case it may be better for him to use a strategy better designed for the single Applicant.

OPTIONS FOR THE SINGLE APPLICANT

Spend-down may not be the best strategy for the single Applicant with significant assets such as a father who has $100,000. Sure he can make his funeral arrangements; but that will only use up a small portion of his assets. He could buy an expensive car, but what good would that be if he needs to enter a nursing home? The Medicaid Annuity is a possibility, but if he has a progressive, long term disease such as Alzheimer's or Parkinson, and needs to go into a facility, he could very well live longer than his life expectancy and all the money invested in the Annuity would be used for his care.

If the Applicant has a medical condition, but he does not expect to need nursing care for several years, he may decide to simply transfer all of his money to his child with the hope that he will not need long term nursing care for at least five years. The five years is the ***Lookback Period*** that HHS uses to investigate the finances of a person who applies for Medicaid. The Lookback Period starts on the date the Applicant enters the nursing home and applies for Medicaid and goes back five years from that date (42 U.S.C. 1396p(c)).

If the HHS determines that the Applicant, or his spouse, made an ***uncompensated transfer*** during the Lookback Period, the HHS will impose a PENALTY PERIOD. An uncompensated transfer is one in which the Applicant gets nothing in return for the transfer (love and affection don't count).

The ***Penalty Period*** is a *Period of Ineligibility* during which the Applicant is disqualified from receiving Medicaid benefits. The Period of Ineligibility used to begin on the day the transfer was made. But under the Budget Deficit Reduction Act, the disqualification begins on the day the Applicant applies for Medicaid!

Should the Applicant go this route, the HHS will disqualify the Applicant from receiving Medicaid for a period of time based on amount that was transferred as a gift or for a price that is less than the fair market value (GLM 118E:38).

COMPUTING THE PENALTY PERIOD

The Penalty Period is computed by dividing the amount transferred by the average monthly cost of nursing home care in the Commonwealth of Massachusetts. The value for the average monthly cost of nursing care being used by the HHS in the year 2006, is $244 per day or $7,320 for a 30 day month. If the Applicant in the example just given, decided to transfer $100,000 to his child he would be disqualified for almost 14 months:

$100,000/$7,320 = 13.66 months

To figure out the actual time period you would need to count the number of days in the month and multiply it by .66. For simplicity, and to be on the safe side, we will "round up" to the nearest month.

The HHS allows the Penalty Period to be reduced provided the money is returned to the Applicant. For example, suppose our Applicant transferred the $100,0000 and six months later he needs nursing care. If the $100,000 is returned to the father, there will be no Penalty. But this is not a complete solution because the father still has too much to qualify for Medical Assistance. He will need to spend-down his assets (probably on nursing home care) before he can qualify for MassHealth.

THERE IS NO LIMIT ON THE PENALTY PERIOD

Although the HHS will only look back five years for transfers, there is no limit on the Penalty Period imposed for that transfer. For example, suppose the Applicant gives his child $500,000. If he applies for Medicaid within five years from the date of transfer, he can be denied Medicaid benefits for over five and a half years:

$500,000/$7,320 = 68.31 or 69 months

And this is not a game of "Catch me if you can." Under both state and federal law, the Applicant and his spouse (or whoever applies for him) are required to make a full disclosure of transfers made during these periods. Anyone who knowingly makes a false statement in an application for Medicaid can be convicted for Medicaid fraud. Whoever is convicted of Medicaid fraud can be fined up to $500 or imprisoned for up to one year (GLM 118E:39).

UNDUE HARDSHIP — CAUGHT IN THE TRANSITION

In 2006, profound changes were made to the Medicaid law:

** FIVE YEAR LOOK BACK INSTEAD OF THREE
** PENALTY PERIOD STARTS WHEN YOU APPLY
** DENIAL OF MEDICAID IF HOME HAS EQUITY OF $500,000 (OR $750,000) AND NO DEPENDENT LIVES THERE.

Because of a legal challenge to the law, and the fact that state legislators need to pass new rules relating to Medicaid eligibility, it may take several months before the new law is effective. It could be well into 2007 before the states enforce the new law. But the new law, as written, can be applied retroactively, back to the time it became law on February 8, 2006.

The federal government recognized that the transition from the old law to the new could cause ***undue hardship,*** so they included the following provision to 42 U.S.C. 1396p:

> Each State shall provide for a hardship waiver process ...
> (1) under which an undue hardship exists when application of the transfer of asset provision would deprive the individual —
> (A) of medical care such that the individual's health or life would be endangered; or
> (B) of food, clothing, shelter, or other necessities of life; and
> (2) which provides for —
> (A) notice to recipients that an undue hardship exemption exists;
> (B) a timely process for determining whether an undue hardship waiver will be granted; and
> (C) a process under which an adverse determination can be appealed.

In other words, the state may not deny the Applicant Medical Assistance if to do so will be dangerous to his health, or deprive him of food, clothing, shelter and other necessities. Although the definition of undue hardship seems clear enough, applying it is complicated. It may take the efforts of an experience Elder Law attorney to convince the HHS that a particular case meets the definition.

For example, suppose a father set up a Medicaid Qualifying Plan under the old law. He kept enough money to pay for his nursing care for three years, and transferred $100,000 to his son. When the father applies for Medicaid, the HHS will look back five years and see the transfer. They will deny him Medical Assistance for close to 14 months, beginning on the day he applied for Medicaid. If the son refuses to return the money, and the father has no other way to pay for the care he needs, will the HHS consider this a case of undue hardship?

A father, in another state, with a similar set of circumstances was denied Medicaid. The state decided that this was not a case of undue hardship because the father gave away the money of his own free will.

The reader may be thinking "Yes, but if I come down with an illness that I know will cause me to deteriorate over a period of time, all I need to do is give all my money to my child and be sure to wait five years. My child will keep my money safe. Should I need that money, my child will return as much as I need to me. Money that I don't use will be protected for my child."

The Medicaid Qualifying Plan of giving away all assets and waiting five years is allowed under current law, but this is a "brute force" approach to the problem. It is a drastic step to take and fraught with peril. Once the money is transferred, a completed gift is made. The child becomes the legal owner of the money and with all of the obvious "what ifs."

- What if the child becomes bankrupt?
- What if he dies?
- What if the child is sued? Will a Court order the child to use the money you gave to pay the judgment?
- What if the child is divorced? Will a judge decide that your child's spouse is entitled to half of that money?

And what if you give the money away and never need long term nursing care? The medical field is advancing with amazing speed. Although few cures have been found for mankind's ills, there have been many breakthroughs in treatment. With modern drugs, many patients are able to function on their own. Even those who have been diagnosed with a progressive disease may not need nursing care for several years — maybe not at all. Meanwhile, your money is gone, and your independence along with it.

Being impoverished at a time in your life when you are unable to supplement your income, and when your health is declining, can lead to much sadness. Imagine going to your child and asking for money. Imagine the child thinking, or worse yet, asking: "What's the money for?"

Many of these concerns can be remedied by a transfer into an Irrevocable Trust with the understanding that you will not be able to apply for Medicaid for at least five years. But even that has its risks. A lot can happen in five years. The federal law could change the Lookback period to six years — or more. You could require full nursing care the day after you transfer your assets into the Trust. The Trust assets could be depleted in less than five years, yet you will not be able to apply for Medicaid because of the transfer.

For those in good health, an alternative is to do nothing until you actually need nursing home care and then implement a Medicaid qualifying strategy at that time. Of course, there is the chance that you take suddenly ill, say with a stroke, and are unable to implement a Medicaid Qualifying plan. A Durable Power Of Attorney that is properly drafted and signed while you have capacity should solve the problem. You can appoint someone to be your Agent to implement a Medicaid Qualifying plan for you.

It is important that the Durable Power of Attorney be properly drafted. In December 2002, A New Jersey Court refused to allow a son to transfer property on behalf of his incapacitated mother for the purpose of qualifying for Medicaid. Although his mother gave him a Power of Attorney authorizing him to apply for Medicaid on her behalf, the Court refused to allow the transfer because the Power of Attorney "... did not provide for him to make gifts on her behalf to himself or anyone else, either to qualify her for Medicaid or for any other reason" (*In the Matter of Mildred Keri*, Superior Court of New Jersey, Appellate Division, A-5949-01T5).

This case was reversed by the New Jersey Supreme Court and eventually the son was able to transfer the assets on behalf of his mother. But a transfer of property under an improperly drafted Power of Attorney can still be challenged.

HHS may challenge transfers made under a Power of Attorney that does not give the Attorney-In-Fact specific authority to implement a Medicaid Qualifying plan. It is important that your Power of Attorney be drafted by an Elder Law attorney who knows what provisions to include in the document so that it will stand up to HHS scrutiny.

CAUTION THE ONLY THING CERTAIN IS CHANGE

Profound changes were made in 2006 to the Medicaid law. This is not the end of changes to the Medicaid law. There is a proposal in the federal government to give states new powers to reduce, eliminate or increase Medicaid benefits within the state. Under this proposal, benefits for welfare recipients, poor children and other groups who are automatically eligible for Medicaid would remain regulated by federal law. The state would be given autonomy to administer the Medicaid program for other groups; and in particular for the elderly in need of nursing care. Proponents of state autonomy explain that with autonomy, the state could increase benefits, but in these days of budget deficits, more likely the states will opt to decrease Medicaid benefits to the elderly.

If states are given autonomy in administering the long-term nursing care program, uniformity would no longer be imposed by the federal government. Medicaid benefits for the elderly could vary significantly state to state. Not only would there be variation state to state, there could be variation within the state. State programs could be administered with different eligibility criteria county to county. There could even be a difference in benefits county to county!

The point is that there is no certainty when it comes to future Medicaid qualifying options.

But we did not write this chapter to give the reader a definitive Medicaid Qualifying strategy. Rather, it was to give the reader an understanding of the law as it relates to qualifying for Medicaid; and to let the reader know that under current law, options are available should the need for long-term nursing care arise.

We also wrote this chapter to let the general public understand how this federal program is administered here in the state of Massachusetts. And, incidentally, we touched only on the basics. There are other, more sophisticated, Medicaid Qualifying options available that an experienced Elder Law attorney can explain to you. The prudent thing to do is to visit an Elder Law attorney if and when you become concerned about a long term care problem. He can explain current law to you as it relates to qualifying for Medicaid. He can suggest the best path for you to follow, given your set of circumstances.

It is also important to keep up with changes in policy both in the state and federal government; and to let your legislators know how you feel about such changes.

Protecting the Homestead 11

As explained in Chapter 10, whether a home in the name of the Applicant counts as an Asset for purposes of qualifying for Medicaid depends on his equity in the home, and if over $500,000 (or $750,000) whether his spouse or a dependent family member is living there. Even if no family member is living in the home, the Applicant cannot be denied Medical Assistance, provided his equity in the home is less than the state limit, and he says he intends to return home. Once on Medicaid, the state has the right to have a physician determine whether he can reasonably be expected to return home within a year. If not, the state has a right to place a TEFRA Lien on the property for money spent on his behalf. TEFRA stands for TAX EQUITY AND FISCAL RESPONSIBILITY ACT, a federal law. A home encumbered by a TEFRA lien cannot be sold or transferred until the money spent by the state for the care of a MassHealth Member are paid (42 U.S.C. 1396p(a)(1)(B), 130 CMR 520.007(G)(12)).

Even if the state does not place a lien on his home during his lifetime, if the Member received Medical Assistance after age 55, the state can place a TEFRA Lien on the property to seek recovery from the sale of his home once the home is sold or he dies (42 U.S.C. 1396a(1)(B)). The state will not seek recovery from a home owned by a deceased Recipient while his spouse, or minor or disabled child are living there. However, once the child reaches 22, or the spouse and disabled child are deceased, whoever inherits the home will need to pay off the lien or the state can force the sale of the property and take the money from the proceeds of the sale (42 U.S.C. 1396p). In this chapter we discuss ways to protect the home from a ***TEFRA Lien.***

Protecting the homestead is easy to do if the Medicaid Recipient is married. Under state and federal law, the Applicant can transfer his home to the Community Spouse without penalty. He can make the transfer either before or after he applies for Medicaid (42 U.S.C. 1396p (c) 2A),130 CMR 520.019).

If the home is in the name of the Member only, he can sign a deed transferring the property to his spouse. If he and the Community Spouse own the property jointly, they can sign a deed transferring his interest to his Spouse. It is important to make the transfer of the Recipient's interest — otherwise the state can place a TEFRA lien on the property, and seek recovery for medical assistance given to the Member, once both husband and wife are deceased.

Protecting the home is more of a problem for the aged, single parent; and it is a problem for aging parents who both are not in the best of health. Who knows which of them will require long term nursing care? Maybe both will need such care. Maybe neither of them will require nursing care.

Many parents want to have their children inherit the one thing the parent has of value, namely his home. Parents fear that if they ever need Medicaid benefits, their home will be sold to reimburse the state. This idea is so distressing to some people that even though they are in relatively good health, they may decide to transfer their home to a child with the understanding that the parent will continue to live there for the rest of his life.

Those planning such a move need to understand that they are trading one risk (need to apply for Medical Assistance) for several other risks.

⌧ RISK OF LOSS

Once you transfer the property to your child it becomes his property and that property can be lost or used to pay for his debts just like anything else he owns. Your child could run into serious financial difficulties. Your child could be sued. This is especially a risk if your child is a professional (doctor, nurse, accountant, financial planner, attorney, etc.). If your child is found to be personally liable for damages, your home could become part of the settlement of that law suit.

If your child is (or gets) married, then this complicates matters even more. If the child divorces, the value of your home might be included as part of the property settlement agreement. This may be to your child's detriment because the child may need to share the value of the property with his/her former spouse. If you do not transfer the property, it cannot become part of his marital equation.

Even if your child is single there is a risk of loss. Your child may want to take out a business loan. If the loan is significant, the lender will want to include everything your child owns as collateral (security for the debt). If the lender learns that you are occupying the house, he will especially want to include your house as collateral because that will motivate your son to repay the loan.

The point is, transferring the house to your child could be bad for both of you. And that is not the only downside.

⮽ LOSS OF HOMESTEAD TAX CREDIT

In Massachusetts, homeowners' tax exemptions are allowed for any number of reasons such as the owner being blind, or a disabled veteran, or the surviving spouse of a blind person or a disabled veteran (GLM 59:5). If you are eligible for a tax exemption and you transfer your home, you will lose your right to receive the tax breaks.

⮽ LOSS OF HOMESTEAD EXEMPTION

As explained in Chapter 5, up to $500,000 of the value of your homestead is protected from creditors during your lifetime. With the exception of property taxes and the loan on your homestead, your creditors cannot force the sale of your property (GLM 188:1; 188:2, 188:4). If you simply transfer your homestead to a child, you lose your Homestead Exemption. If you are married, it is a double loss of creditor protection. Not only do you lose protection for yourself, you lose it for your spouse as well.

If the child does not occupy that property as his home, there is no homestead creditor protection whatsoever. The child's creditors can force the sale of the property (that's your home) for relatively small amounts of unpaid debts.

⮽ POSSIBLE CAPITAL GAINS TAX

Although Congress has expressed its intent to phase out the Estate Tax, there is no discussion to do away with the Capital Gains Tax. If you gift the property to the child during your lifetime, when he sells the property he will pay a Capital Gains Tax on the increase in value from the price you paid for your home to the selling price at the time your child sells the property. If you do not make the gift during your lifetime, the child will inherit the property with a step-up in basis, i.e., he will inherit the property at its market value as of the date of your death.

Under today's tax structure and continuing through 2009, that step-up in basis is unlimited. If your child sells the property when he inherits it, he will pay no Capital Gains Tax, regardless of how large the step-up in basis. In 2010, there will be a limit on the amount that can be inherited free of the Capital Gains Tax, but that limit is quite high, so for most of us this is not a concern.

⌦ POSSIBLE GIFT TAX

A Gift Tax needs to be paid if the value of the equity in your home (plus the value of all the gifts you gave over your lifetime in excess of the Annual Gift Tax Exclusion) exceeds the lifetime Gift Tax Exclusion. The current lifetime Gift Tax Exclusion is $1,000,000, so for most of us, this is not a problem. Yet there still is the hassle of filing a Gift Tax return.

⌦ POSSIBLE LOSS OF GOVERNMENT BENEFITS

If you are married and you, or your spouse, make an uncompensated transfer, both you and your spouse could be denied Medical Assistance if you apply within five years from the date of transfer of the property. It could happen that during that period of time, one of you takes suddenly ill and requires long-term nursing care. Why jeopardize your right to receive Medicaid for both of you? Owning a home will not disqualify you from receiving Medicaid, but transferring it may make you and your spouse ineligible for a long time.

The elderly parent, who is single, may not be convinced that gifting the house is a bad idea. He may be thinking "By giving my home to my child, I risk not being able to qualify for MassHealth for five years. If I don't make the gift and need Medicaid at any time during the rest of my lifetime, the state will get the house for sure." But there are better Estate Plans than the outright gift. The Life Estate strategy may be one of them.

You can give the property to your child, and keep a Life Estate for yourself. Your child will have no right to your homestead while you are alive so you have no fear that the property can be lost or taken from you during your lifetime. Upon your death, your child will own the property 100%, and without the need for Probate.

Depending on the value of your home, this Life Estate approach might allow you to shorten the Medicaid transfer Penalty Period, because you are not giving your child the full value of your home, you are just giving away the value of the ***Remainder Interest*** i.e., what is left of the property after your death.

More importantly, a gift of the Remainder Interest results in a reduction of your equity in the property. This reduction in equity may bring the value of the portion of the residence "owned" by you as a life tenant to less than $500,000. Should you transfer the Remainder Interest, and need nursing care once five years from the date of transfer has passed, the value of your home should not bar you from being eligible for Medicaid.

DETERMINING THE VALUE OF THE REMAINDER INTEREST

The value of the Remainder Interest depends on your life expectancy. A gift of a Remainder Interest when you are 90 is worth more to your child than when you are 50. The Centers for Medicare and Medicaid Services publishes a table of values for the Life Estate Interest and the Remainder Interest based on the age of the Grantor at the time of the transfer (State Medicaid Manual, Part 3 (SM3 3258.9) LIFE ESTATE AND REMAINDER INTEREST TABLE).

You can find excerpts from this table, at the Public Information section of the Eagle Publishing Company Web site. http://www.eaglepublishing.com

Fortunately, this table goes up to age 109, so the value they assign to the remainder interest is relatively low. For example, according to this table, if a 70 year old makes a transfer to his son and keeps a Life Estate for himself, his Life Estate is equal to 61% of the value of the property. The remainder interest is worth only 39%.

The actual percentage given in the table for the Remainder Interest is .39478. If the home is worth $600,000 it means the value of the gift of the Remainder Interest is $236,868.

$600,000 X .39478 = $236,868

The value of your Life Estate Interest as of the date of transfer is $363,132: $600,000 - 236,868 = $363,132
This is well under the $500,000 limit.

Remember that the Penalty Period for the transfer of the Remainder Interest ($236,868/$7,320 = 32.36 months) will be enforced if you apply for MassHealth at any time during the five years after the date of transfer.

And that is not the only problem:

CONTROL

You will not be able to sell your home, or get a mortgage on the property, without permission from your child.

TAX ISSUES

And, as explained at the end of Chapter 2, if you sell the home, you or your child might need to pay a Capital Gains Tax.

RECOVERY BY THE STATE

Under federal law, the state has the right to recover monies spent on your behalf if you received nursing care under Medicaid after the age of 55. Monies can be recovered from property you owned at the time of your death. This includes property you own jointly with another, and property in which you own a Life Estate interest (42 U.S.C. 1396p(b)(4)(B), 130 CMR 520.007(G)(12)). On September 1, 2003, the state of Massachusetts began seeking recovery from property in which the recipient of Medicaid benefits owned a Life Estate interest. There are efforts to protect up to $300,000 from such recovery. But right now the state is following federal law.

THE REVERSE MORTGAGE

Another possible solution to the problem of owning a home whose equity exceeds the state limit is the REVERSE MORTGAGE. A *Reverse Mortgage* is a mortgage such that the lender gives the borrower a certain amount of money, with the agreement that the loan does not need to be repaid until the house is sold or the borrower dies. The money may be given as a lump sum or the borrower may opt to receive a certain amount of money each month based on his life expectancy.

For example, suppose a couple with low monthly income own a home with equity that exceeds the state limit. If they have a child who earns has a substantial income, the couple may take out a Reverse Mortgage with their son as lender. The son will pay his parents a certain amount of money each month. Because the parents are getting value from the transaction, no Penalty Period will be imposed should either parent need to apply for Medicaid at any time.

Meanwhile, the parents are receiving a regular income that will enable them to increase their standard of living, and pay for home health care, if it is needed.

The mortgage on the property reduces the equity in the home, so should one parent die, and the other parent need to apply for Medicaid, the $500,000 (or $750,000, depending on state law) limit may not be a problem. Of course, should either parent become a MassHealth Member, the state can place a TEFRA lien on the property, but that lien cannot be paid until both parents are deceased, and their lender son is fully paid. This is one way to protect the equity in the home for their child.

If the child does not have sufficient income to become the lender of a Reverse Mortgage, the parent can take out a Reverse Mortgage with a lending institution. A single Applicant whose equity in his home is greater than $500,000 (or $750,000) may be able to reduce his equity in the home by taking a Reverse Mortgage, but there are downsides for the single Applicant:

ABSENCE FROM HOME MAY RESULT IN FORECLOSURE

The lender may require the homestead to be occupied by the borrower. The mortgage agreement may allow the lender to foreclose in the event the borrower/MassHealth Member does not occupy his home for 365 days or more.

STATE REIMBURSED FROM SALE PROCEEDS

The state has the right to place a TEFRA lien on the property. Once the property is sold, the Reverse Mortgage will be paid from the proceeds of the sale. The state will be reimbursed from whatever remains of the net proceeds of the sale. It could happen that there will be nothing left for the Member's child to inherit.

TRANSFERS THAT PROTECT

As explained, you can own a home and still qualify for Medicaid, but there still is the concern that once you become a Member, the state may place a TEFRA Lien on your homestead for monies spent on your behalf. Under current law, there are several ways to protect your home from such lien. For a married person, the home can be protected by transferring it to the Community Spouse.

TRANSFERRING THE HOME TO THE SPOUSE

The Applicant is free to transfer his home to his spouse without penalty, either before or after he qualifies for Medicaid (42 U.S.C. 1396p(C)(2)(A)(i)). Once the house is in the name of the Community Spouse, she can arrange to have it inherited by a family member and not the Masshealth Member.

Should the Applicant be too ill to make the transfer himself, the deed can be signed by his Attorney-In-Fact under a properly drafted Durable Power of Attorney. If he did not give anyone authority to make the transfer, and he is too ill to sign his name, it may be necessary to have a Guardian appointed who can ask the Court for permission to make the transfer.

Establishing a guardianship may be expensive and time consuming, but as explained earlier in this Chapter, it is important that the homestead be transferred to the Community Spouse. The downside is that there is no guarantee that the judge will allow the transfer of the homestead to the Community Spouse. Before you apply for a guardianship it is important to ask your attorney whether such transfers have been allowed in the past.

ONE-THIRD OF THE HOUSE MAY REMAIN UNPROTECTED

Once the homestead is transferred to the Community Spouse, she can arrange to have it inherited by a family member and not the Member. But that can present still another problem. As explained in Chapter 2, a surviving spouse has one-third Life Estate interest in real property owned by a deceased spouse (GLM 189:1). If the Member did not waive (give up) his Dower rights, the state has the right to require the Member to assert his right in the homestead of his deceased spouse. Again, it is important to consult with an experienced Elder Law attorney to examine all of the aspects of a transfer of the homestead to the Community Spouse.

TRANSFERRING THE HOME TO A SIBLING

Under state and federal law, if an Applicant owns his home together with a sibling and the sibling lived with the Applicant for at least one year before entering the nursing facility, then the Applicant can transfer the home to the sibling without a Medicaid transfer penalty (42 U.S.C. 1396). This law presents an opportunity for an unmarried Applicant who has a brother or sister to protect the homestead. The only question is how the sibling becomes co-owner. If the Applicant and his sibling purchased the property together, and the sibling lived in the home for a year prior to the Applicant entering the nursing home, then the sibling's interest in the property is protected. The Applicant can transfer his share of the homestead to his sibling without penalty, and that will protect the entire homestead.

If the house is in the Applicant's name only, it is important to consult with an Elder Law attorney to determine the best way for the sibling to become part owner of the home. Federal law only requires that the sibling have an ***equity interest*** in the property.

An equity interest could be joint ownership or a Tenancy In Common or a Remainder Interest in the homestead. An Elder Law attorney will be able to suggest a method of transferring an equity interest to the sibling that will result in a short Penalty Period. Remember, the Penalty Period does not begin until the homeowner applies for Medicaid.

The attorney will also assist with preparing documentation to present to HHS to verify that:

- ⇨ the sibling owns an equity interest in the home
- ⇨ the sibling occupied the home for a year prior to the Applicant entering the nursing home.

TRANSFER TO A CAREGIVER CHILD

A law similar to the transfer to a sibling applies to the Medicaid recipient who owns his home and wants to transfer it to his child. The federal law allows a transfer of the homestead to the child without penalty, provided the child lived with and took care of his parent for at least two years before the parent entered the nursing home.

There is no requirement that the child own an equity interest in the property; but the federal statute does require that the state verify that the child lived in the home and provided care to the parent for the two years; and that this care enabled the parent to remain at home rather than be placed in a nursing home (42 U.S.C. 1396p(c)(2)(A)(iv)).

It is important to consult with an Elder Law attorney, preferably prior to the two year period. The attorney will explain how to document that care over the two year period so that the information can be presented to the HHS when the parent applies for Medical Assistance.

The attorney may suggest that parent and child sign a Caretaker's Agreement that sets out the terms and conditions of the transfer; i.e., what care the child promises to give to the parent over the next two years in exchange for the transfer of the homestead to the child.

The attorney will explain how to document that care over the two year period so that the information can be presented to HHS when the parent applies for Medicaid. Some of the things HHS will want to know are:

- ⇨ the Applicant's medical condition during the two year period
- ⇨ whether the child lived in the home for the required time period
- ⇨ what care was provided by the child that enabled the parent to remain at home
- ⇨ how many hours per day were spent by the child in caring for his parent
- ⇨ whether the child worked outside of the home during the two year period; and if so, who cared for the parent while the child was at work.

The HHS will want a physician to verify that the care provided by the child delayed the parent's entry into the nursing home for at least two years. Once it is established by the HHS that federal requirements are satisfied, the property can be transferred to the child without affecting the right of the Applicant to receive MassHealth benefits.

TRANSFER TO A DISABLED CHILD

In Massachusetts, the Applicant or his spouse may transfer their home or any other of their assets to a child (minor or adult) who is blind, or disabled without penalty (42 U.S.C. 1396p(c)(2A),130 CMR 520.019). In the event the child does not have a determination of blindness or disability from the Social Security Administration, the HHS will review the child's medical records to determine whether the child is blind or disabled.

If the child is receiving Social Security disability benefits, the parent can transfer their home or other assets to a Supplemental Needs Trust for the child (see Chapter 7). This transfer will not disqualify the child (or the parent) from receiving government benefits, provided the Trust is drafted according to state and federal law.

IMPACT OF DEFICIT REDUCTION ACT

Laws relating to the transfers of the home to the spouse, sibling and child were enacted prior to the Deficit Reduction Act. Whether these laws will still apply if the home is worth more than $500,000 (or $750,00, depending on state law) is unknown as of the time we went to print in 2006.

CAUTION DON'T TRY THIS ON YOUR OWN

A Medicaid Qualifying Plan is not something to attempt on your own. The Medicaid program is complex and volatile. There are many levels of law that govern Medicaid. There are the federal statutes (Social Security Act Title XIX/P.L. 89-97); the U.S. Code of Federal Regulations (42 CFR 430-435) and the Centers for Medicare and Medicaid Services State Medicaid Manual, Part 3 that say how the federal statutes are to be administered in the United States.

There are the Massachusetts Medicaid statutes (Title XVII Public Welfare); and the Massachusetts Administrative Code (Title 130) that say how the Medicaid program is to be administered in this state. These five different sets of laws and regulations constantly change — often with little or no notice to the general public.

In addition to changes to the state and federal law, several times each year, the Commissioner of the Health and Human Services issues *Eligibility Operations Memos* and *Eligibility Letters.* These Memos and Letters are provided to the workers at each MassHealth Enrollment Center. The workers use the regulations to implement the MassHealth program.

These Memos and Letters are available to the general public at the Health and Human Services section of the Massachusetts Web site.

http://www.mass.gov/

Trying to read the laws relating to Medicaid is an exercise for even the most talented legal scholar. A federal judge criticized the structure of the laws regulating Medicaid: "The Social Security Act is among the most intricate ever drafted by Congress. Its Byzantine construction ... makes the Act 'almost unintelligible to the uninitiated.' ... The District Court ... described the Medicaid statute as 'an aggravated assault on the English language, resistant to attempts to understand it'." (*Schweiker v. Gray Panthers*, 453 U.S. 34 (1981)).

In *Rehabilitation Association of Virginia v. Kozlowski*, 42 F.3d 1444, 1450 (4th Cir 1994), the Court had nothing but sympathy for officials who must interpret or administer these ever changing laws "... (the laws) are among the most completely impenetrable texts within human experience. Indeed, one approaches them ... with dread, for not only are they dense reading of the most tortuous kind, but Congress also revisits the area frequently, generously cutting and pruning in the process and making any solid grasp of the matters addressed merely a passing phase."

Even with the Commissioner's Memos and Letters available to the workers who administer Medicaid, because of the complexity of the law, there is variation in the way the law is applied. A Medicaid qualifying option may be accepted in one county and challenged in another.

If HHS decides to challenge a particular strategy, even though that strategy is based on federal or state law, you will have no choice but to appeal the ruling.

An Applicant who is denied Medicaid benefits will receive notice from Health and Human Services that he has the right to appeal (130 CMR 516.007 (D)).

The first step in the appeal process is for the Applicant, or someone acting on his behalf, to request an administrative review called a "Fair Hearing." The *Board of Hearings* is the unit within Health and Human Services responsible to conduct the Fair Hearing (130 CMR 456.402). The Board will appoint a hearing officer. The hearing officer is called a *Referee* (GLM 118E:47, 103 CMR 601.012).

Even though a Fair Hearing is an informal proceeding, it is, none-the-less, a complex legal proceeding. To win you will need have a complete understanding of all applicable law. You will need to know how to discover and present evidence to prove your case. It is important that you have an attorney present at the hearing to represent you. If you cannot afford to employ an attorney, ask Legal Aid for assistance. See Page xii for the Legal Aid office nearest you.

It is important to seek legal counsel just as soon as you determine that the Applicant has been denied benefits. If it is necessary to present evidence to support your position, you will need to request an *Evidentiary Hearing* at the same time you request the hearing. You will need to justify your reason for requesting an Evidentiary Hearing (105 CMR 100.981, 130 CMR 610.05).

Few Applicants have the necessary knowledge and skills to support even this initial stage of requesting an Evidentiary Hearing. They don't know what is involved in an Evidentiary Hearing, none-the-less knowing how to justify the request.

If you are serious about challenging the decision of the HHS, consultation with an experienced Elder Law Attorney is a must.

The Referee may subpoena witnesses, administer oaths, take testimony, and examine written evidence, before deciding the case. The person appealing has the right to cross-examine witnesses and to question or challenge evidence presented at the hearing. In other words, this is much the same procedure as a trial (GLM 118E:48).

The decision must be issued within 90 days from the day the appeal was filed. If the Commissioner disagrees with the decision he can direct the Board of Hearings to conduct a re-hearing using the same, or a different Referee. If the Applicant disagrees with the Referee's decision he can ask for a re-hearing, however, the Commissioner will not order a re-hearing unless he disagrees with the Referee's decision (106 CMR 343.710, GLM 118E:47).

In other words, if you win, the Commissioner can order still another Fair Hearing. If you lose, you can ask for a re-hearing, but the Commissioner is under no duty to order a re-hearing unless he agrees with your position. Considering that the Commissioner believed you were not entitled to MassHealth in the first place, it is not likely he will disagree with the Referee's decision

If you lose at this administrative level, you can take the case to the Superior Court in the county where the Applicant lives, or you can file it in Suffolk County (106 CMR 343.720). The Superior Court will take a broad look at the picture and consider state and federal law, as well as the Constitutional rights of the Applicant. If you are turned down in Superior Court, you can take the appeal to the Massachusetts Supreme Judicial Court, or you can appeal to a federal court — all the way up to the United States Supreme Court.

As you can see, appealing the DMA'S decision is complicated, and time consuming. It is important to employ an attorney to help with the appeal and that can be expensive. In Chapter 10 we presented many different options that are legally available to the Applicant at this time. The goal is to get the Applicant qualified for Medicaid as quickly as possible, and with the least amount of hassle. It is better to choose a strategy that has been allowed in the past, rather than chance a denial of the application and be forced to appeal the decision.

An experienced Elder Law attorney can explain what strategies have been allowed in the past in your county and which strategies are likely to be challenged. The key word is "experienced." Before employing an attorney, determine what percentage of his practice is devoted to Medicaid eligibility; how long he has practiced Elder Law in that county; and whether he is familiar with the appeals process, should the need arise.

Guiding Those You Love 12

Once you are satisfied with your Estate Plan, then the final thing to consider is whether your heirs will be able to locate your assets after you're gone.

Most people have their business records in one place, their Will in another place, car titles and deeds in still another place. When someone dies, their beneficiaries may feel as if they are playing a game of "hide and seek" with the decedent. The game might be fun were it not for the fact that unlocated items may be forever lost. For example, suppose you die in an accident and no one knows you are insured by your credit card company for accidental death in the amount of $25,000. The only one to profit is the insurance company, which is just that much richer because no one told them that you died as a result of an accident.

And how about a key to a safe deposit box? Will anyone find it? Even if they find the key, how will they locate the box?

It is not difficult to arrange things so that your affairs are always in order. It amounts to being aware of what you own (and owe) and keeping a record of your possessions. A side benefit is that by doing so, you will always know where all your business records are. If you ever spent time trying to collect information to file your taxes or trying to find a lost stock or bond certificate, you will appreciate the value of organizing your records.

POINTING THE WAY

Heirs need all the help they can get. It is difficult enough dealing with the loss, without the frustration of trying to locate important documents. Your heirs will have no problem locating your assets if you keep all of your records in a single place. It can be a desk drawer or a file cabinet or even a shoe box. It is helpful if you keep a separate file or folder for each type of investment. You might consider setting up the following folders:

THE BANK & SECURITIES FOLDER

Store your original certificates for stocks, bonds, mutual funds, certificates of deposit, in a folder labeled BANK & SECURITIES FOLDER. In addition to the original certificate include a copy of the contract you signed with each financial institution. The contract will show where you have funds and who you named as beneficiary or joint owner of the account. If someone owes you money and has signed a promissory note or mortgage that identifies you as the lender, then you can store these documents in this folder as well.

If you have a safe deposit box, keep a record of its location and the number of the box, in this folder. Keep a copy of all of the items stored in the box in this folder. If you have an extra key to the box, put it in this folder.

E-bank Accounts

If you are doing your banking on-line, it is important to leave a record of your passwords so that your family can access the account in the event of your incapacity or death. The same applies if you have on-line brokerage or installment loan accounts. Keep a paper record of these accounts in your Bank & Securities Folder.

THE INSURANCE FOLDER

The INSURANCE FOLDER is for each insurance policy that you own, be it life insurance, car insurance, homeowner's insurance or health care insurance. If you purchased real property, you may have received a title commitment at closing and the original title insurance policy some weeks later when you received your original deed from recording. If you cannot locate the title insurance policy, contact the closing agent and have them send you a copy of your title insurance policy.

THE PENSION AND ANNUITY FOLDER

Put all of the documents relating to your pension or annuity in this folder. Include the telephone number and/or address of the person to contact in the event of your death.

FOR FEDERAL RETIREES

If you are a Federal Retiree, you should have received your **P**ERSONAL **I**DENTIFICATION **N**UMBER (**PIN**) and the person who will inherit your pension (your ***survivor annuitant***) should have received his/her own PIN as well. It is relatively simple to obtain this during your lifetime, but it may be difficult and/or stressful for your survivor annuitant to work through the system once you are gone.

Survivor annuitant benefits are not automatic. Your survivor annuitant must apply for them by submitting a death claim to the Office of Personnel Management. Your survivor needs to know that it is necessary to apply and also how to apply. You can call the Office of Personnel Management at (888) 767-6738 to get printed information that you can keep in this folder to guide your survivor annuitant through the process. You can also download information from their Web site: http://www.opm.gov

THE DEED FOLDER

Place the original deed (or a copy if the original is in a safe deposit box) in a separate DEED FOLDER. Include cemetery deeds, condominium deeds, timesharing certificates, deed to out of state property, etc. Also include a copy of related documents such as an Abstract of Title, or a recorded condominium approval. If you have a title insurance policy, put the original in the insurance folder, and a copy in this folder. If you own several properties, you may want to have a separate folder for each property which includes all of the closing documents for that parcel of land.

If you have a mortgage on your property, put a copy of the recorded mortgage and promissory note in a separate LIABILITY FOLDER. Once the mortgage is paid off, the lender should give you a Release of Mortgage. The Release needs to be recorded in the county where the property is located. Keep the recorded Release together with the deed to the property. Remember to remove the paid mortgage from your Liability Folder.

LOCATING REAL PROPERTY

If you own a vacant lot, your beneficiaries will find the deed (or a copy) in this folder but that deed will not contain the address of that property because it doesn't have one. The post office does not assign a street address until there is a building on the site. Your beneficiary could get the location of the property from city or county records. But why make things hard for them? Include a simple handwritten note in this folder that tells them exactly how to locate the property.

THE LIABILITY FOLDER

The LIABILITY FOLDER should contain all loan documents of debts that you owe. For example, if you purchased real property and have a mortgage on that property, put a copy of the mortgage and promissory note in this folder. If you owe money on a car, put the loan documents here. A lease is a liability, because you have contracted to pay a certain amount for the period of the lease, so include a copy of any lease agreement in this Liability Folder. If you have a credit card, put a copy of the contract you signed with the credit card company in this folder. By having a record of your assets and outstanding debts, you can calculate your net worth (what you own less what you owe) whenever you wish.

THE TAX RECORD FOLDER

Your Personal Representative (or next of kin) will need to file your final income tax returns. Keep a copy of your tax returns (both federal and state) for the past three years in your Tax Record Folder. As explained in Chapter 3, beginning in 2010, there will be a cap on the step-up basis to 4.3 million dollars for property inherited by your spouse and 1.3 million for property inherited by anyone else. It is important to keep a record of the basis of your property, not only for your heirs, but for yourself should you decide to sell the property during your lifetime.

If you purchase real property, you need to keep a record of the purchase price as well as money you paid to improve the property. For condominium units, that will include special assessments for improvements to the property. You need these records to determine whether a Capital Gains Tax is due on the transfer. Your accountant can help you set up a bookkeeping system to keep a running record of your basis in everything you own of value.

THE PERSONAL PROPERTY FOLDER

MOTOR VEHICLES

Put all motor vehicle titles in a Personal Property Folder. This includes cars, mobile homes, boats, planes, etc. If you owe money on the vehicle, the lender may have possession of the title certificate. If such is the case, put a copy of the title certificate and registration in this folder and a copy of the loan documents in a separate liability folder. If you own a boat or plane, identify the location of the motor vehicle. For example, if you are leasing space in an airplane hangar or in a marina, keep a copy of the leasing agreement in this folder.

JEWELRY

If you own expensive jewelry, keep a picture of the item together with the sales receipt or written appraisal in this folder.

COLLECTOR'S ITEMS

If you own a valuable art or coin collection, or any other item of significant value, include a picture of the item in this folder. Also include evidence of ownership of the item, such as a sales receipt or a certificate of authenticity, or a written appraisal of the property.

THE PERSONAL RECORDS FOLDER

The PERSONAL RECORDS FOLDER should include documents that relate to you personally, such as a birth certificate, naturalization papers, marriage certificate, divorce papers, military records, Social Security card; etc.

THE ESTATE PLANNING DOCUMENT FOLDER

WILL/TRUST

Place your Will and/or Trust in a separate folder. If the original document is in a safe deposit box, then place a copy of the document in this folder together with instructions about how to find the original. If you placed your Will with the Registry of Probate, you should have a Certificate of Receipt (GLM 191:10). Put the Certificate in this folder, together with a copy of the Will.

It is important to keep a copy of your Will or Trust because over the years you may forget what provision you made. Keeping a copy in your home may save you the time and effort to retrieve the document, just to determine whether it needs to be updated.

MARITAL AGREEMENTS

Antenuptial or Postnuptial agreements generally provide for the disposition of your property upon your death, so a copy of the agreement should be included in this folder.

OTHER ESTATE PLANNING DOCUMENTS

You can include the original or a copy of other Estate Planning Documents in this folder such as your:

- ⇨ Power of Attorney
- ⇨ Health Care Proxy
- ⇨ Living Will
- ⇨ Pre-need Funeral Contract.

Many do not have the time, nor inclination, to "play" with all these folders. They do not anticipate an immediate demise. Getting hit by a truck, or dying in a fiery plane crash is not something to think about, much less prepare for. But consider that death is not the only problem. You could take suddenly ill (say with a stroke) and become incapacitated. Even the most time-starved optimist should have a murmur of concern that his loved ones will be left with a mess should something unforeseen happen.

If you do not feel like doing a complete job of organizing your records at this time, consider an abridged version. You can set up a single folder and place all of your important papers in that folder. You need to make the folder easily accessible to whomever you wish to manage your affairs in the event of your incapacity or death. You can do this by letting that person know of the existence of the folder and how to get it in an emergency.

You can keep the folder in an easily accessed place in your home with the folder identified as containing important papers. We labeled it "THE QUICK-FIND FOLDER" because the folder gives you and your family easy access to important information and/or documents. But you can create your own heading such as: "MY IMPORTANT PAPERS" or if you want a particular person to access the folder, you might label it: "RECORDS FOR MY SON, ROBERT"

It is helpful if you include a list of all you own and the location of each item in that folder.

WHEN TO UPDATE YOUR ESTATE PLAN

We discussed people's natural disinclination to make an Estate Plan until they are faced with their own mortality. Many believe that they will make just one Will and then die (maybe that's why they put off making a Will). The reality is, most people who make a Will, change it at least once before they die. If you have an Estate Plan, it is important to update it when any of the following events take place:

✍ CHANGE IN MARITAL STATUS

GETTING MARRIED

Unless you enter a marriage with no property and no children, it is fool-hardy to marry without signing an Antenuptial (i.e., Premarital) Agreement. The example given in the stepchildren section of Chapter 7 shows how the lack of planning on the part of a parent who remarries can be to the detriment of his children. An Antenuptial Agreement could have provided for a fair distribution of his property.

Hopefully, your marriage will prosper and you along with it. You should review your Agreement on a regular basis as your finances change or as you have children. With the consent of your spouse, you can amend your Antenuptial Agreement. If it needs a complete revision, you can revoke the agreement, and replace it with a Post-nuptial (i.e., Marital) Agreement.

Changes to the Antenuptial Agreement need to be prepared and signed in the same manner as your original agreement. There must be full disclosure by both parties as to the extent of their wealth. Each of you should be represented by your own attorney.

GETTING A DIVORCE

If you get divorced, there are certain changes that take place by law. For example, if you divorce and then die before you get around to changing your Will, any provision that you made for your former spouse in the document will be read as if your former spouse died before you (GLM 191:9). But it is important to not just rely on the law. Best to change all documents after a divorce. This includes a Health Care Proxy, Durable Power of Attorney, as well as bank accounts, insurance policies, etc.

In addition, you need to notify anyone who might rely on these documents of the divorce. For example, suppose you gave your spouse a Power of Attorney and your spouse used that document after the divorce to sell your securities. You could sue your spouse for doing so, but not your broker, unless you gave the broker written notice that you revoked the Power of Attorney.

SEPARATION HAS NO LEGAL EFFECT

A Decree of Separation does not terminate the marriage. Your Will is not changed as described above because of the separation. If you expect the separation to be permanent, you need to change your Will, Trust, insurance policies, etc. on your own. However, you will not be able to change title to real property that you own together with your spouse, unless your spouse agrees to the change.

NOTIFY EMPLOYER OF CHANGE

If you change your marital status (either marry or divorce) you need to tell your employer of the change so that the employer can change your status for purposes of paycheck tax deductions. If you have a health insurance plan or a pension plan, that provides benefits to your spouse, these need to be changed as well.

If you die without a Will, your employer can transfer up to $100 of your unpaid wages to your surviving spouse, or if no spouse to your adult child. If you are without spouse or child, the wages can be transferred to your parent (GLM 149:178A). This law does not apply to employees of the Commonwealth. If you are employed by a private company, tell your employer, in writing, who is to receive your unpaid wages in the event of your death.

✍ A CHANGE IN RELATIONSHIP

Getting married, separated or divorced; having a child; having a beneficiary of your Estate die, are all profound changes in one's life. When the dust settles, it is important to examine your Estate Plan to see if it needs revision. If you have a Trust, you can change it by having your attorney prepare an *amendment* to the Trust. If you have a Will, your attorney can prepare a *codicil* (a supplement) to the Will.

It is important to have changes made by a properly drafted and signed document. If you make changes by crossing things out or writing over your Will, or Trust, the validity of the document can be challenged once you die.

If you simply rip up the old Will, that will effectively revoke the Will (GLM 191:8). But it could happen that someone (perhaps your attorney) has a copy of the Will. If no one knows that you revoked the Will, they may think the Will is lost and then offer the copy of the Will for Probate. If you draft a new Will, the first paragraph should say, "I revoke all prior Wills ..." This makes it clear that you want the new Will to replace all other Wills.

CAUTION NEW SPOUSE OR CHILD CAN CHALLENGE OLD WILL

CHALLENGE BY SURVIVING SPOUSE

Under Massachusetts law, any Will made prior to marriage is revoked by law when the Will maker marries, unless the Will indicates that it shall continue to be effective after the marriage (GLM 191:9). If you marry and "forget" to change the Will you prepared prior to your marriage, your spouse has a right to challenge your Will.

CHALLENGE BY CHILD

If you make a Will and fail to provide for an adopted child or a child who was born either before or after your death, the child is entitled to as much as he would have inherited had you died without a Will — unless:

⇨ the Will indicates that the omission was intentional; i.e., that you wanted to omit the child from inheriting your property - or -

⇨ you made other provisions for the child during your lifetime (GLM 191:20).

The same rule applies to the descendants of a deceased child, i.e., if your child dies before you, his descendants (your grandchildren) are entitled to an Intestate share of your Estate unless you intentionally omitted them from your Will or made other provision for the child.

If your spouse, child (or grandchild) successfully challenges your Will, the beneficiaries named in your Will need to contribute part of their inheritance to make up for the share given to the omitted spouse or child.

The laws relating to an omitted spouse or child are complex, and could lead to disagreement and hard feelings for those forced to contribute part of their inheritance. It is better to change your Will when you marry or a child is born to you, or adopted by you, so that your spouse or child receive no more and no less than you intended.

✍ BENEFICIARY DIES

Most of us remember to name an alternate beneficiary in their Will in the event a beneficiary dies before we do. If you have not made such provision, and your beneficiary dies, then under Massachusetts law, if the beneficiary is your relative, the share intended for the deceased beneficiary will go to his descendants (GLM 191:22).

✍ BENEFICIARY MOVES

It is important that your beneficiary's address be available to those in charge of distributing funds upon your death. Many life insurance proceeds are never paid because the company cannot locate the beneficiary. The Actuarial Office of the Federal Employees' Group Life Insurance Program reported that as of September, 2003, they had over 55.8 million dollars in unpaid benefits, mostly because they could not locate the beneficiary at the last given address.

✍ RELOCATION TO A NEW STATE OR COUNTRY

There is no need to change your Estate Plan for a move within the state of Massachusetts. There is much to check out if you are moving to another state. If you deposited your Will with the Registry of Probate, you need to retrieve your Will and deposit it with the Registry of Probate in the county of your new residence. If you are moving out of state, you need to take the Will with you.

Not all states allow a Will to be deposited with the Court prior to the death of the Will maker. You may need to make other arrangements for the storage of your Will in the new state. If your attorney has your original Will or any other original of your Estate Planning documents, then unless you plan to continue to employ him, you need to retrieve these items to take with you to the new state.

You need to determine whether your Will conforms to the laws of the state of your new residence. Most states will honor a Will drafted according to Massachusetts law, however, the rights of a spouse vary considerably state to state. Massachusetts has rights of Dower, but many states have replaced their Dowers statutes with certain minium amounts to be inherited by the surviving spouse.

If you are married and have not provided the minimum amount as required by the laws of the new state, should you die before your spouse, your Will may be challenged on that basis. The same applies to a Trust. Many states allow a surviving spouse to demand funds from the Trust of the decedent spouse, if he did not provide the minimum amount to his spouse as required by the laws of that state.

Most importantly, other states do not recognize a Massachusetts marriage between parties of the same sex. If you go to another state, your same-sex Massachusetts marriage partner will be considered to be your friend. Your spouse will not have any marital rights or responsibilities.

Certain states such as California and Hawaii have laws which give same sex partners rights and responsibilities within the state, provided the partners register their union with the state. In California, they need to register as *Domestic Partners*. In Hawaii, they register as *Reciprocal Beneficiaries*.

If you do not have a Will, this is the time to think about who will inherit your property should you die in the state of your new residence. This is especially important for those who are married. The right of a spouse to inherit property varies significantly from state to state. Spousal rights in a Community Property state (Arizona, California, Idaho, Louisiana, Nevada, New Mexico, Texas, Washington and Wisconsin) are very different from the rights of a spouse in Massachusetts.

OTHER ESTATE PLANNING DOCUMENTS

Massachusetts has laws directing physicians to honor a Health Care Proxy that is properly drafted in another state (GLM 201D:11). But not all states have such laws. Some states will not recognize a Medical or Health Care Directive unless it is drafted according to the laws of that state. But even if the laws of the state honor your Massachusetts Health Care Proxy, consider drafting another in the new state. Medical Directives vary significantly state to state. Other states may have laws that enable you to appoint someone with powers similar to a Health Care Agent, but the laws of the state may refer to such person as a *Patient Advocate* or a *Health Care Surrogate* or a *Health Care Representative.*

It is best to sign a new Health Care Proxy using the form and terminology recognized in the new state, rather than chance any confusion should you become ill and find yourself in an emergency situation. Similarly, if you have appointed someone to handle your finances under a Power of Attorney, you may want to have another prepared in conformity with the laws of the new state, so there will be no question of the right of your Attorney-In-Fact to conduct business on your behalf.

TRANSFER PRE-NEED PLAN

If you have a Pre-need Funeral plan, and do not plan to return to Massachusetts, you need to transfer your funeral plan to the state of your new residence. Under Massachusetts law, you have the right to assign your funeral contract to a new firm, provided the new firm agrees, in writing, to honor your Massachusetts contract (239 CMR 4.06).

TAX CONSIDERATIONS

You need to check out the taxes of the new state. Each state has its own tax structure. Some states have an inheritance tax, or a transfer tax on all inherited property. If state taxes are high, you may need an Estate Plan that will minimize the impact of those taxes.

CREDITOR PROTECTION

Creditor protection is another item that is significantly different state to state. If you have much debt, determine what items can be inherited by your family free of your debts in that state.

RELOCATING THE MEMBER OF MASSHEALTH

If your family member is a Member of MassHealth, and you want to move him to another state, you need to check out whether he will continue to be eligible for Medicaid in that state. As explained in Chapter 10, Medicaid is both a state and federal program. A MassHealth Member can be transferred to a nursing home in another state; provided he qualifies under that state's Medical Assistance Program. Eligibility for Medical Assistance varies significantly state to state. For example, Massachusetts does not have an upper limit for income, but other states do. If the Member has an income that exceeds the limit in a state with an *income cap*, he may be refused Medicaid benefits in that state.

If you plan to move a Member to another state, it is important to first check with an Elder Law attorney in that state who can explain the Medicaid eligibility laws of the state to you. He will be able to tell you what needs to be done in order to have the Member qualify for Medicaid in that state.

As you can see, state law has an important impact on your Estate Plan. When moving to another state, you need to educate yourself about the laws of the state, or consult with an attorney who can assist you in reviewing your Estate Plan to see if that plan will accomplish your goals in that state.

✍ A SIGNIFICANT CHANGE IN THE LAW

We pay our legislators (state and federal) to make laws and, if necessary, change those in effect. We pay judges to interpret the law and that interpretation may change the way the law operates. The legislature and the judiciary do their job and so laws change frequently. Tax laws are particularly volatile. The 2001 change in the federal Estate Tax law gradually increases the Exclusion amount so that by 2010 no federal Estate Tax will be due regardless of the value of your Estate.

You may be thinking that there is no need for an Estate Tax plan because you don't intend to die prior to 2010. But any certainty relating to death and taxes is false security (especially taxes, in this case). As explained in Chapter 3, the federal Estate Tax law passed in 2001, is effective only until December 31, 2010. If lawmakers do nothing, on January 1, 2011, the federal Estate Tax goes back into effect; and Estates that exceed one million dollars will once again be subject to federal Estate Taxes.

And that is not the only uncertainty. Each state has its own Estate Tax structure. It remains to be seen how each state will react to the position taken by the federal government in 2010. If federal Estate Taxes are phased out altogether, some states may follow the lead of the federal government and dispense with Estate Taxes. However, with states struggling to balance the budget, more likely they will see this as an opportunity to increase their Estate Taxes, so Estate Taxes that would have been paid to the federal government will be paid to the state.

You need to keep up with the news to learn about changes in the law that affect your Estate Plan. It is a good idea to check with your attorney on a regular basis to see if any change in the state or federal law affects your current Estate plan. And also check out the Eagle Publishing Company Web site for changes we will post to keep this book fresh. http://www.eaglepublishing.com

SPRING CLEAN YOUR RECORDS

Used to be, that housewives did a once a year, floor to ceiling, "spring housecleaning." We know of no survey telling whether today's houseperson conducts an annual purge of dirt and clutter. We suspect it went by the wayside when housewives entered the work force as full time employees. But it was a good practice. In many cases, it was the only time of the year when the house was truly clean and tidy. It is a good idea to apply that old-fashioned housecleaning practice to your financial records and clean them up on a regular basis. There is no need to keep the deed to real property that you have long since sold; a lease agreement to an apartment you no longer rent; a credit card to a closed account, etc.

Many hesitate to toss out some scrap of paper for fear it will not be available for future reference. There are documents you may need to keep for a lengthy period of time to establish a basis for tax purposes. You can avoid the problem of keeping too much, or not enough, by taking your box (or folder) of records with you the next time you visit with your accountant or attorney. You can ask your advisor to help you organize your records and assist with your "housecleaning."

Keys are another item to keep up to date. You may have a sentimental reason to keep old keys, but there is no business reason to keep a key to a car you no longer own, a safe deposit box you no longer lease, etc. Keeping such keys can only cause confusion should you become disabled or die. Whoever takes possession of your property will be left with mysterious keys. He will probably think the keys are protecting something of value.

Unless you enjoy picturing an heir's frustration as he seeks an imaginary treasure, pitch the key.

Glossary

ABSTRACT OF TITLE An ***Abstract of Title*** is a condensed history of the title to the land. It consists of a summary of all the documents recorded with the County Registry that affect the land, including mortgages.

ACTUARIAL TABLE An ***actuarial table*** is a table organized according to statistical data that indicates the life expectancy of a person.

ADDENDUM An ***addendum*** to a contract is an addition to the contract.

ADMINISTRATION The ***administration*** of a Probate Estate is the management and settlement of the decedent's affairs. There are different types of administration. See SUMMARY ADMINISTRATION.

ADMINISTRATIVE CODE The ***Administrative Code*** is the set of rules used by governmental agencies to apply laws enacted by the legislature. The Administrative Code interprets the law and describes the agency's requirements to implement that law. See *CFR.*

AFFIANT An ***Affiant*** is someone who signs an affidavit and swears or acknowledges that it is true in the presence of a notary public or other person with authority to administer an oath or take acknowledgments.

AFFIDAVIT An ***Affidavit*** is a written statement of fact made by someone voluntarily, under oath, or acknowledged as being true, in the presence of a notary public or someone else who has authority to administer an oath or take acknowledgments.

AGENT An ***Agent*** is someone who is authorized by another (the principal) to act for or in place of the principal.

AMENDMENT An ***amendment*** to a Trust is an addition to the Trust that changes the provisions of the Trust.

ANATOMICAL GIFT An ***anatomical gift*** is the donation of all or part of the body of the decedent for a specified purpose, such as transplantation or research.

ANCILLARY ADMINISTRATION An ***Ancillary Administration*** is a Probate procedure that aids or assists the original (primary) Probate proceeding. Ancillary administration is conducted to determine the beneficiary of the decedent's property located within that state, and to determine whether the property is taxable in that state.

ANNOTATED STATUTE A statute that is ***annotated*** is a statement of the law followed by cases which illustrate or explain the statute.

ANNUAL GIFT TAX EXCLUSION The ***Annual Gift Tax Exclusion*** is the amount a person can gift to another each year without being required to file a federal Gift Tax Return. The Annual Gift Tax Exclusion is currently $11,000, but is expected to increase to $12,000 in the year 2006.

ANNUITANT An ***Annuitant*** is someone who is entitled to receive payments under an annuity contract.

ANNUITY CONTRACT An ***annuity contract*** is a contract that gives someone (the annuitant) the right to receive periodic payments (monthly, quarterly) for the life of the annuitant or for a given number of years.

ANTENUPTIAL AGREEMENT An ***Antenuptial Agreement*** (also known as a *Prenuptial or Premarital Agreement*) is an Agreement made prior marriage to take effect once a couple marry. The Agreement states how the couple's property is to be managed during their marriage and how their property is to be divided should either die, or they later divorce.

ASSET An ***asset*** is anything owned by someone that has a value, including personal property (jewelry, paintings, securities, cash, motor vehicles, etc.) and real property (condominiums, vacant lots, acreage, residences, etc.).

ASSIGN To ***assign*** is to transfer one's rights in or to something to another. For example, a person who has the right to receive income from a partnership may assign that right to another person.

ATTORNEY or ATTORNEY AT LAW An ***attorney***, also known as an ***Attorney at law***, or a ***lawyer***, is someone who is licensed by the state to practice law in that state.

ATTORNEY-IN-FACT An ***Attorney-In-Fact*** is someone appointed to act as an Agent for another (the Principal) under a Power of Attorney.

BASIS The ***basis*** is a value that is assigned to an asset for the purpose of determining the gain (or loss) on the sale of the item or in determining the value of the item in the hands of someone who has received it as a gift.

BENEFICIARY A ***beneficiary*** is one who benefits from the act of another or from the transfer of property. In this book we refer to a beneficiary as someone named in a Will, Trust, or deed to receive property, or someone who inherits property under the Laws of Intestate Succession.

BENEFICIARY ACCOUNT A ***beneficiary account*** is a bank account with a named beneficiary. The owner of the funds in the account directs the bank to give the funds remaining in the account to the named beneficiary upon the death of all of the owners of the bank account. *Pay On Death* and *In Trust For* accounts are beneficiary accounts.

BONA FIDE A ***bona fide*** act is something that is done in good faith; honestly, openly and without deceit or fraud.

BURDEN OF PROOF The ***burden of proof*** is the duty of one of the parties in a dispute to establish the facts in the case. Who has the burden of proof is established by law.

BY REPRESENTATION ***By representation*** is a method of distributing property to a group of people such that if one of them dies before the gift is made, then the deceased person's share goes to his/her descendants.

CAPITAL GAINS TAX A ***Capital Gains Tax*** is a tax on the amount the net sales proceeds exceeds the basis of a capital asset sold by a taxpayer.

CASH SURRENDER VALUE The ***Cash Surrender Value*** of a life insurance policy is the amount of money the insurance company will pay to the owner of an insurance policy in the event the owner cancels the policy before the death of the person who is insured under the policy.

CFR The ***Code of Federal Regulations ("CFR")*** is the annual cumulation of regulations set by federal executive agencies combined with previous regulations that are still in effect. The CFR contains the general body of laws that govern the practices and procedures of federal administrative agencies.

CHARITABLE REMAINDER ANNUITY TRUST A ***Charitable Remainder Annuity Trust*** is a Trust that pays an annuity to a beneficiary (the *Annuitant*) for a certain period of time or until his death. Once the annuity is paid, whatever remains in the Trust is donated to a tax exempt charity.

CLAIM A ***claim*** against the decedent's Estate is a demand for payment. To be effective, the claim must be filed with the Probate court within the time limits set by law.

CLOSE CORPORATION A ***Close Corporation*** is a corporation whose voting shares are held by a single shareholder or a small, closely-knit, group of shareholders.

CMR The ***Code of Massachusetts Regulations ("CMR")*** are the rules of an administrative office that are used to apply Massachusetts laws.

CODE A ***Code*** is a body of laws arranged systematically for easy reference e.g. the Internal Revenue Code.

CODICIL A ***codicil*** to a Will is an addition to the Will that changes or replaces certain parts of the Will.

COLUMBARIUM A ***columbarium*** is a vault with niches (spaces) for urns that contain the ashes of cremated bodies.

COMMON LAW MARRIAGE A ***Common Law marriage*** is one that is entered into without a state marriage license or any kind of official marriage ceremony. A Common Law marriage is created by an agreement to marry, followed by the two living together, and telling everyone they know that they are husband and wife. Massachusetts does not recognize a Common Law marriage unless it was entered into in another state that considers the union to be a valid marriage.

COMMUNITY PROPERTY Certain states (Arizona, California, Idaho, Louisiana, Nevada, New Mexico, Texas, Washington, and Wisconsin) have laws stating that property acquired by husband or wife, or both, during their marriage is ***Community Property*** and is owned equally by both of them.

CONFLICT OF INTEREST A ***conflict of interest*** is a conflict between the official duties of a fiduciary (guardian, Trustee, attorney, etc.) and his own private interest. For example, it is a conflict of interest for a Successor Trustee to use Trust property for his own personal profit.

CONSERVATOR A ***Conservator*** is someone appointed by the Probate Court to manage, protect and preserve the property of someone who is unable to care for his property because of mental illness or mental retardation.

CORPORATION A ***Corporation*** is a company created by one or more persons according to the laws of the state. The company is owned by the *shareholders* or *stockholders*. Each owner has limited liability. See LIMITED LIABILITY.

COUNTABLE ASSET See RESOURCE.

COURT The ***Court*** as used in this book is the Court that handles Probate and guardianship matters. When referring to an order made by the Court, the term is synonymous with "judge," i.e., an "order of the Court" is an order made by the judge of the Court.

CREDITOR A ***creditor*** is someone to whom a debt is owed by another person (the *debtor*).

CURTESY ***Curtesy*** is the right of a husband, upon the death of his wife, to a Life Estate in real property she owned during their marriage, provided they had a surviving child who could inherit the property. This English Common Law has been abolished in most states. In Massachusetts, it has been replaced by a Right of Dower which is a one-third Life Estate interest in real property owned by the deceased spouse.

CUSTODIAN A ***Custodian*** under the ***Massachusetts Uniform Gifts to Minors Act*** is a financial institution or person who accepts responsibility for the care and management of property given to a minor child.

DAMAGES ***Damages*** is money that is awarded by a Court as compensation to someone who has been injured by the action of another.

DEBTOR A ***debtor*** is someone who owes payment of money or services to another person (the *creditor*).

DECEDENT The ***decedent*** is the person who died.

DESCENDANT A ***descendant*** is someone who descends from a common ancestor. There are two kinds of descendants: a *lineal descendant* and a *collateral descendant*. The lineal descendant is one who descends in a straight line such as father to son to grandson. The collateral descendant is one who descends in a parallel line, such as a cousin. In this book, unless otherwise stated, the term *descendant* refers to a *lineal descendant*. The word ***issue*** has the same meaning as the word descendant.

DISTRIBUTION The ***distribution*** of a Trust or Probate Estate is the giving to the beneficiary that part of the Estate to which the beneficiary is entitled.

DOWER ***Dower*** is the right of a wife, upon the death of her husband, to a Life Estate in one-third of all real property that he owned during their marriage. This English Common Law has been abolished in most states. Massachusetts has modified this Common Law to include rights for the husband and wife. Dower rights in Massachusetts are limited to a one-third Life Estate interest in real property owned by the deceased spouse at the time of his/her death

DURABLE As used in the Power of Attorney, the word ***durable*** means that the Power of Attorney will remain in effect in the event that the principal (the person giving the Power of Attorney) becomes incapacitated.

ELECTIVE SHARE The ***Elective Share*** is the minimum amount of the decedent's Estate that a surviving spouse is entitled to receive under law. In Massachusetts, that amount depends on whether the decedent left surviving descendants or other next of kin.

ELIGIBILITY REPRESENTATIVE The ***Eligibility Representative*** is someone who applies for Medical Assistance in the Commonwealth of Massachusetts on behalf of an Applicant who is too ill to apply himself.

EMERGENCY GUARDIANSHIP PROXY An ***Emergency Guardianship Proxy*** is someone appointed by a minor's parent(s), to care for the child, for up to 60 days, in the event that neither of the child's parents are able to do so.

ENTITLEMENT An ***entitlement*** is a legal right to receive a benefit of income, property or services.

EQUITY The ***equity*** in a home is the market value of the home less monies owed on the property (mortgages, tax liens, etc.)

EQUITY INTEREST An ***equity interest*** is an ownership interest. It is the value of the ownership interest over and above monies owed on the property.

ESTATE A person's ***Estate*** is all of the property (both real and personal property) owned by that person. The decedent's Estate may also be referred to as his *Taxable Estate* because all of the decedent's assets must be included when determining whether Estate Taxes are due. Compare to PROBATE ESTATE.

ESTATE OF HOMESTEAD In Massachusetts, An ***Estate of Homestead*** is created by a statement on the deed that the Grantee is taking the property as his Estate of Homestead, or by filing a Declaration of Homestead with the Registry of Deeds. An Estate of Homestead has creditor protection and the surviving spouse of the owner has a Life Estate in the property.

EXECUTOR An ***Executor*** (feminine *Executrix*) is a legal term found in many Wills. The term refers to the person named by the Will maker to carry out directions given in the Will. In modern Wills, that person is referred to as the *Personal Representative*.

FACE VALUE The ***face value*** of a life insurance policy is the value stated on the insurance certificate or policy. It is the amount to be paid upon the death of the insured person.

FAIR HEARING A ***Fair Hearing*** is an administrative procedure. It is the first step in the appeals process for someone who has been denied Medical Assistance. In Massachusetts, the Fair Hearing is conducted by the *Board of Hearings*.

FIDUCIARY A ***Fiduciary*** is one who takes on the duty of holding property in Trust for another or acting for the benefit of another, such as a Personal Representative, Trustee, Guardian etc.. A fiduciary relationship is also one that is developed out of trust and confidence. For example, an attorney has a fiduciary relationship with his client.

FORECLOSURE ***Foreclosure*** is a court proceeding in which a creditor either takes title to, or forces the sale of, property owned by the borrower, in order to satisfy the debt.

GLM ***GLM*** is the abbreviation for the ***General Laws of Massachusetts.***

GRANTEE The ***Grantee*** of a deed is the person who receives title to real property from the *Grantor*.

GRANTOR The ***Grantor*** is someone who transfers property. The Grantor of a deed, is the person who transfers real property to a new owner (the Grantee). The Grantor of a Trust is someone who creates the Trust and then transfers property into the Trust. Also see SETTLOR

GUARANTOR A ***Guarantor*** is someone who promises to pay a debt or perform a contract for another in the event that person does not fulfill his obligation.

GUARDIAN A ***Guardian*** is someone who has legal authority to care for the person or property of a minor or for someone who has been found by the Court to be incapacitated.

GUARDIAN AD LITEM A ***Guardian Ad Litem*** is a special Guardian appointed by the Court to represent the interests of a minor, or someone who is incapacitated, during a Court proceeding.

HEALTH CARE AGENT A ***Health Care Agent*** is someone who is appointed by another (the *Principal)* to authorize medical treatment for the Principal, in the event the Principal is to too ill to do so himself.

HEALTH CARE PROXY A ***Health Care Proxy*** is a document in which someone (the **Principal**) gives another (his *Health Care Agent*) authority to make medical decisions on behalf of the Principal.

HEIR An ***Heir*** is anyone entitled to inherit the decedent's property under the Laws of Descent and Distribution in the event that the decedent dies without a valid Will.

HOLOGRAPHIC WILL A ***Holographic Will*** is a Will written, dated and signed by the hand of the Will maker himself. Many states refuse to admit a Holographic Will into Probate unless it is witnessed according to the laws of the state.

HOMESTEAD The ***homestead*** is the dwelling that is owned, and occupied, in the state of Massachusetts, as the owner's principal residence.

HSS The Massachusetts ***Health and Human Services ("HHS")*** is the agency that administers the Medicaid program in the Commonwealth of Massachusetts.

INCAPACITATED The term ***incapacitated*** is used in two ways. A person is *physically incapacitated* if he lacks the ability to perform certain tasks. A person is *legally incapacitated* if a Court finds that he is unable to care for his person or property.

INFORMAL ADMINISTRATION An ***Informal Administration*** is a simplified and/or shortened Probate procedure that is available in Massachusetts for Probate Estates of $15,000 or less.

INTER VIVOS TRUST An ***Inter Vivos Trust*** (also known as a *Living Trust*) is a Trust that is created and becomes effective during the lifetime of the Grantor (or Settlor) as opposed to a Trust that he includes as part of his Will to take effect upon his death.

INTESTATE ***Intestate*** means not having a Will or dying without a Will. ***Testate*** is to have a Will or dying with a Will.

IRREVOCABLE CONTRACT An ***irrevocable contract*** is a contract that cannot be revoked, withdrawn, or cancelled by any of the parties to that contract.

IRREVOCABLE TRUST An ***Irrevocable Trust*** is a Trust that cannot be changed, cancelled or terminated until its purpose is accomplished.

IRREVOCABLE INSURANCE TRUST An ***Irrevocable Insurance Trust*** is a Trust that is set up to purchase life insurance. The proceeds of the life insurance policy can be used to pay taxes that may be due upon the death of the insured person.

ISSUE The decedent's ***issue*** are his descendants, children, grandchildren, great-grandchildren, etc.
See DESCENDANT.

IRA ACCOUNT An ***Individual Retirement Account ("IRA")*** is a retirement savings account in which income taxes on certain deposits and interest to the account are deferred until the monies are withdrawn from the account.

JOINT AND SEVERAL LIABILITY If two or more people agree to be ***jointly and severally liable*** to pay a debt, then each individually agrees to be responsible to pay the debt, and together they all agree to pay for the debt.

JOINT TENANCY In Massachusetts, a ***Joint Tenancy*** means that each tenant owns an equal share of the property with right of survivorship; i.e., should one Joint Tenant die the remaining tenants own the property.

KEOGH PLAN A ***Keogh Plan*** (named for its author, Eugene Jones Keogh) is a retirement plan available to self-employed taxpayers. Certain tax benefits are available such as tax deductions for annual contributions to the plan.

KEY MAN INSURANCE ***Key man insurance*** is a disability and life insurance policy designed to protect a company from economic loss in the event that an important employee of the company becomes disabled or dies.

KINDRED ***Kindred*** are those related by blood. They are also referred to as *Kinsfolk*.

LAWS OF DESCENT AND DISTRIBUTION The ***Laws of Descent and Distribution*** are the laws of the state that determine who is to inherit the decedent's Probate Estate if the decedent died without a valid Will. In some states, these laws are called the *Laws of Intestate Succession*.

LEGALESE ***Legalese*** refers to the use of legal terms and confusing text used by some attorneys when drafting legal documents.

LETTERS ***Letters*** is a document, issued by the Probate court, giving the Personal Representative authority to take possession of and to administer the Estate of the decedent.

LIEN A ***lien*** is a charge against a person's property as security for a debt. The lien is evidence of the creditor's right to take the property as full or partial payment, in the event that the debtor defaults in paying the monies owed.

LIFE ESTATE A ***Life Estate*** interest in real property is the right to possess and receive the income from that property for so long as the holder of the Life Estate lives. A one-third Life Estate interest means the person can occupy one-third of the property or receive one-third of the income generated by that property.

LIMITED ACCESS DEPOSIT ACCOUNT A ***Limited Access Deposit Account*** is a bank account in which the owner of the funds in the account authorizes another to make bank transactions as his Agent.

LIMITED LIABILITY ***Limited Liability,*** as related to a corporation or other company created according to state law, means that a shareholder of the company generally is not responsible to pay the debts of the company beyond the amount that he/she invested in the company.

LIMITED LIABILITY COMPANY A ***Limited Liability Company*** is a company created according to the laws of the state. In Massachusetts, it can be organized to conduct any lawful business. All of the members of the company have limited liability.

LIMITED PARTNERSHIP A ***Limited Partnership*** is a partnership created according to the laws of the state. Each *Limited Partner* has limited liability. Each *General Partner* has control of the business and is personally liable for all of the debts of the company. (See Limited Liability).

LINEAL DESCENDANT See ***descendant*.**

LITIGATION ***Litigation*** is the process of carrying on a lawsuit, i.e., to sue for some right or remedy in a court of law. A Litigation Attorney is one who is experienced in conducting the law suit and in particular, going to trial.

LIVING WILL A ***Living Will*** is a Health Care Directive that gives instructions to the physician about whether life support systems should be withheld or withdrawn in the event that the person who signs the Living Will is terminally ill or in a persistent vegetative state and unable to speak for himself.

LOOKBACK PERIOD The ***Lookback Period*** is a period of consecutive months that can be reviewed for transfers of Resources to determine whether a period of ineligibility should be imposed for the Medicaid Applicant.

MASSHEALTH See MEDICAID.

MEDICAID ***Medicaid*** is a medical assistance program sponsored jointly by the federal and state government to provide health care for people with low income and limited resources. In Massachusetts, the program is also referred to as *MassHealth.*

MEMBER ***Member*** is the name used by the Commonwealth of Massachusetts to refer to a person who is a recipient of MassHealth; i.e., the state's Medical Assistance Program.

NET WORTH A person's ***net worth*** is the value of all of the property that he owns less what he owes.

NEXT OF KIN ***Next of kin*** has two meanings in law: *next of kin* refers to a person's nearest blood relation or it can refer to those people (not necessarily blood relations) who are entitled to inherit the property of a person who dies without a valid Will.

NONCOUNTABLE ASSET A ***Noncountable Asset*** is property owned by a person (or his spouse) that does not count towards the Asset Limit when determining whether that person qualifies for MassHealth.

NON-PROBATE TRANSFER A ***Non-Probate Transfer*** is a transfer made to a beneficiary of the decedent without going through a Probate procedure. This includes transfers from a joint account, a Trust, a Pay On Death account, a Transfer On Death security, etc.

PARTNERSHIP A business ***partnership*** is an agreement between two or more persons to use their assets, expertise and/or labor to carry on a business for profit as co-owners.

PERSONAL EFFECTS ***Personal effects*** is personal property that is kept for one's personal use such as clothing, jewelry, books, and other items generally found in the home.

PERSONAL PROPERTY ***Personal property*** is all property owned by a person that is not real property (real estate). It includes personal effects, cars, securities, bank accounts, insurance policies, etc.

PERSONAL REPRESENTATIVE The ***Personal Representative*** is someone appointed by the Probate Court to settle the decedent's Estate and to distribute whatever is left to the proper beneficiary.

PETITION A ***Petition*** is a formal written, request to a Court asking the Court to take action or issue an order on a given matter; e.g. a request to appoint a Guardian.

POSTNUPTIAL AGREEMENT A ***Postnuptial agreement*** is an Agreement made by a couple after marriage to decide their respective rights in case of a dissolution or the death of a spouse.

POWER OF ATTORNEY A ***Power of Attorney*** is a document in which someone (the *Principal*) gives another person (his *Agent* or *Attorney-In-Fact*) authority to do certain things on behalf of the Principal.

PRENUPTIAL AGREEMENT See ANTENUPTIAL AGREEMENT.

PRINCIPAL OF A POWER OF ATTORNEY The ***Principal*** of a Power of Attorney is someone who gives another (his *Agent*) authority to act on his (the Principal's) behalf.

PRINCIPAL OF A TRUST The ***Principal of a Trust*** is the Trust property. The Trust income is the money that is earned on the Trust Principal.

PROBABLE CAUSE ***Probable cause*** exists if it is reasonable to believe certain facts. Mere suspicion is not enough. For probable cause to exist, there must be more evidence for the facts than against.

PROBATE ***Probate*** is a Court procedure in which a Court determines the existence of a valid Will. The Decedent's Estate is settled by the Personal Representative who pays all valid claims and then distributes whatever remains to the proper beneficiary.

PROBATE ESTATE The ***Probate Estate*** is that part of the decedent's Estate that is subject to a Probate procedure. It includes property that the decedent owned in his name only. It does not include property that was jointly held by the decedent and someone else. It does not include property held in trust for someone.

PRO BONO The term ***Pro Bono*** means "for the public good." When an attorney works Pro Bono, he does so voluntarily and without pay.

REAL PROPERTY ***Real property***, also known as ***real estate,*** is land and anything permanently attached to the land such as buildings and fences.

REFEREE A ***Referee*** is someone appointed by the Massachusetts Board of Hearings to conduct an administrative hearing. He has authority to administer oaths, take testimony, and then decide the facts of the case. Although the Referee can decide the facts of the case, the final outcome of the hearing is decided by Commissioner of the Division of Medical Assistance.

REMAINDER INTEREST A ***Remainder Interest*** in real property is the property that passes to a beneficiary at the end of the life interest i.e. the property that passes to the beneficiary once the owner of the Life Estate dies.

RESIDUARY BENEFICIARY A ***Residuary Beneficiary*** of a Will is a beneficiary who is entitled to whatever is left of the Probate Estate once specific gifts have been distributed and the decedent's bills, taxes and costs of Probate have been paid. Unless the Will makes some other provision, Residuary Beneficiaries share equally in the Residuary Estate.

RESIDUARY ESTATE The ***Residuary Estate*** is whatever is left of the Probate Estate once specific gifts made in the Will have been distributed and the decedent's bills, taxes and costs of Probate have been paid.

RESOURCE A ***Resource*** for purposes of determining Medicaid eligibility, is an asset owned by the decedent, or his spouse, that can be converted into cash to meet their needs. Federal statute 42 U.S.C. 1382b identifies what counts (and does not count) as a Resource.

REVERSE MORTGAGE A ***Reverse Mortgage*** (also known as a ***Reverse Annuity Mortgage)*** is a mortgage whose loan proceeds are paid to the borrower incrementally over a period of time. The loan is not repaid until the borrower dies or the property is sold.

REVOCABLE TRUST A ***Revocable Trust*** is a Trust which can be amended or revoked by the Grantor or Settlor during his lifetime.

REVOCABLE LIVING TRUST A ***Revocable Living Trust*** (also known as an ***Inter Vivos Trust***) is a Revocable Trust that is created and becomes effective during the lifetime of the Grantor or Settlor.

SELF PROVED WILL A ***Self Proved Will*** is a Will that eliminates some of the formalities of proof in a Probate procedure. The Will is Self Proved if signed by the witnesses in the form as required by the statute.

SETTLOR A ***Settlor*** or a ***Trustor*** is someone who creates a Trust.

SIBLING A ***sibling*** is one of two or more people born of the same parents; i.e., a brother or a sister. Unless, otherwise noted, we used the term to include those who have only one parent in common; i.e. a half brother or a half sister.

SOLE PROPRIETORSHIP A ***Sole Proprietorship*** is a form of business ownership in which one person owns all of the assets of the business and that person is personally liable for all of the debts of the business.

SOLEMNIZE To ***solemnize*** a marriage is to enter into the marriage publicly, before witnesses, in contrast to a secretive or Common Law marriage.

SPECIFIC GIFT A ***Specific Gift*** is a gift of a specific item of the Will maker's Estate that is made to a named beneficiary of the Will.

SPENDTHRIFT A ***Spendthrift*** is someone who wastes money and/or spends lavishly.

SPENDTHRIFT TRUST A ***Spendthrift Trust*** is a Trust created to provide monies for the living expenses of a beneficiary, and at the same time protect the monies from being taken by the creditors of the beneficiary.

SPRINGING POWER OF ATTORNEY A ***Springing Power of Attorney*** is a Power of Attorney that is not operational until, and unless, the Principal is incapacitated.

STANDBY GUARDIANSHIP PROXY A ***Standby Guardianship Proxy*** is someone appointed by a parent to take over the care of a minor child in the event that both parents are unable to care for the child. Within 90 days of assuming care for the child, the Proxy must petition the Court to be appointed as the child's legal Guardian.

STATUTE OF LIMITATION A ***Statute of Limitation*** is a federal or state law that sets maximum time periods for taking legal action. Once the time set out in the statute passes, no legal action can be taken.

STATUTORY CUSTODIANSHIP TRUSTEE A ***Statutory Custodianship Trustee*** is someone who is given property to hold and manage in Trust for another according to Massachusetts law.

STEPPED-UP BASIS A ***stepped-up basis*** is the fair market value placed on property that is purchased or inherited from another. The "step-up" refers to the increase in value from the basis of the former owner (usually what he paid for it), to the basis of the new owner (usually the market value when the transfer is made).

SUCCESSOR TRUSTEE A ***Successor Trustee*** is someone who takes the place of the Trustee.

SUMMARY ADMINISTRATION A ***Summary Administration*** is a simplified and/or shortened Probate procedure.

SURETY BOND A ***Surety Bond*** is a bond in which a company (the *Surety*) agrees to pay if the *Principal* defaults on his obligation. For example, the Court may order the Personal Representative to be bonded for the value of the Probate Estate. If the Personal Representative does not perform his duties and the Estate loses money, the Court can require the Surety to pay for the lost funds.

SURROGATE A ***Surrogate*** is a substitute; someone who acts in place of another.

TEFRA LIEN ***TEFRA*** is the abbreviation for the TAX EQUITY AND FISCAL RESPONSIBILITY ACT. It is a federal law that allows states to place a lien on real property owned by those who receive Medicaid benefits after age 55.

TENANCY BY THE ENTIRETY A ***Tenancy by the Entirety*** is the name of a form of ownership of real property held by a husband and wife. It is a joint tenancy with right of survivorship, modified by the common law theory that the husband and wife are one.

TENANCY IN COMMON ***Tenancy In Common*** is a form of ownership such that each tenant owns his share without any claim to that share by the other tenants. There is no right of survivorship. Should a Tenant In Common die, his share belongs to the tenant's Estate and not to the remaining owners of the property.

TERM LIFE INSURANCE POLICY A ***Term Life Insurance policy*** insures the life of a person for a certain period of time. No insurance proceeds are paid unless the insured person dies within the given period of time. The monies paid for the policy are not refundable, so a Term Life Insurance policy has no cash surrender value.

TITLE INSURANCE ***Title Insurance*** is a policy issued by a title insurance company after searching title to the property. The insurance covers losses that result from a defect of title, such as unpaid taxes, or a claim of ownership of the property.

TRUST AGREEMENT A ***Trust Agreement*** is a document in which someone (the Settlor) creates a Trust and appoints a Trustee to manage property placed into the Trust. The usual purpose of the Trust is to benefit persons or organizations named by the Settlor as beneficiaries of the Trust.

TRUSTEE A ***Trustee*** is a person, or institution, who accepts the duty of managing Trust property for the benefit of another.

TRUSTOR A ***Trustor***, also known as as ***Settlor,*** is someone who creates a Trust.

UNASSIGNABLE ANNUITY An ***unassignable annuity*** is an annuity that cannot be assigned; i.e., the annuitant's benefits cannot be transferred to another.

UNDUE INFLUENCE ***Undue influence*** is pressure, influence or persuasion that overpowers a person's free will or judgment, so that a person acts according to the will or purpose of the dominating party.

VOID PROVISION A ***void provision*** is one that is not legally enforceable. For example, if a Will provision makes a gift and the Court finds that provision to be void, then the beneficiary has no legal right to receive that gift.

WAIVER A ***waiver*** is the intentional and voluntary giving up of a known right.

WARRANTY DEED A ***Warranty Deed*** is a deed in which the Grantor warrants (promises) that the property he is transferring has good and clear title; i.e., that no one else has rights in the property. This is different than a ***Quit-claim Deed*** where the Grantor says, in effect, "I am releasing any interest I have in this property to you, but I make no guarantees about anyone else's right to this property."

INDEX

A

B

C

I

J

K

L

M

T

WEB SITES

PAGE		WEB SITE
x	Federal Statutes	http://www4.law4.law.cornell.edu/uscode
xi	Massachusetts Bar Association	http://www.massbar.org
197	Massachusetts Health and Humber Services	http://www.mass.gov
191	Massachusetts Division of Insurance	http://www.mass.gov/doi
x	Massachusetts Statutes	http://www.mass.gov/legis/
192	NARFE	http://www.narfe.org
168	Registry Organ Donor Program	http://massrmv.com
191	US Office Personnel Mgmt	http://www.opm.gov
158	Veteran's Admin. Cemetery	http://www.cem.va.gov

189 Massachusetts Statutes and Regulations
are referenced in
A Will Is Not Enough In Massachusetts

Each state has its own set of laws relating to the control, and protection of a person's Estate. The laws of Massachusetts relating to Guardianship, Probate and especially Medicaid are very different from the laws of other states.

The author is in the process of "translating" *A Will Is Not Enough* for the rest of the states; that is, writing state specific books that explain how to set up an Estate Plan for the given state and how to qualify for MEDICAID in that state.

A Will Is Not Enough is now available for:
ARIZONA, CALIFORNIA, CONNECTICUT
COLORADO, FLORIDA, GEORGIA, HAWAII
INDIANA, ILLINOIS, MARYLAND, MICHIGAN
MASSACHUSETTS, NEBRASKA
NEW JERSEY, NEW MEXICO, NEW YORK
OREGON, PENNSYLVANIA, TEXAS
VIRGINIA, WASHINGTON, WISCONSIN.

To order any of these books call (800) 824-0823, or visit our Web site for a 20% discount.
http://www.eaglepublishing.com

OTHER BOOKS BY AMELIA E. POHL

How To Defend Yourself Against Your Lawyer

is a book about the unhappy experiences people have with their lawyers, beginning with that of the author AMELIA E. POHL. She became involved in a law suit and found herself in the role of client, rather than lawyer. She become concerned about lawyers who do not provide their clients with loyalty and respect. This book is a result of those concerns.

The book is divided into chapters that cover the most common problems that take people to a lawyer: divorce, probate, criminal, personal injury, starting a business, making a Will, buying a house, etc. Each chapter tells of the misadventures of the unwary as they sought the services of a lawyer without a clue as to what they were "buying." This book is funny, sad, interesting, but most of all informative. It tells the reader how to become a savvy consumer, i.e., how to find the right lawyer for the right job. If you ever find the need to employ a lawyer, you will be glad you read this book.

Copyright 2004 272 pages 6" X 9" soft cover

$20 includes Shipping and Handling

BOOK REVIEW

TED KREITER of the SATURDAY EVENING POST said "Horror fans, forget about those tawdry tales of ghosts and vampires. Pick up Amelia E. Pohl's *How To Defend Yourself Against Your Lawyer* to read some really scary stuff. Like the story . . . of the grieving widow, Ethel, whose husband died shortly after a lawyer drafted a sweetheart will for the two of them. . . . Six months in attorney's fees later, Ethel learned that she already had her husband's money because it never needed to go through probate! . . Ethel then went out and found a good lawyer for $1,000 who was able to get her $5,000 back. You do the math. . . Following Pohl's useful advice could save a person much more than money."

Guiding Those Left Behind In . . .

Amelia E. Pohl has written a series of books explaining how to settle an Estate. Each book is state specific, telling how things are done in that state. Each book explains:

- ✧ who to notify
- ✧ how to locate the decedent's property
- ✧ how to get possession of the inheritance
- ✧ when you do, and do not, need an attorney
- ✧ the rights of a beneficiary, and much more.

Each book is written with the assistance of an experienced attorney who is licensed and is practicing in that state.

The ***Guiding*** series is currently available for the following states: ALABAMA, ARIZONA, ARKANSAS, CALIFORNIA CONNECTICUT, FLORIDA, GEORGIA, HAWAII, ILLINOIS INDIANA, IOWA, KANSAS, KENTUCKY, LOUISIANA, MASSACHUSETTS, MARYLAND MICHIGAN, MINNESOTA, MISSOURI MISSISSIPPI, NEW JERSEY, NEW YORK NORTH CAROLINA, OHIO, OKLAHOMA PENNSYLVANIA, SOUTH CAROLINA, TENNESSEE TEXAS, VIRGINIA, WASHINGTON, WISCONSIN

To order any of these books call (800) 824-0823, or visit our Web site for a 20% discount.

http://www.eaglepublishing.com

BOOK REVIEWS OF *Guiding Those Left Behind*

ARIZONA

Ben T. Traywick of the Tombstone Epitaph said "This book is an excellent reference book that simplifies all the necessary tasks that must be done when there is a death in the family. There is even an explanation as to how you can arrange your own estate so that your heirs will not be left with a multitude of nagging problems." "The reviewer has been going through probate for two years with no end yet in sight. This book at the beginning two year ago would have helped immensely."

CALIFORNIA

Margot Petit Nichols of the Carmel Pine Cone called it a ". . .TRULY RIVETING READ." " . . . I could scarcely put it down." "This is a book that we should all have, either on our book shelves or thoughtfully placed with our important papers."

FLORIDA

Maryhelen Clague of the Tampa Tribune Times wrote "Amelia Pohl has created a handy, self-help guide that illustrates the necessary steps that must be taken when someone dies, a guide that is easy to read, extremely clear and simple to refer to when the need arises."

NEW YORK

Saul Friedman of NEWSDAY said "And one section that should be read by readers of any age, suggests and describes how to create an 'If I Die' file to point the way to your vital papers and policies, to minimize the problems and costs for your survivors. Alas, not even you boomers will live forever."

It is the goal of EAGLE PUBLISHING COMPANY to keep our publications fresh.

As we receive information about changes to the federal or Massachusetts law we will post an update to this edition at our Web site.

http://www.eaglepublishing.com